WORLD WAR II SHIPWRECKS OF NEWFOUNDLAND: IN PICTURES

CHRIS POWER

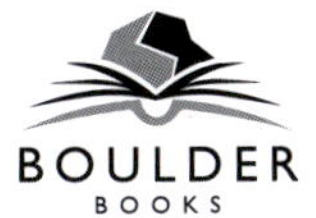

Library and Archives Canada Cataloguing in Publication

Title: World War II shipwrecks of Newfoundland : in pictures / Chris Power.
Names: Power, Chris (Diver and photographer), author, photographer.
Identifiers: Canadiana 20240319494 | ISBN 9781998220144 (hardcover)
Subjects: LCSH: Shipwrecks—Newfoundland and Labrador. | LCSH: Shipwrecks—Newfoundland and Labrador—Pictorial works. | LCSH: Warships—Newfoundland and Labrador—Pictorial works. | LCSH: Merchant ships—Newfoundland and Labrador—Pictorial works. | LCSH: World War, 1939-1945—Naval operations.
Classification: LCC G525 .P69 2024 | DDC 910.4/5209718—dc23

Published by Boulder Books
Portugal Cove-St. Philip's, Newfoundland and Labrador
www.boulderbooks.ca

Design and layout: Tanya Montini
Editor: Stephanie Porter
Copy editor: Iona Bulgin

Printed in China

We acknowledge the financial support of the Government of Newfoundland and Labrador through the Department of Tourism, Culture, Arts and Recreation.

Funded by the Government of Canada | Financé par le gouvernement du Canada | Canada

WORLD WAR II SHIPWRECKS OF NEWFOUNDLAND: IN PICTURES

History at the edge of the Atlantic

Nestled at the edge of the North Atlantic Ocean, the island of Newfoundland is the easternmost point of North America, marked by rugged coastlines and expansive ocean vistas. Due to its location, Newfoundland was strategically important during global conflicts, notably World War II. The island's proximity to the shipping lanes of the Atlantic made it critical for naval operations and a witness to wartime events.

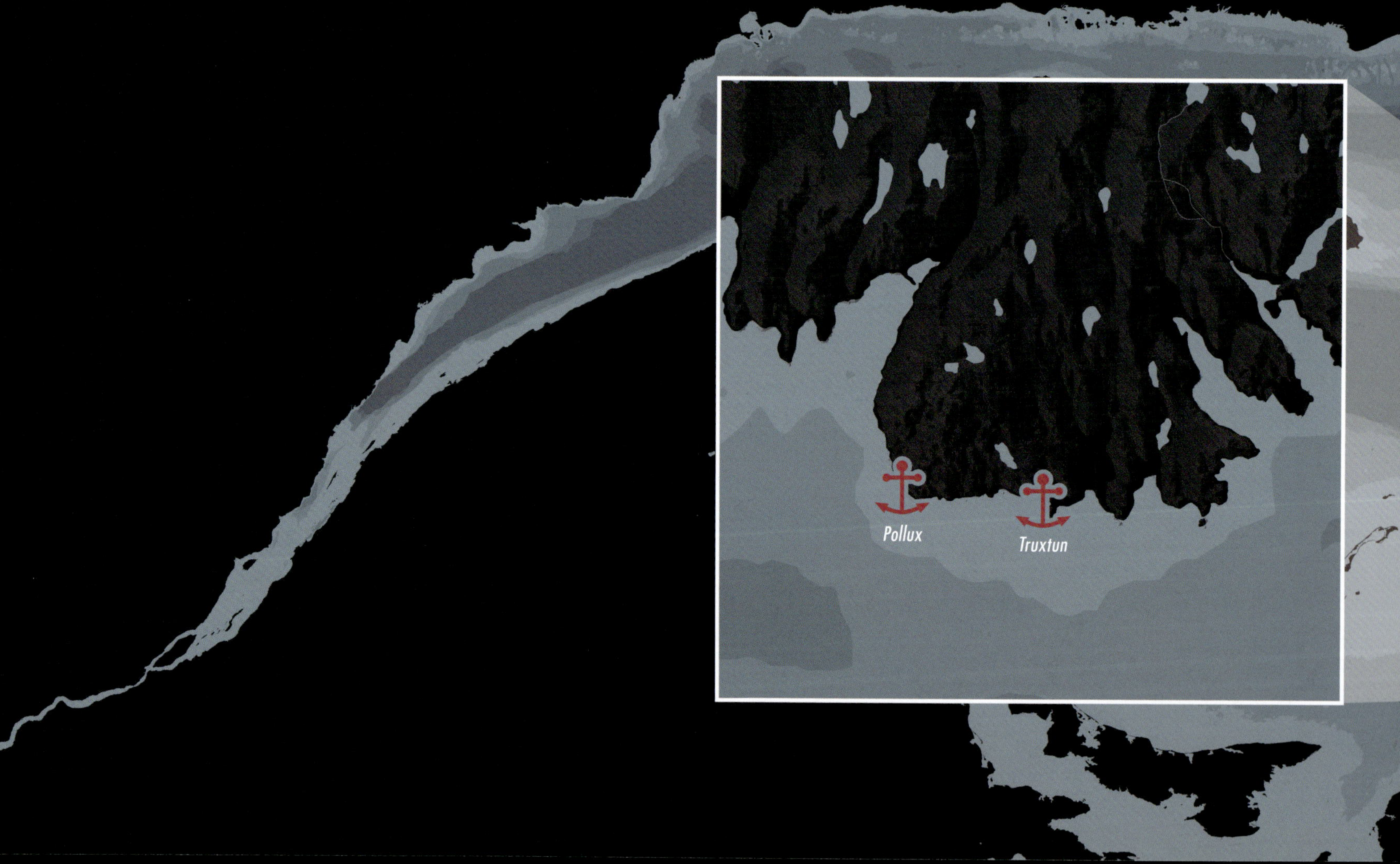

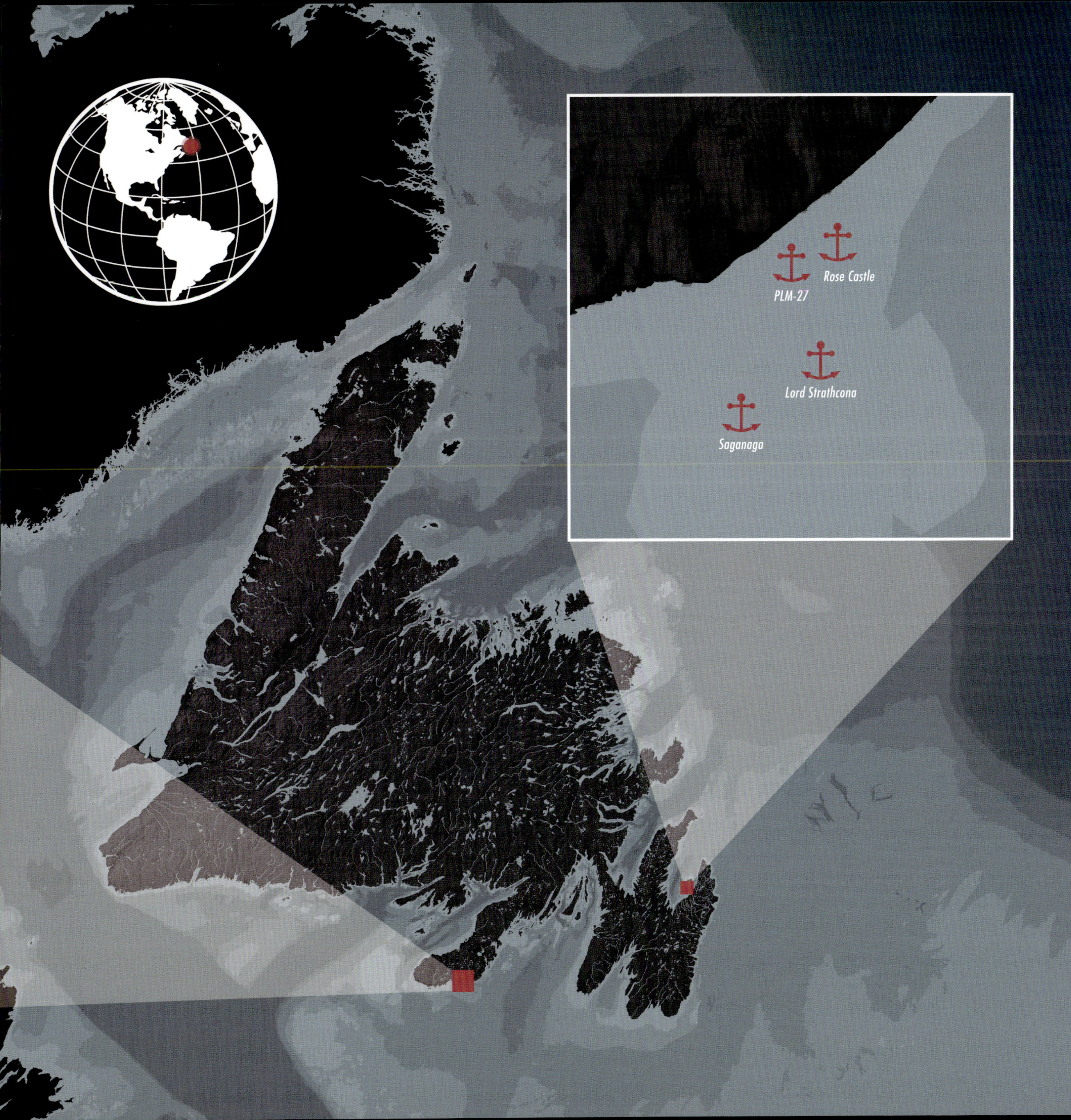
Rose Castle
PLM-27
Lord Strathcona
Saganaga

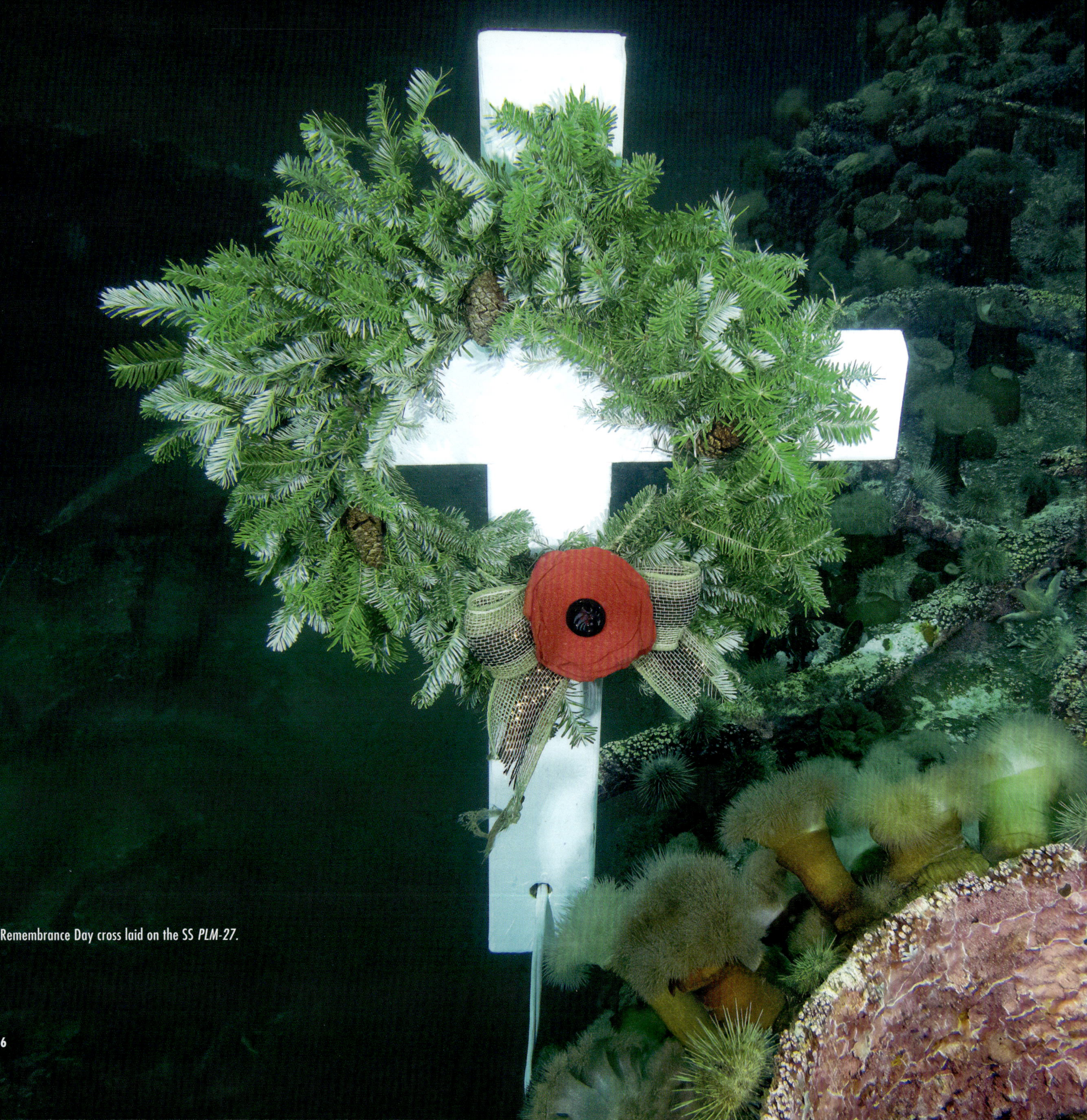

Remembrance Day cross laid on the SS *PLM-27*.

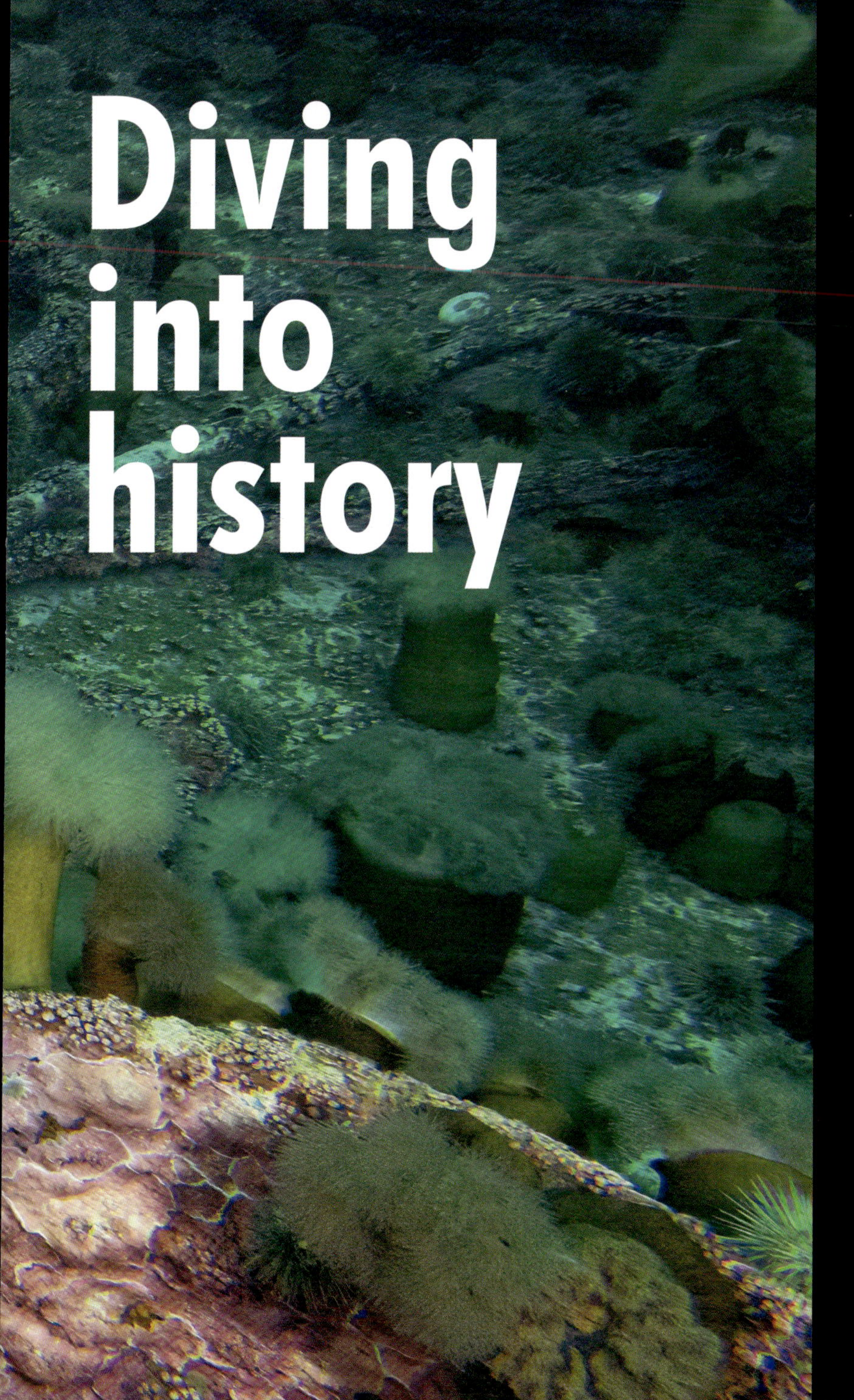

Diving into history

I learned to dive in Nova Scotia in 2007, but I became an avid scuba diver only after moving home to Newfoundland in 2013. Diving the Bell Island shipwrecks captured my imagination and ignited my passion.

Although I grew up in coastal communities across Canada and was a cadet in my youth, I had never known that World War II had come so close to home. When I learned that it came practically to our doorstep, I was eager for the chance to dive any of the war-related wrecks. My first dive to one came on November 11, Remembrance Day. That dive's mission was to place a wreath on the wreck to commemorate the sailors lost. I have been part of many Remembrance Day ceremonies at community cenotaphs but never in a location

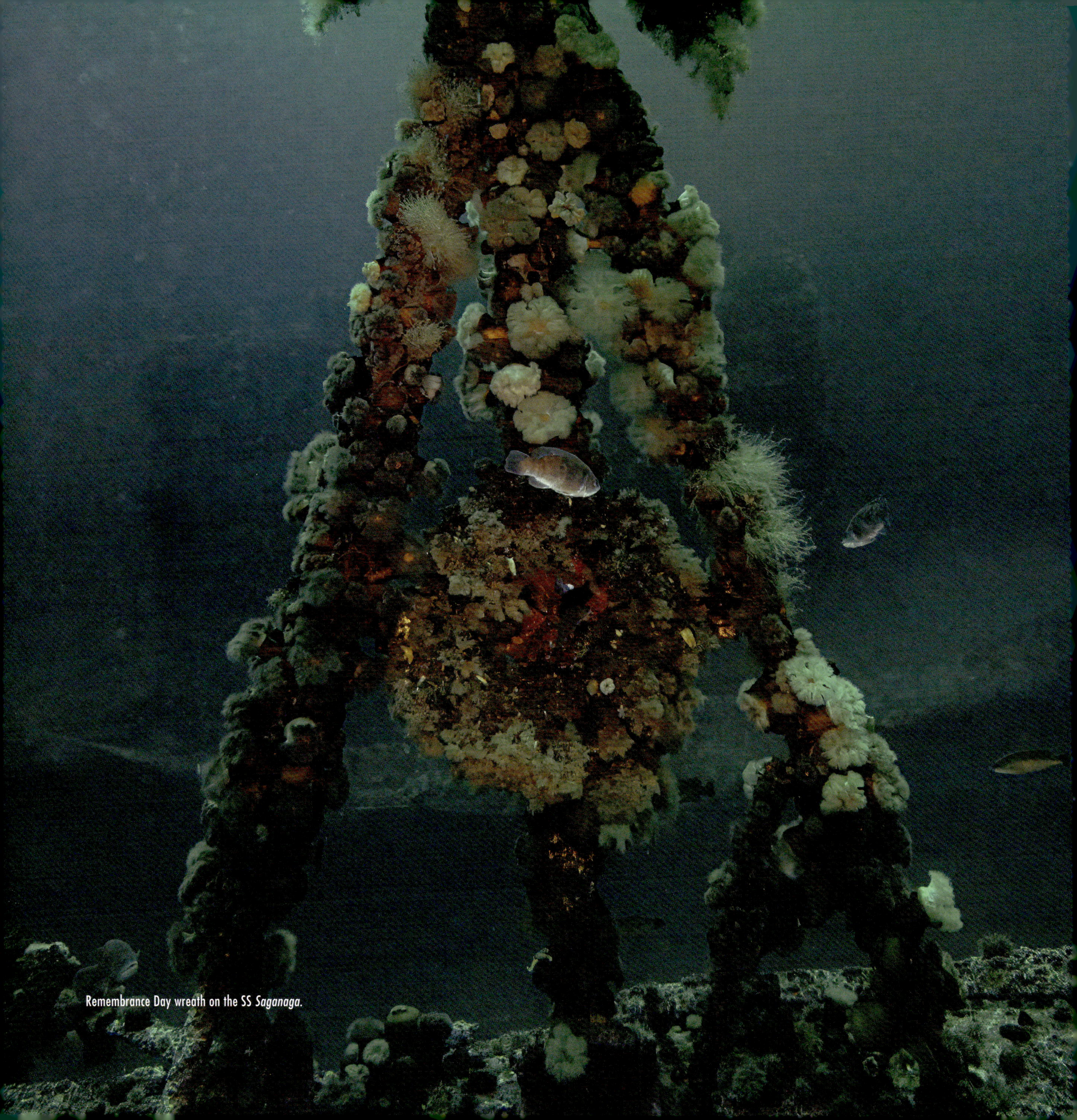

Remembrance Day wreath on the SS *Saganaga*.

touched so directly by the war. I was hooked. That year I completed several advanced scuba courses until I attained my goal of divemaster, helping to teach diving and leading guests on dives.

My mother is the original shutterbug in our family. My own love of photography developed while I was living in Alberta after college, where I spent weekends hiking in the mountains. The only camera I had which could keep up with my diving was an old GoPro, but it did not do justice to what I was actually seeing under water. In 2016, I purchased a dive housing for my camera. Finally, my passion for diving collided with my passion for photography. The aftermath of this collision could best be described as an addiction. To this day, unless I'm teaching others to dive, I am rarely near or in the water without my camera.

In 2017, I travelled to Honduras primarily to become a dive instructor. But I couldn't resist taking an underwater photography course with Ash Kirkham while there, which supercharged the quality of my photographs. Becoming a technical diver extended the depths I could explore with my primary goal of getting a picture of the German torpedo which still lies on the bottom of Conception Bay just off the stern of the *Rose Castle.*

On these pages, I want to bring you under the water to experience my exhilaration each time I explore this part of history.

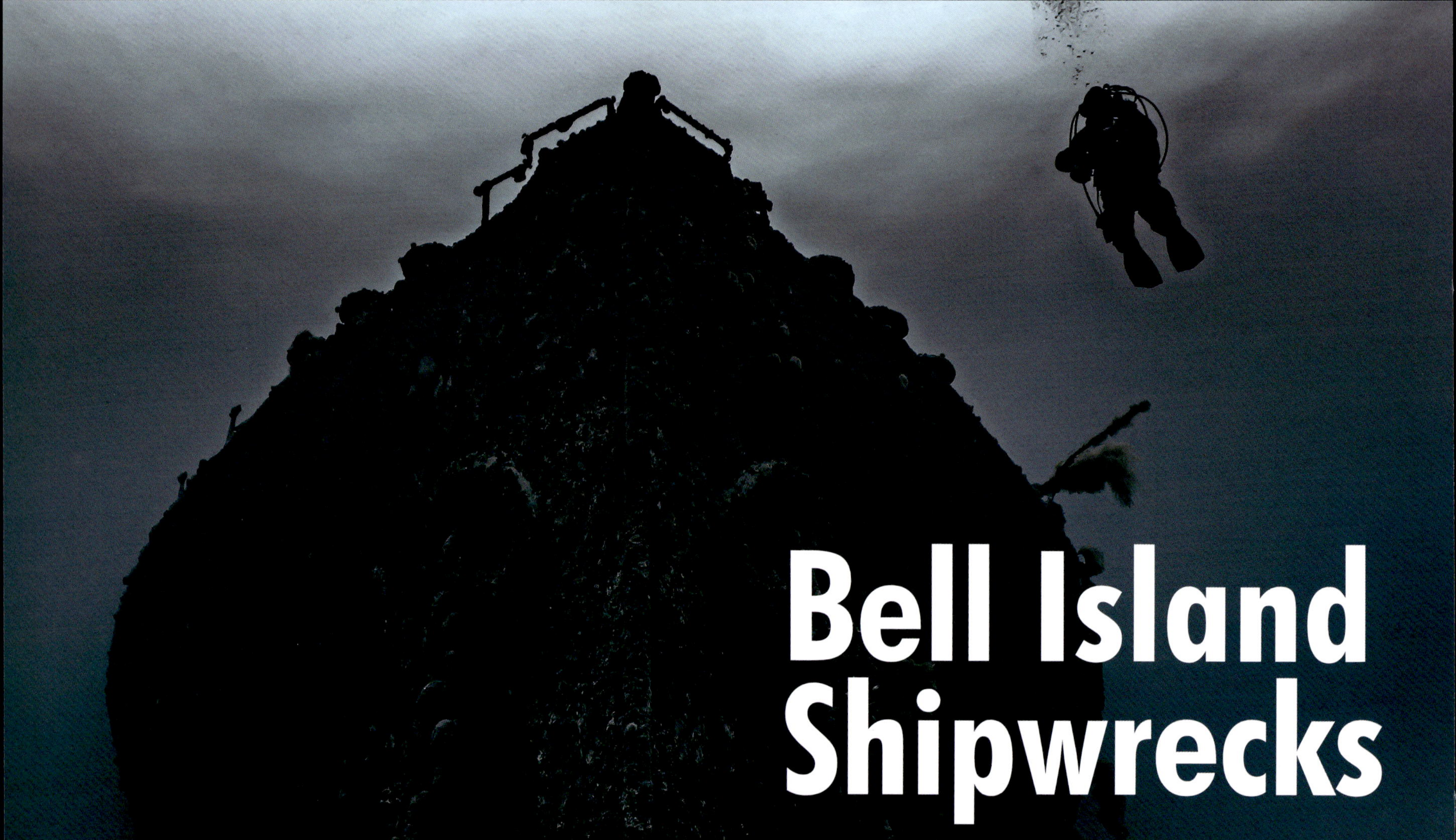
Bell Island
Shipwrecks

The rich culture and history of the island of Newfoundland were forged by the harsh waters of the Atlantic Ocean. Much of the tangible evidence of this maritime legacy rests forever at the bottom of the ocean—countless shipwrecks are found along the coast, many dating to the earliest seafarers. Those artifacts that haven't been lost to time can still be found by those who brave the frigid temperatures and venture to the ocean's depths.

This book is dedicated to exploring World War II shipwrecks in the waters around the island of Newfoundland, as they exist nearly 80 years after coming to rest below the waves. Join me for a diver's-eye view of these ships.

DIVING THE *PLM-27*

This journey begins just off the coast of Bell Island, where four ships were sunk by German U-boats during World War II. These iron ore carriers were part of the Merchant Marines, a civilian fleet that supported the military during the war. The carriers were transporting sought-after iron ore from the Bell Island mines; the ore was a key component in Germany's war machine leading up to the war. The freighters were fully loaded when they were struck by torpedoes, causing them to sink straight to the ocean floor. There they sit, in an upright position, unusual for shipwrecks.

Thanks to the remarkable preservation provided by the

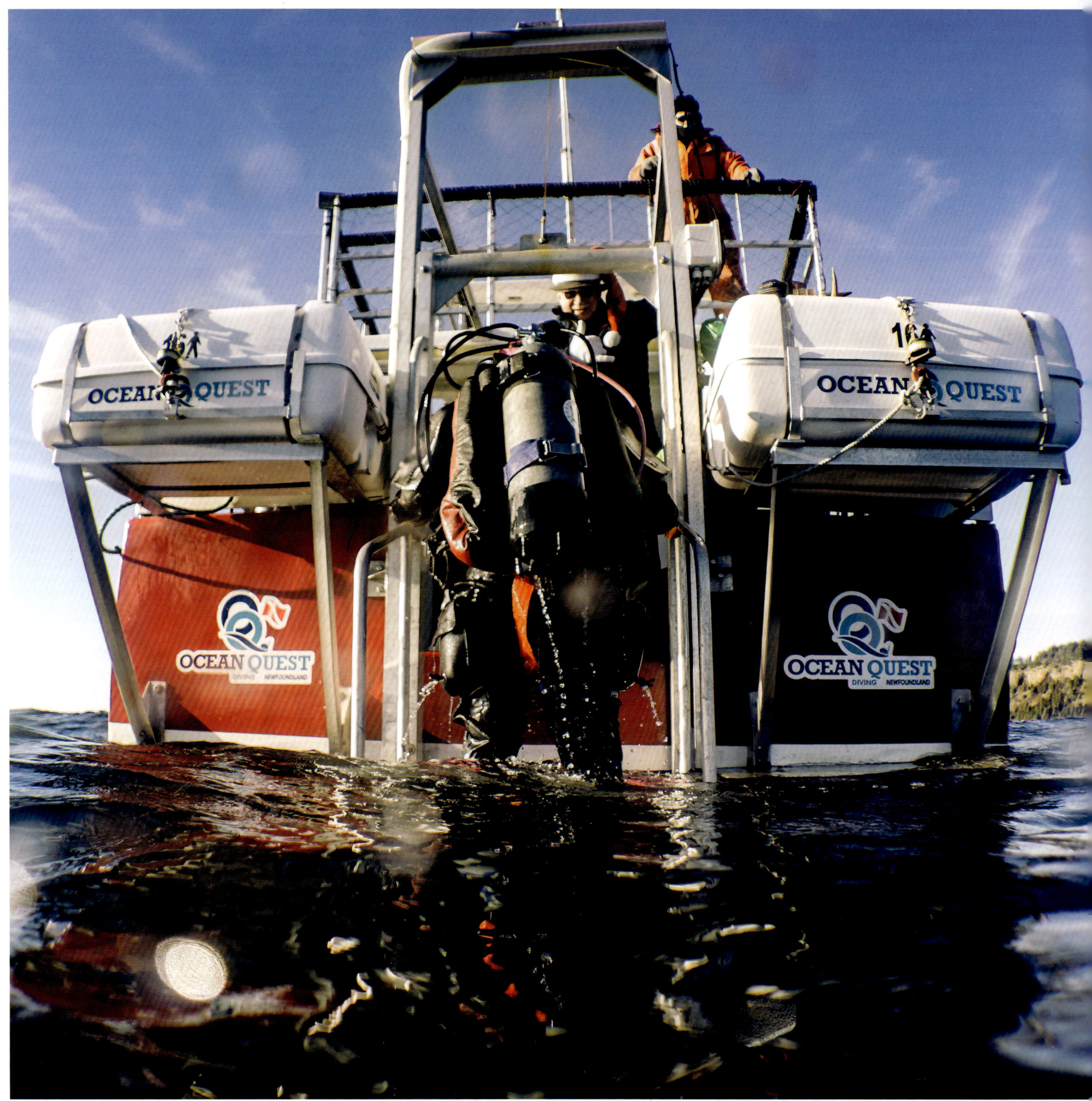

OCEAN QUEST
OCEAN QUEST
OCEAN QUEST
DIVING NEWFOUNDLAND
OCEAN QUEST
DIVING NEWFOUNDLAND

chilly, dark, and relatively calm Atlantic waters near Bell Island, these wrecks have become a must-visit destination for wreck-diving enthusiasts. Divers who travel from around the world to explore these wrecks tend to arrive as guests and leave as family, a testament to the renowned hospitality of the people of Newfoundland. Many choose to stay with the local dive operator Ocean Quest Adventures, which operates dive trips out to the wrecks on their boat the *Mermaid*. Over the years, Ocean Quest has acted as a curator for the protection of these historical monuments.

On board the *Mermaid*, the divers gather for a dive brief from the divemaster, who describes the wreck's history, important information, and highlights. Everybody is in a different state of readiness: some have just finished putting on their warm dive thermals and look like they're ready to explore the Arctic; others are in full drysuits and look ready to explore Mars.

After the briefing, dive buddies pair up, carefully develop their dive plans, and complete final gear checks. Standing at the back of the boat, bent under the weight of their equipment, divers move around only when absolutely necessary. Each diver has donned thousands of dollars' worth of gear, including suits containing technology originally designed by NASA (the metal dry suit zippers were originally designed for space suits) and tanks affixed to their backs with all the air they will breathe once they are under the water.

Divers look down at the ocean surface with wonder—curiosity and excitement never go away, no matter how many dives they've done. What will *this* adventure bring?

A step off the boat and into the water brings a brief sense of freefall. Once wet, the team comes together at the side of the boat. They pull themselves along a guideline, hand over hand, until they arrive at the mooring line. While floating on the surface and holding on to the mooring line, each diver takes a moment to ensure that their air supply is adequate before exchanging a final OK descent hand signal with their dive buddy.

As the divers gaze into the murky depths, the rope vanishes into the blue—or, as is the case in these waters, more of a green hue—and beckons them deeper. The water is typically hazy, not unlike the fog that gives St. John's its nickname of Fogtown. Descent rate is regulated by controlling the air inside the drysuit. Divers pinch their noses to equalize the pressure in their ears with the pressure of the increasing depth—similar to the feeling experienced by many passengers on an airplane's ascent.

As the divers pass depths of 20, 30, 40 feet, the wreck ... the wreck gradually takes shape, emerging like a ghostly apparition. Eventually it solidifies, giving way to the reality of a massive ship that once sailed the world's oceans. It is impossible not to be astounded by the wreck's sheer size and filled with awe for the long-lost vessel.

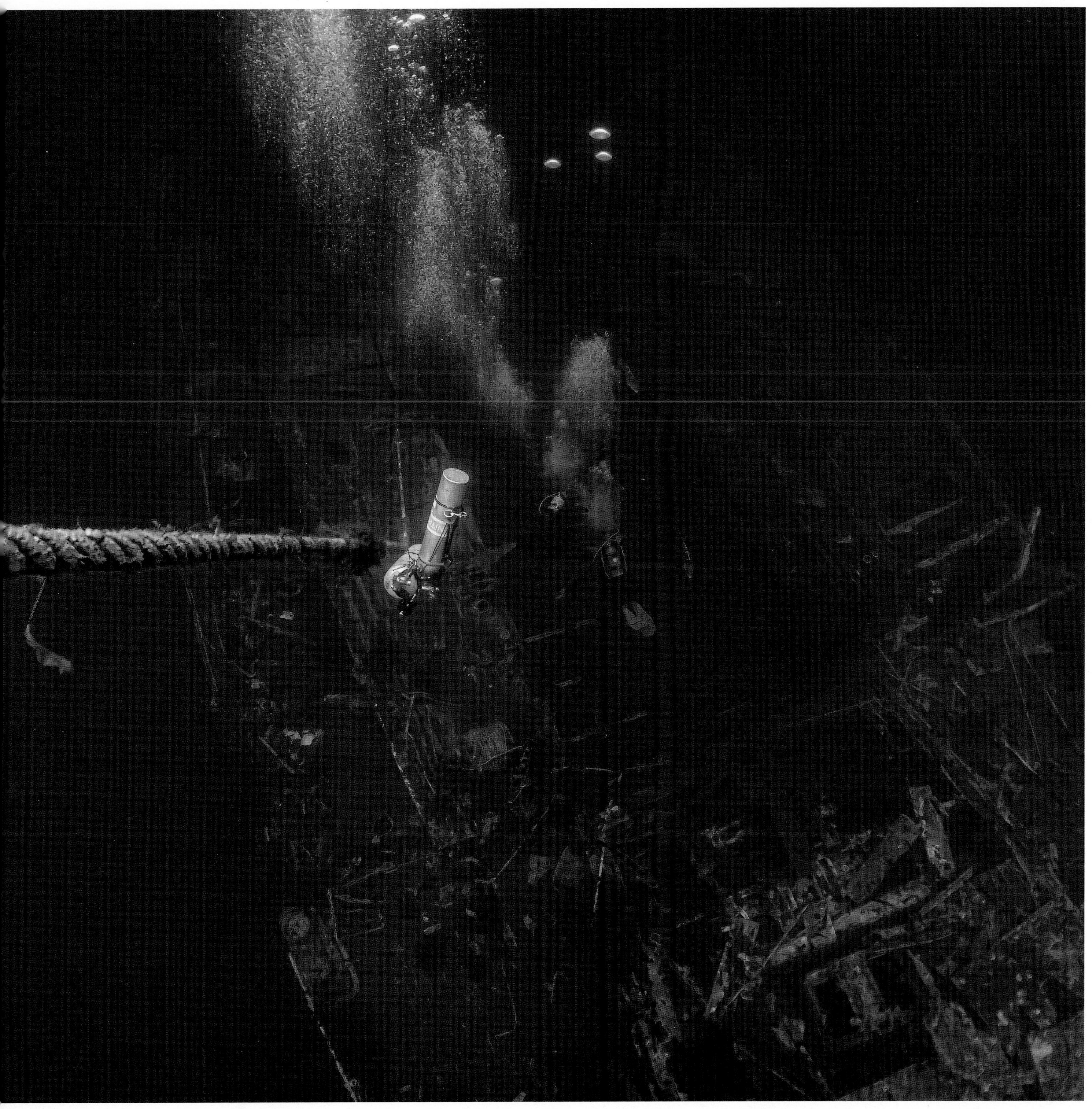

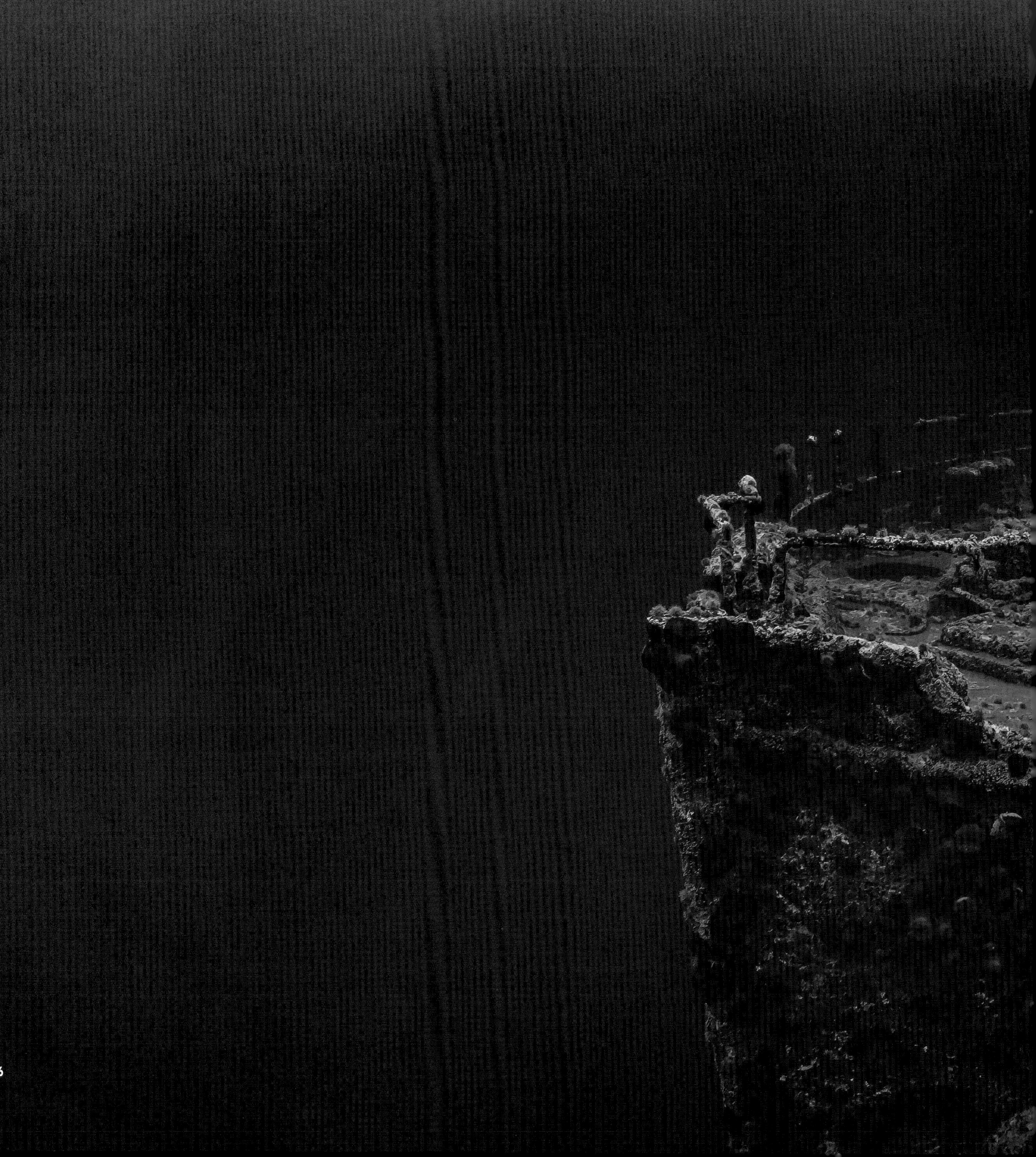

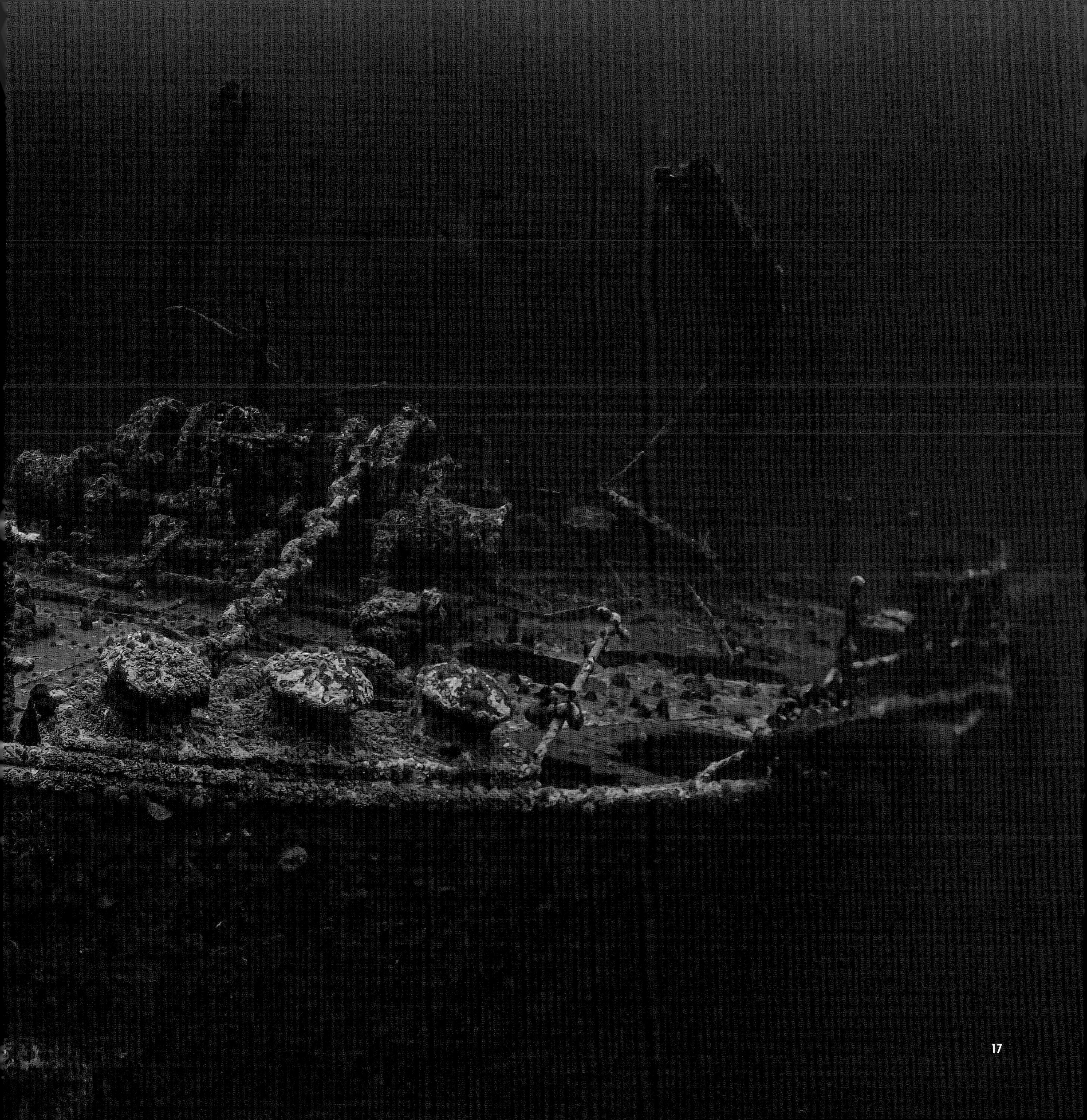

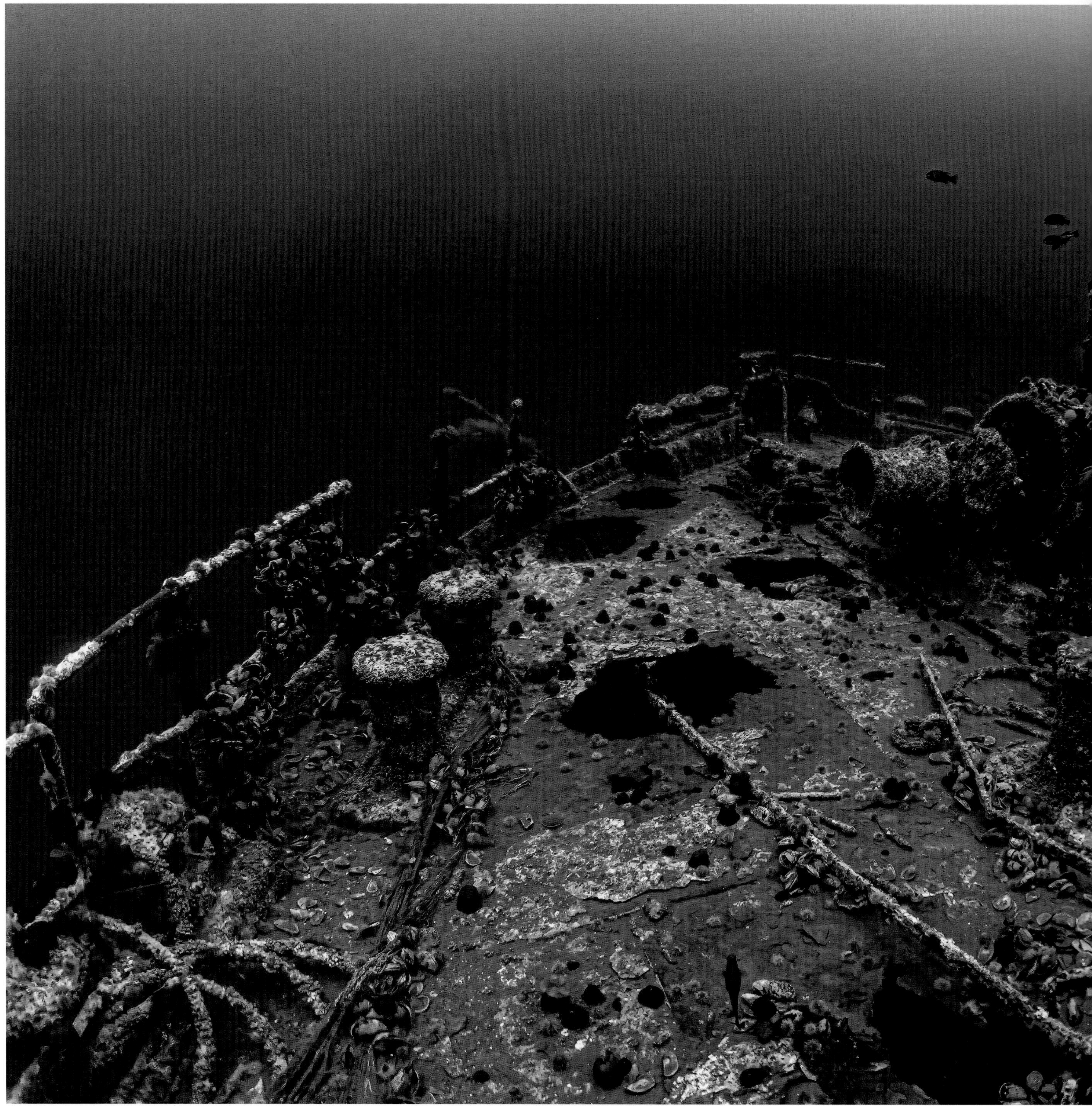

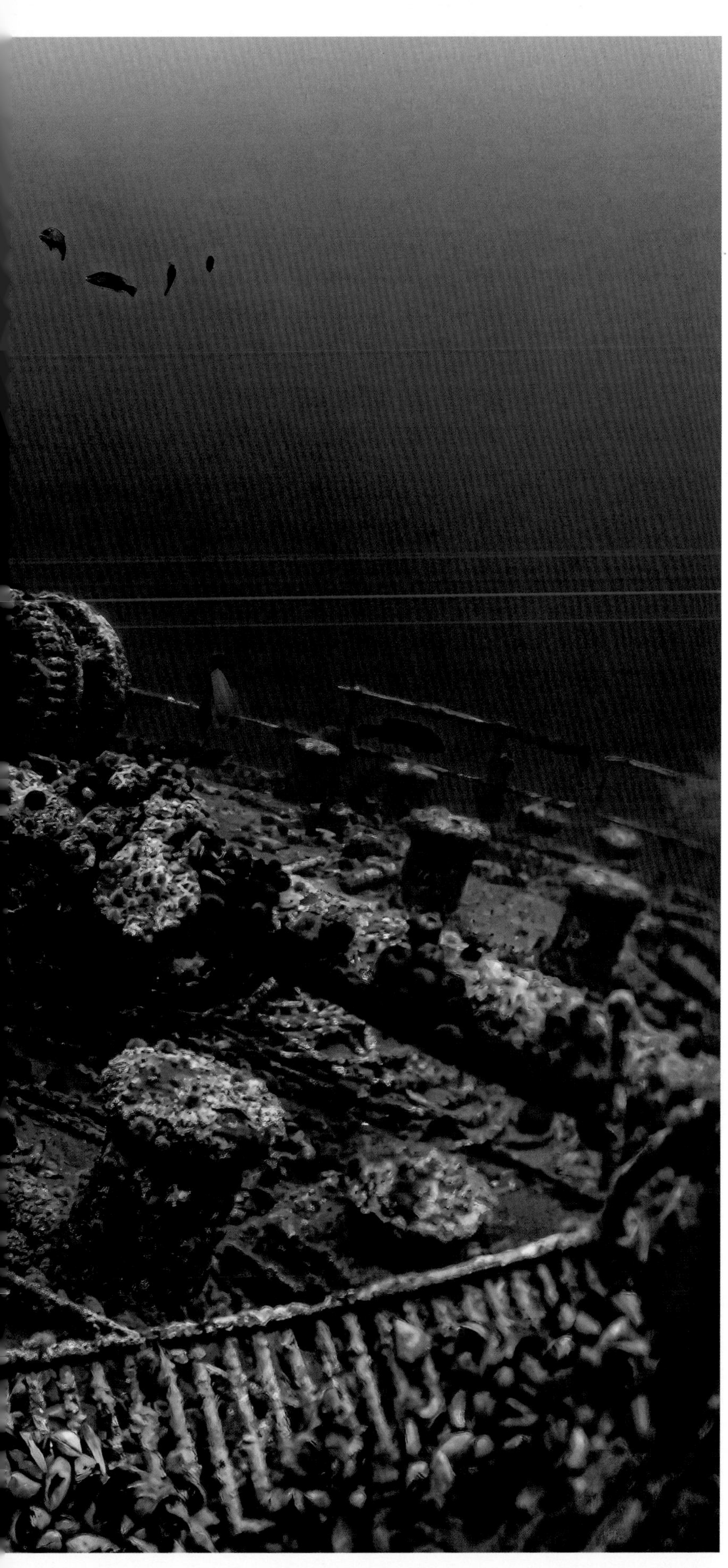

The sea, once it casts its spell, holds one in its net of wonder forever.

—JACQUES COUSTEAU

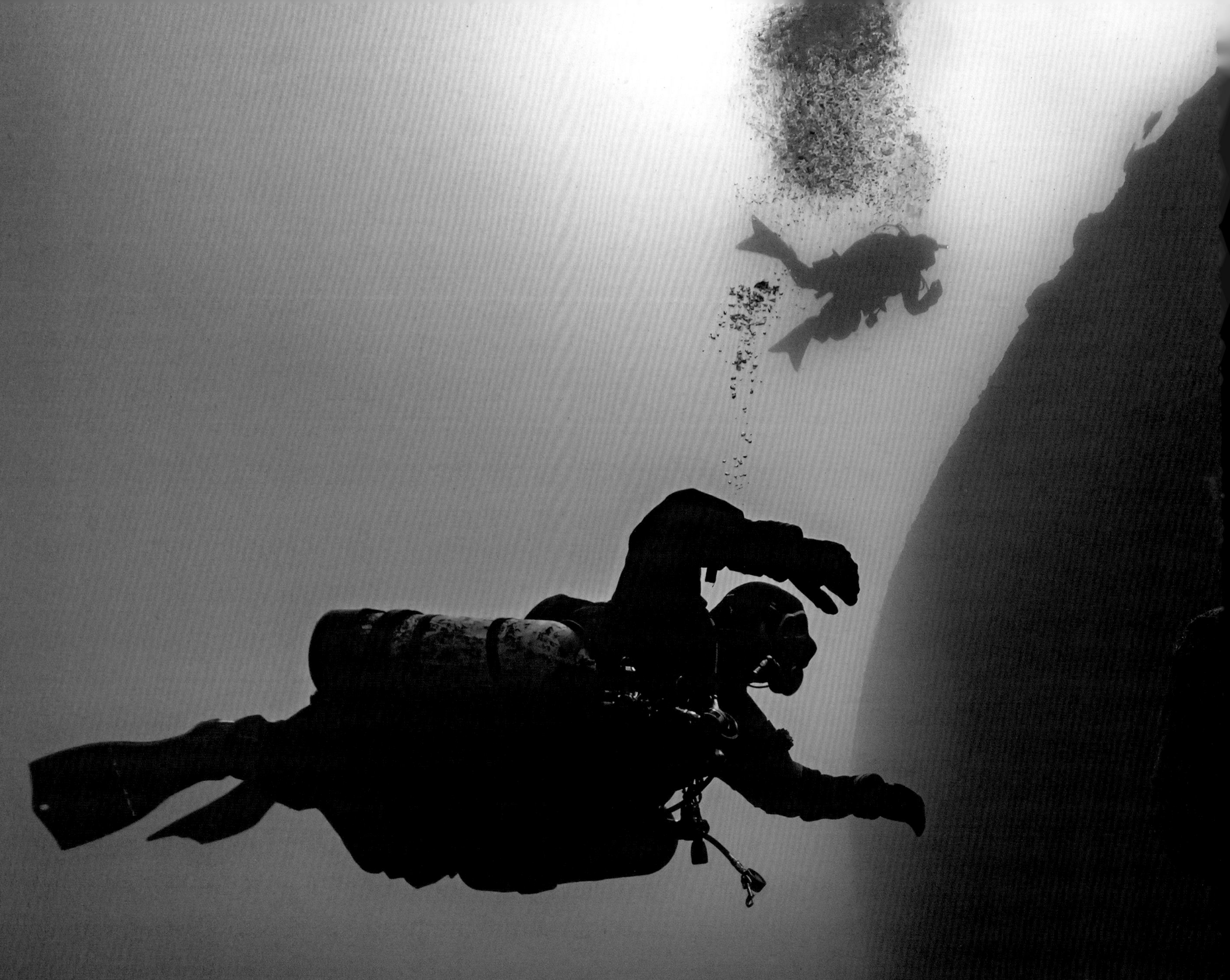

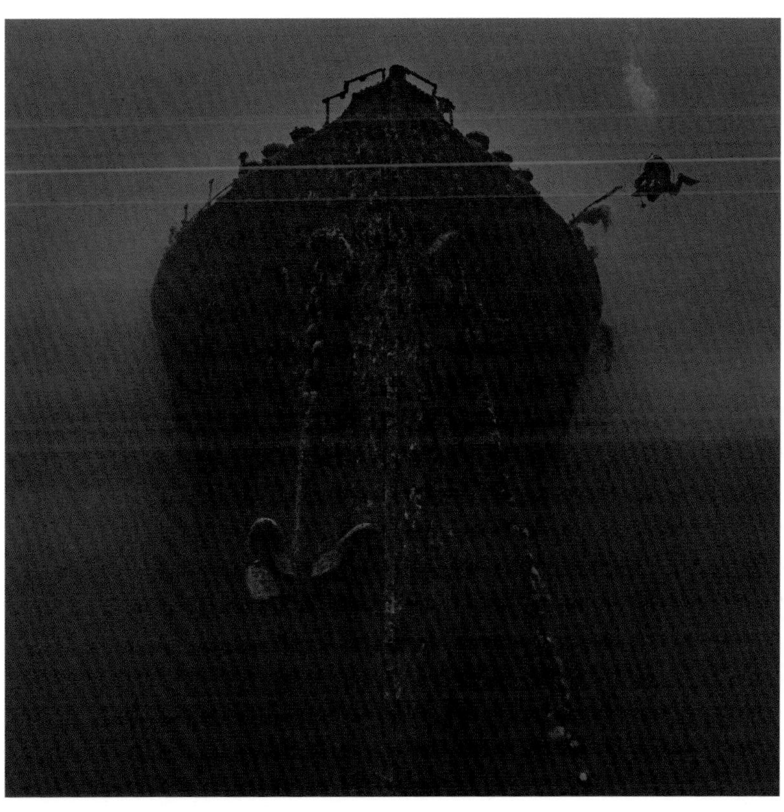

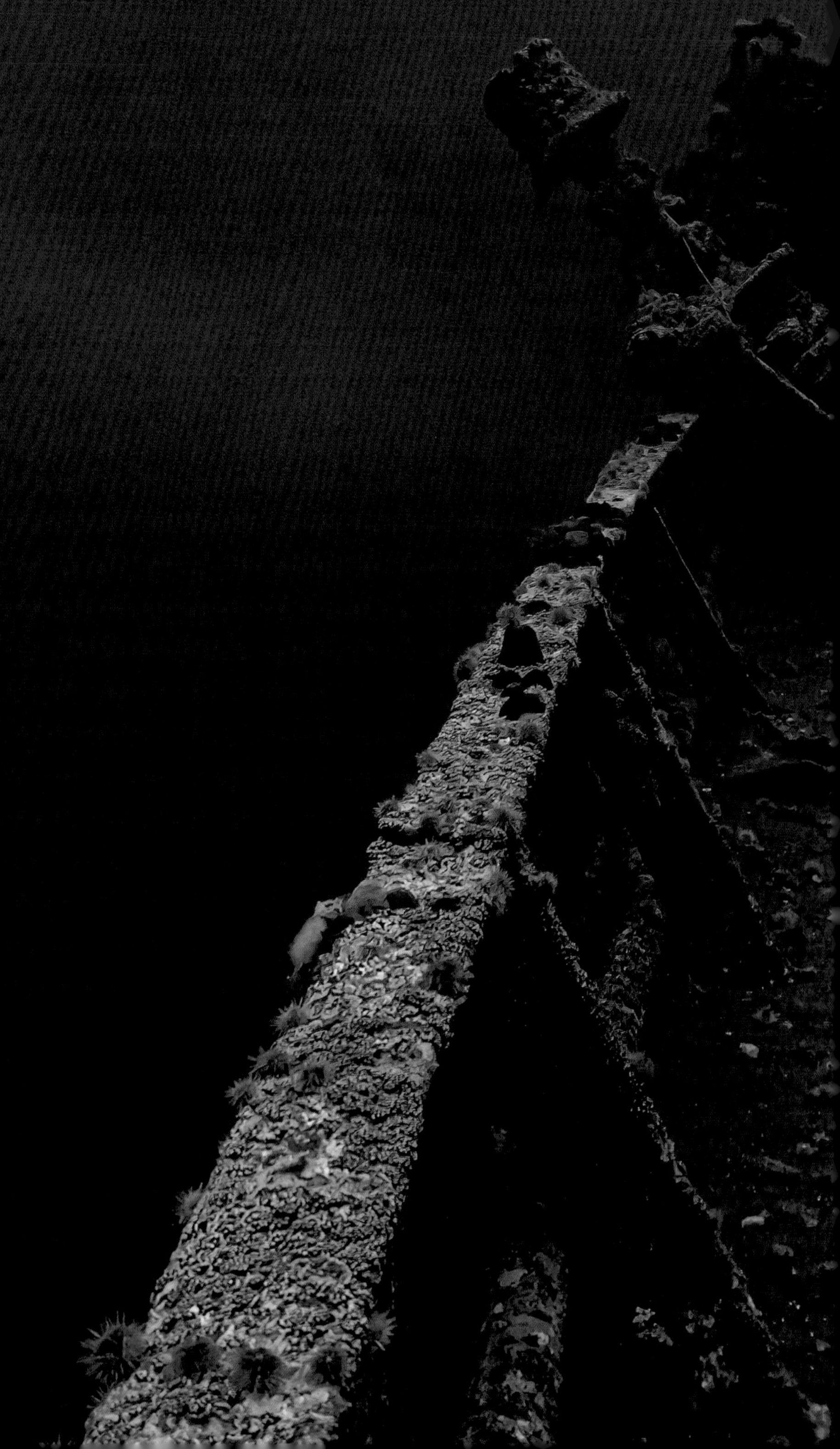

The shallowest of the four wrecks is the *Paris, Lyon, Marseilles 27* (also known as *PLM-27*), a Free French Naval Forces ship. The bow sits at roughly 45 feet deep, with the main deck resting at 60 feet deep and the ocean bottom 35 feet below that. As the divers peer beyond the bow, the enormity of the 400-foot-long ship is evident, as the structure disappears into the murky distance.

Descending to 65 feet reveals the ship's anchor hanging off the starboard side. Looking upward at the bow from this vantage point inspires an appreciation for the engineers and craftsmen who built the vessel.

Back at the bow, it's time to explore the ship. Sticking to the portside, divers pass by the first cargo hold,

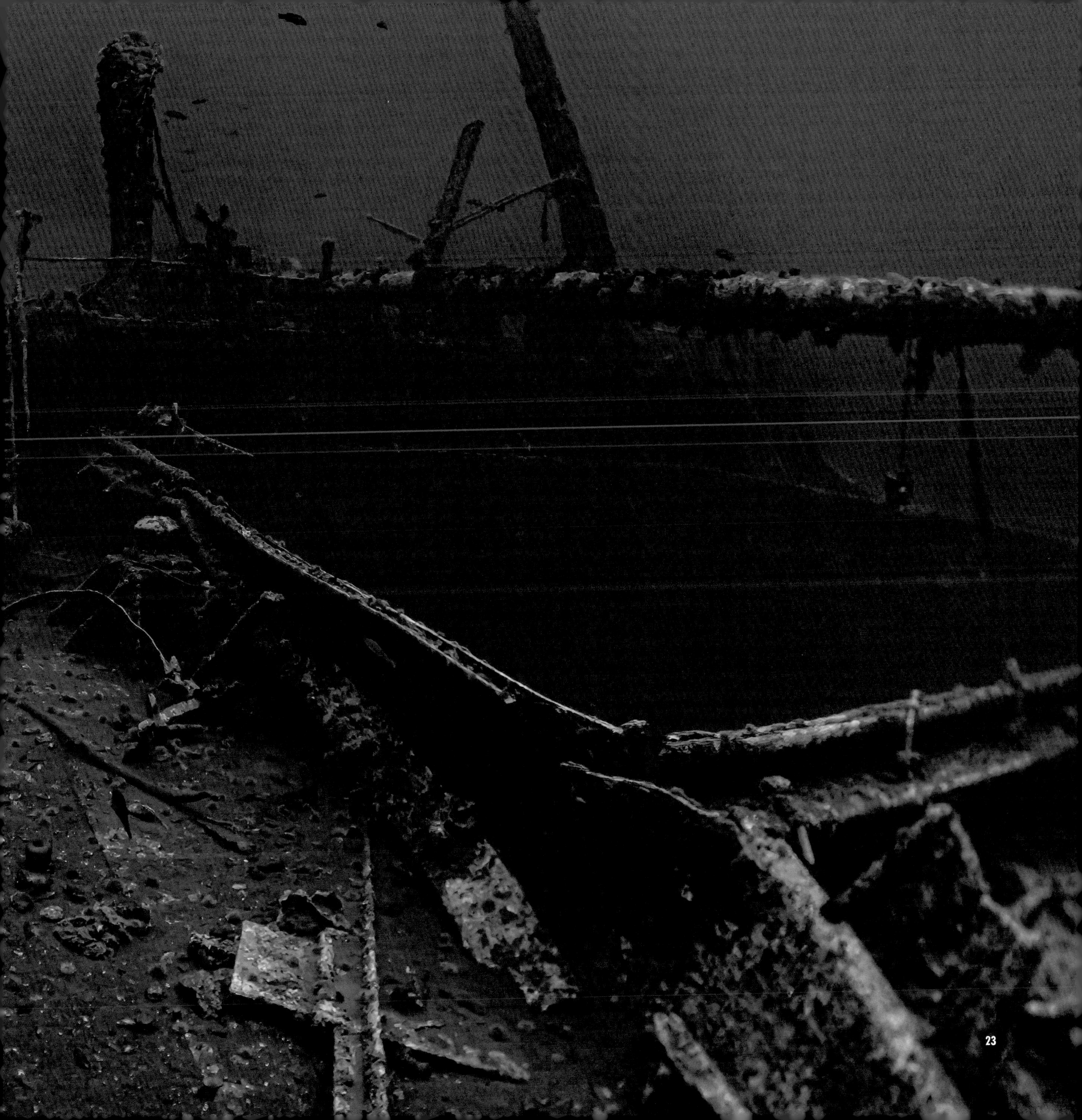

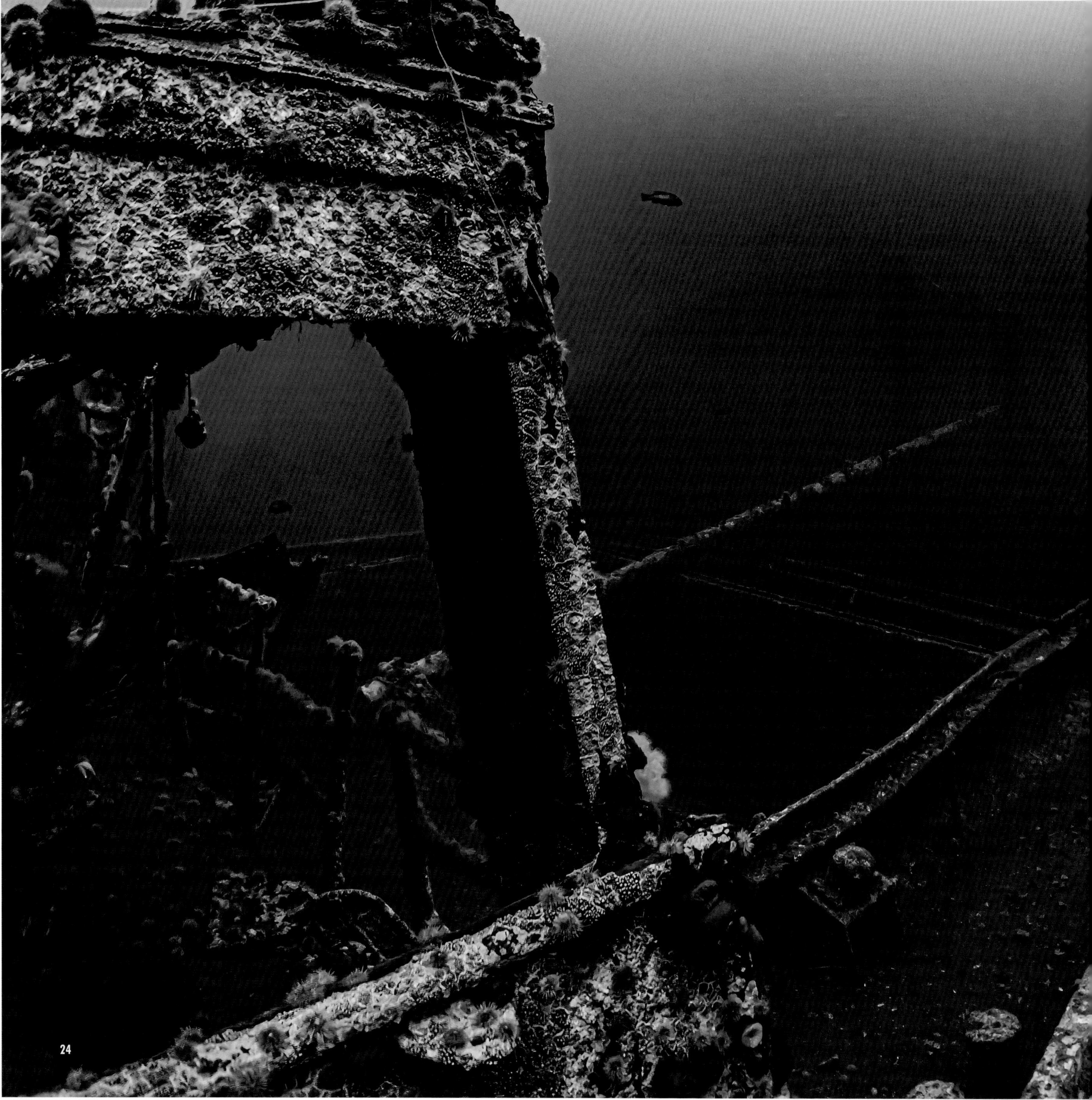

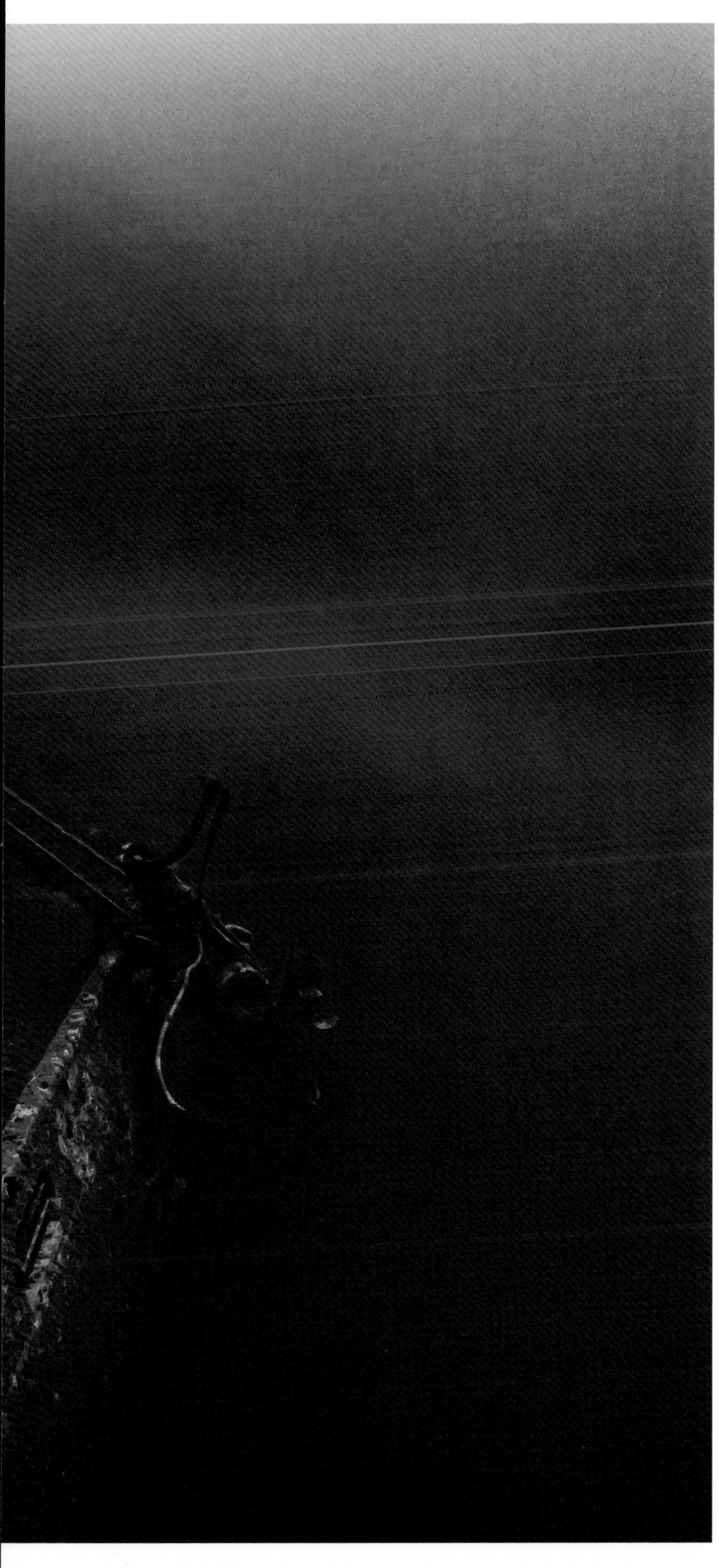

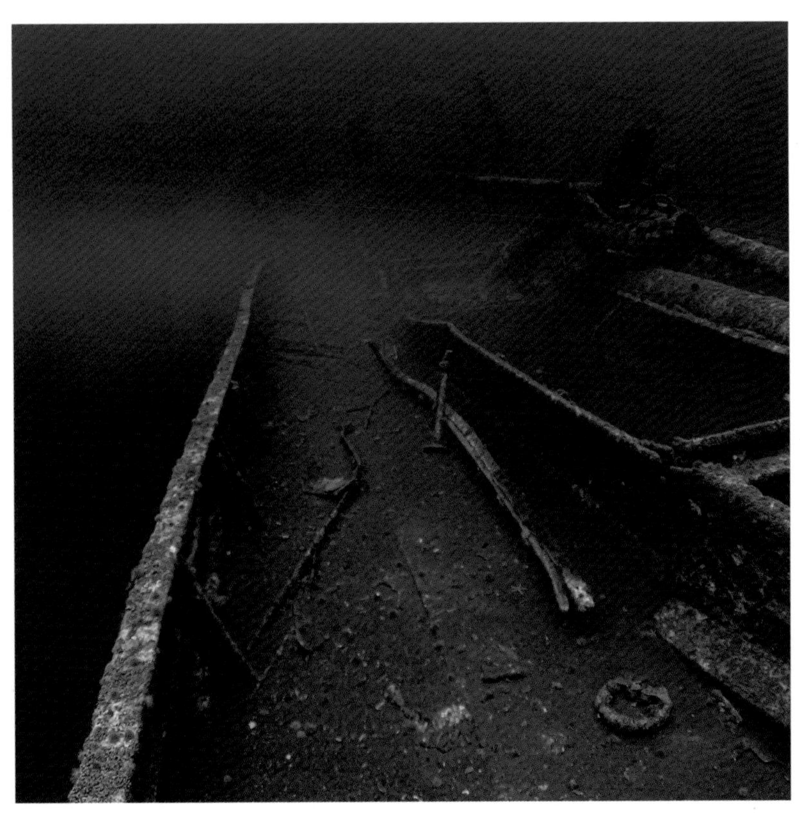

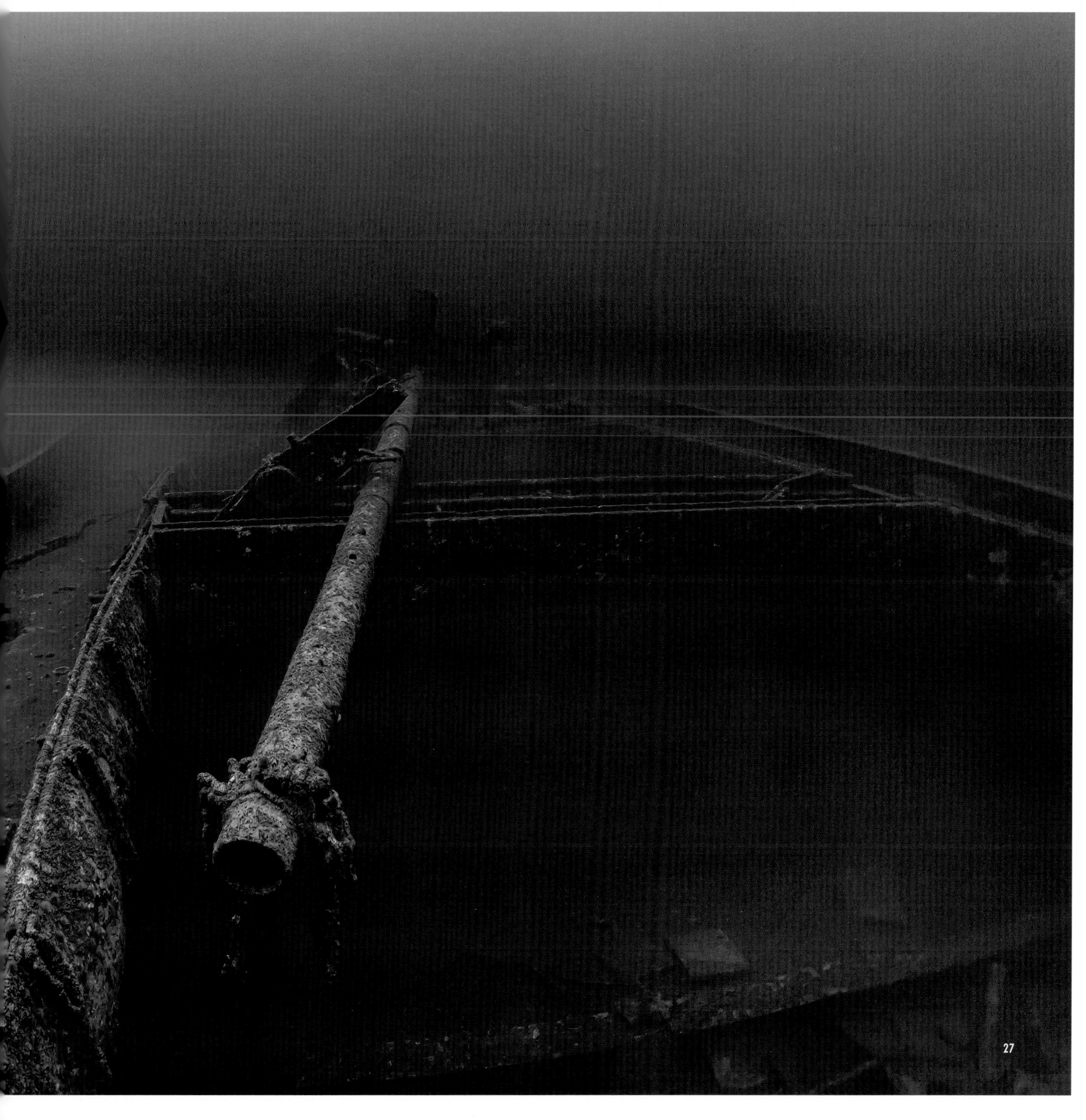

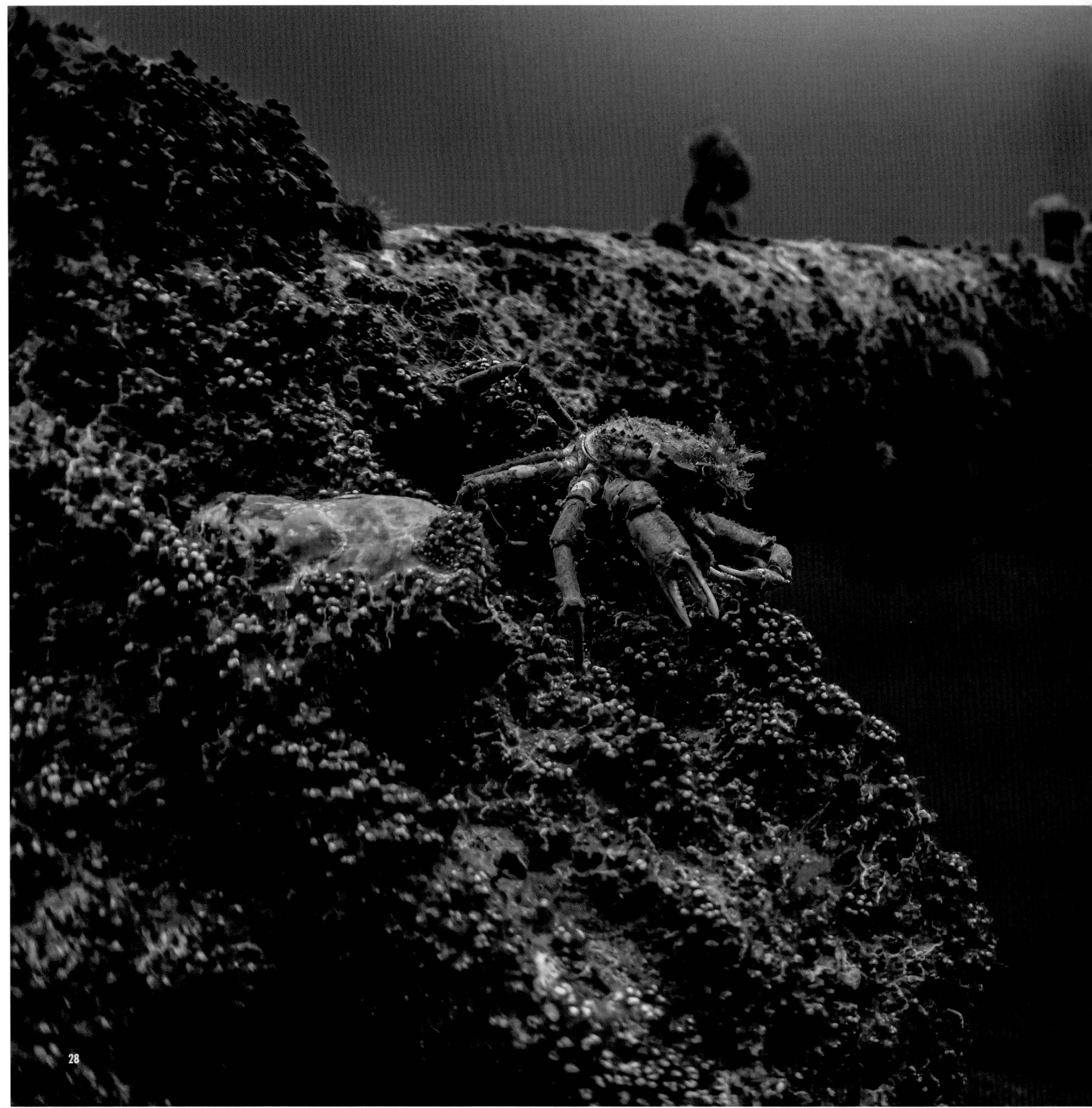

These wrecks have over time become artificial reefs providing habitats for numerous creatures.

peering down to see that it is filled with rusty iron ore rocks—the reason the ship came to Bell Island. Farther ahead, the superstructure that once towered above the main deck lies in ruins. Canadian Navy divers demolished the superstructure after the war to rid the busy waters of the potential collision risk.

At the aft of the ship is a machine gun lying on its handle, with the barrel pointing toward the surface. As it blends in with the deck, most divers don't notice it. Dipping over the edge of the ship offers a view of the massive propeller and rudder below.

Descending to the top of the propeller at 80 feet reveals its considerable size. The gap between the rudder

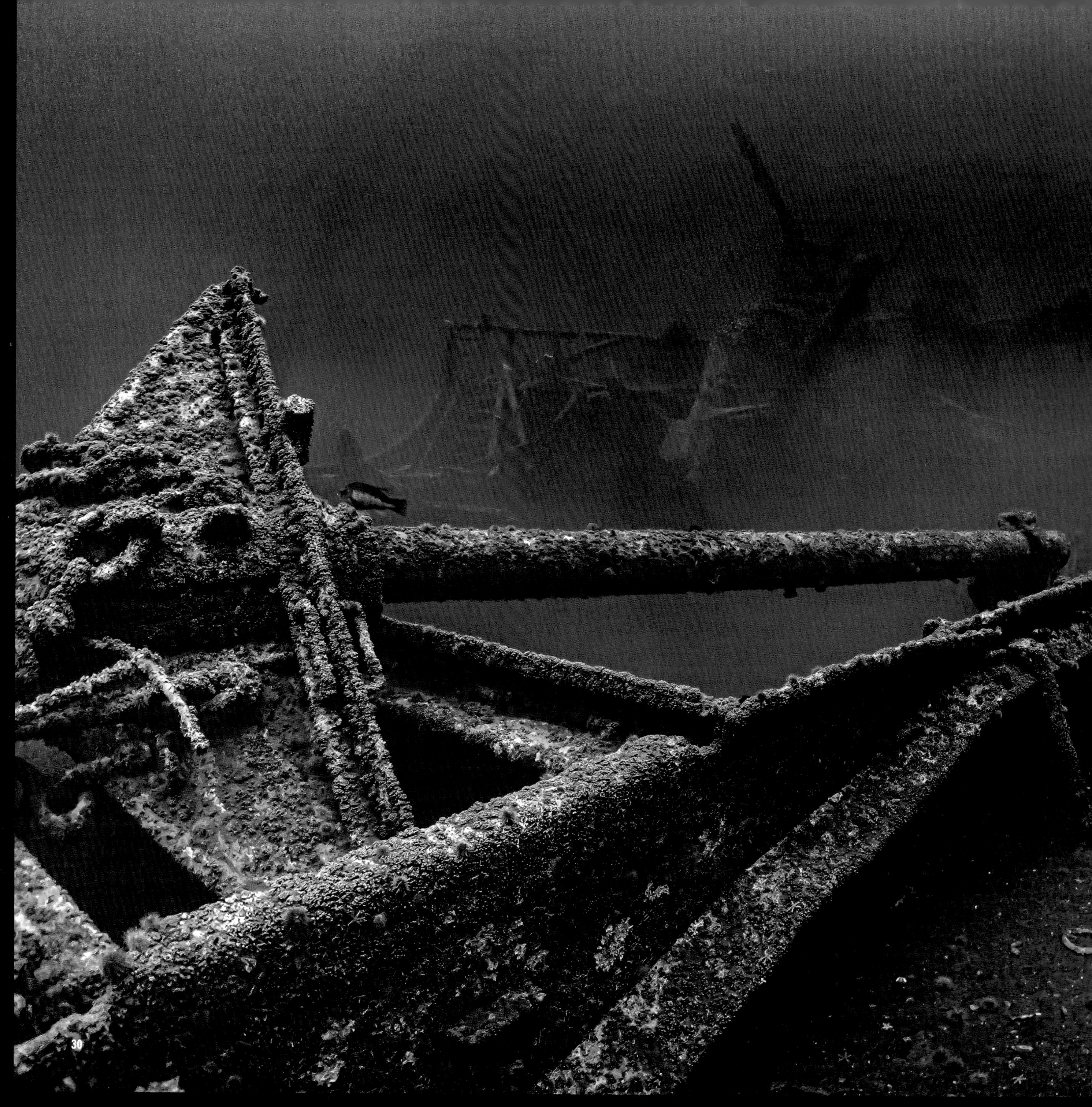

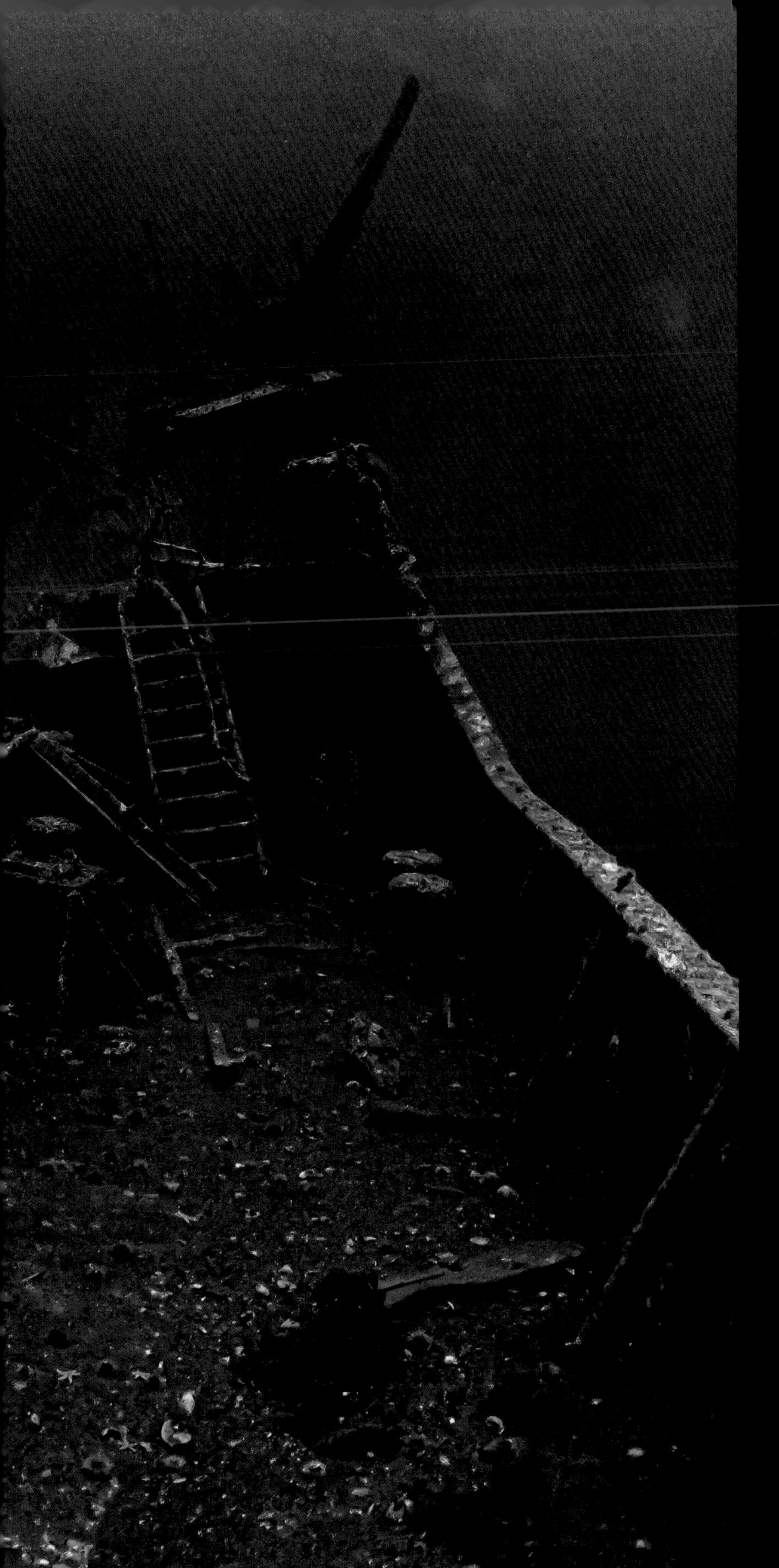

Every time you dive, you hope you'll see something new—some new species. Sometimes the ocean gives you a gift, sometimes it doesn't.

—JAMES CAMERON

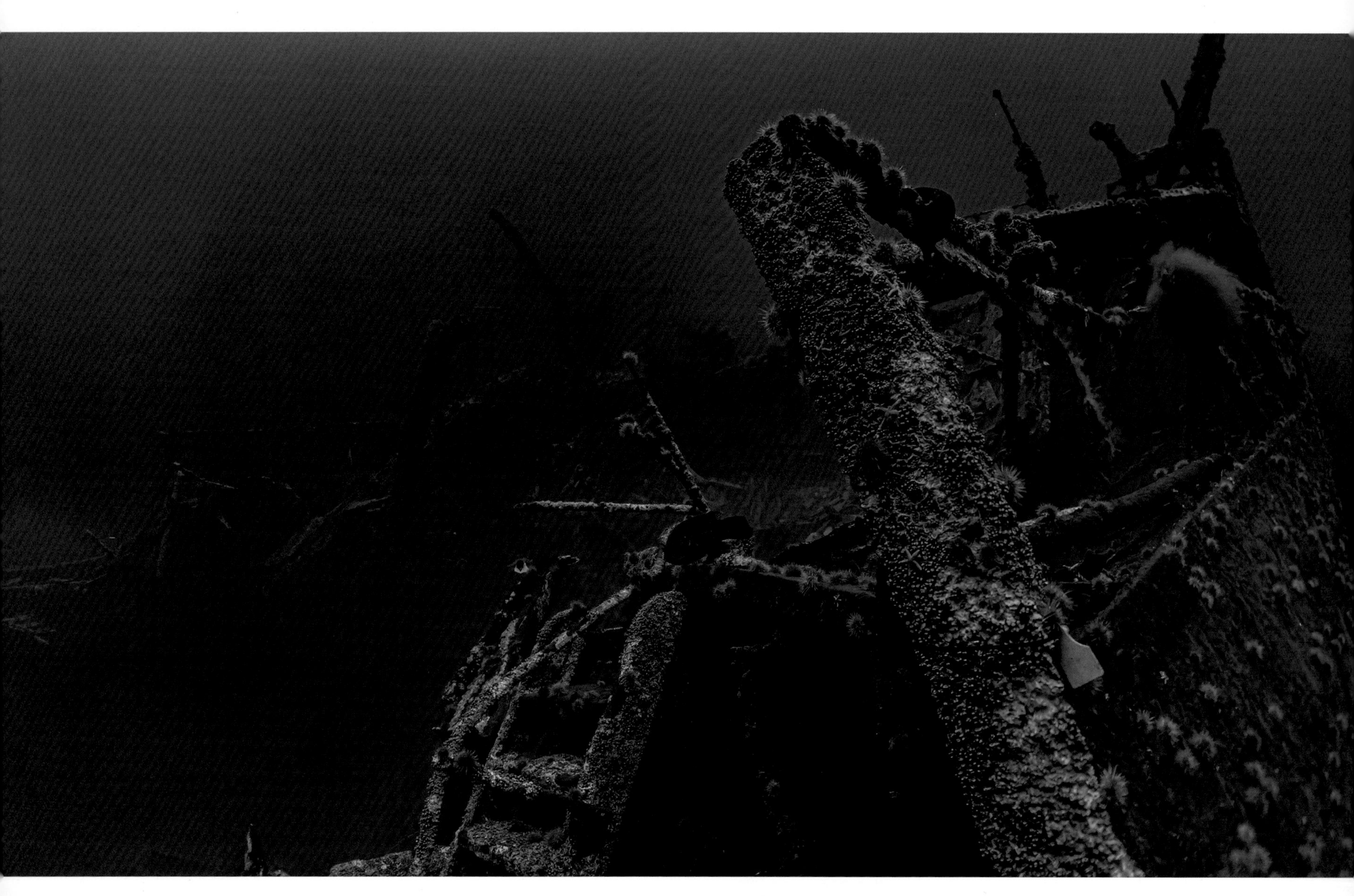

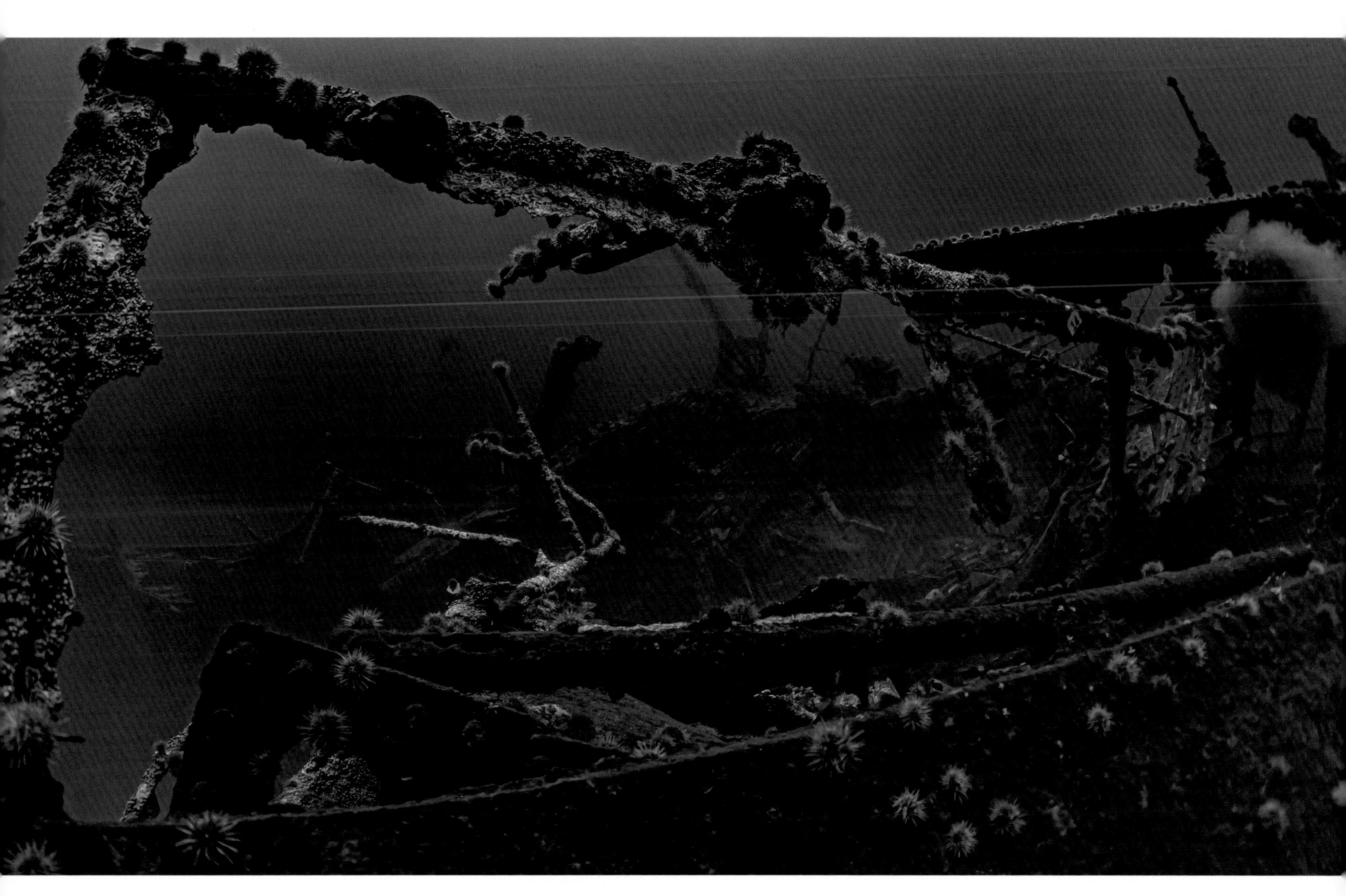

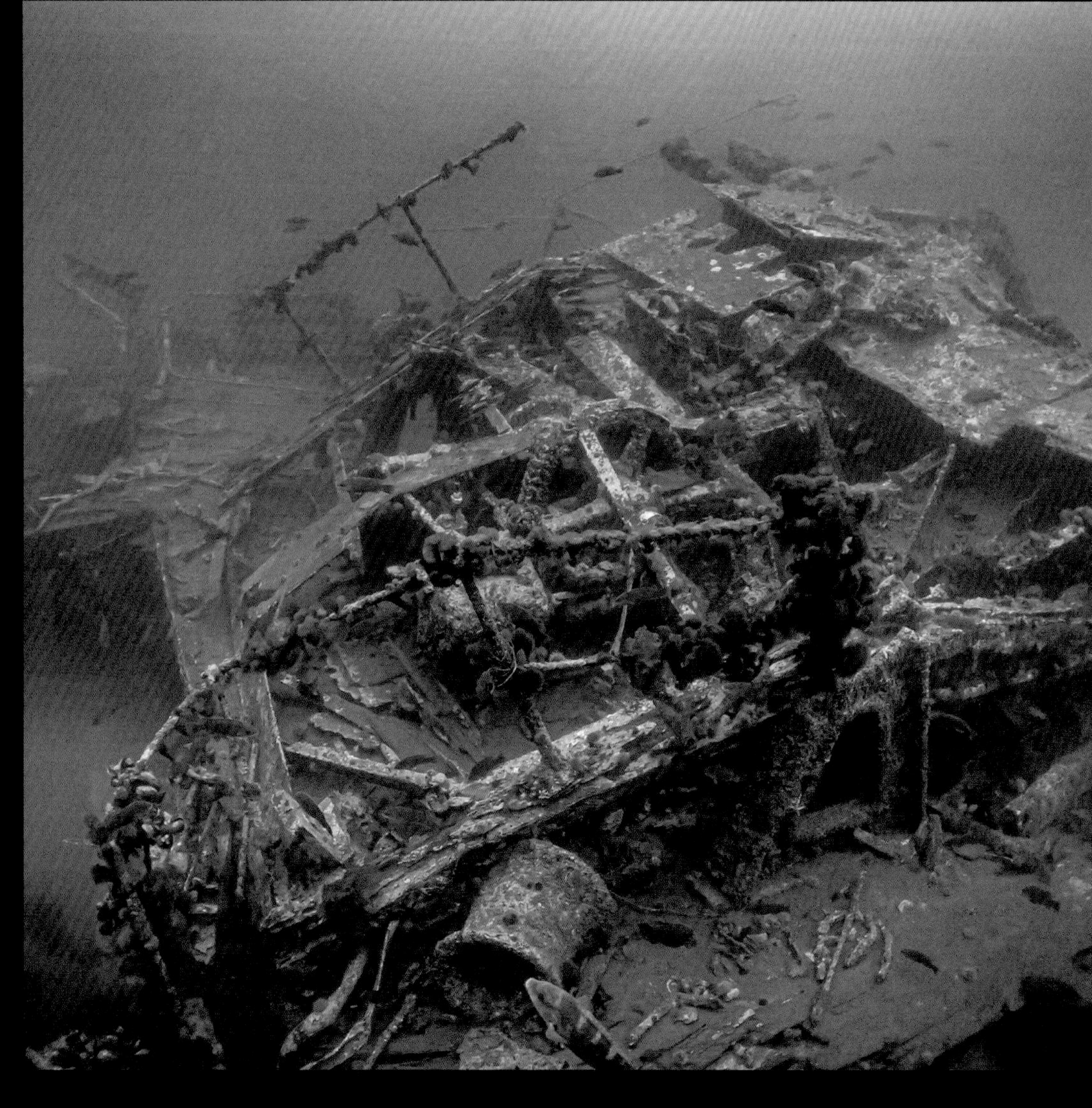

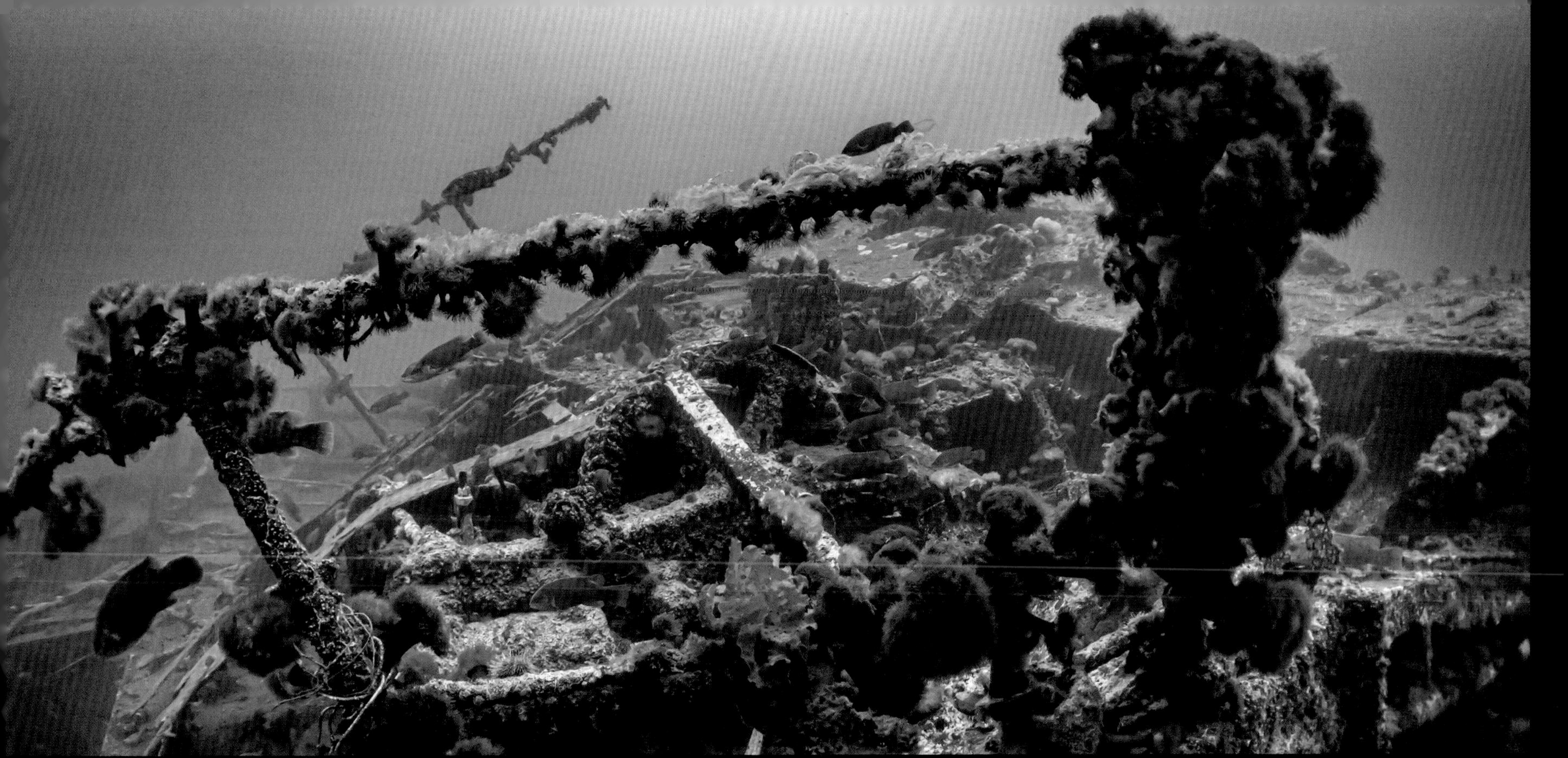

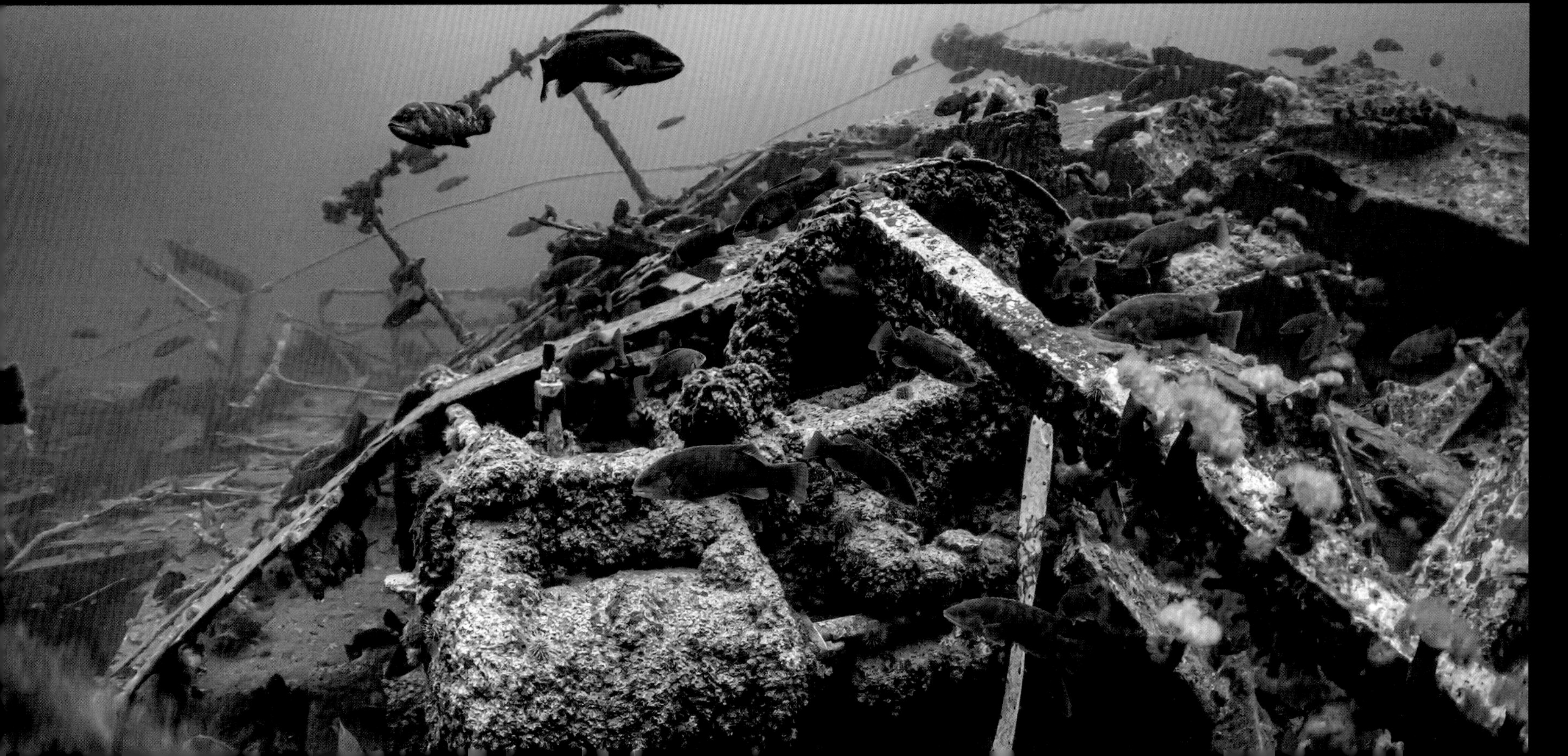

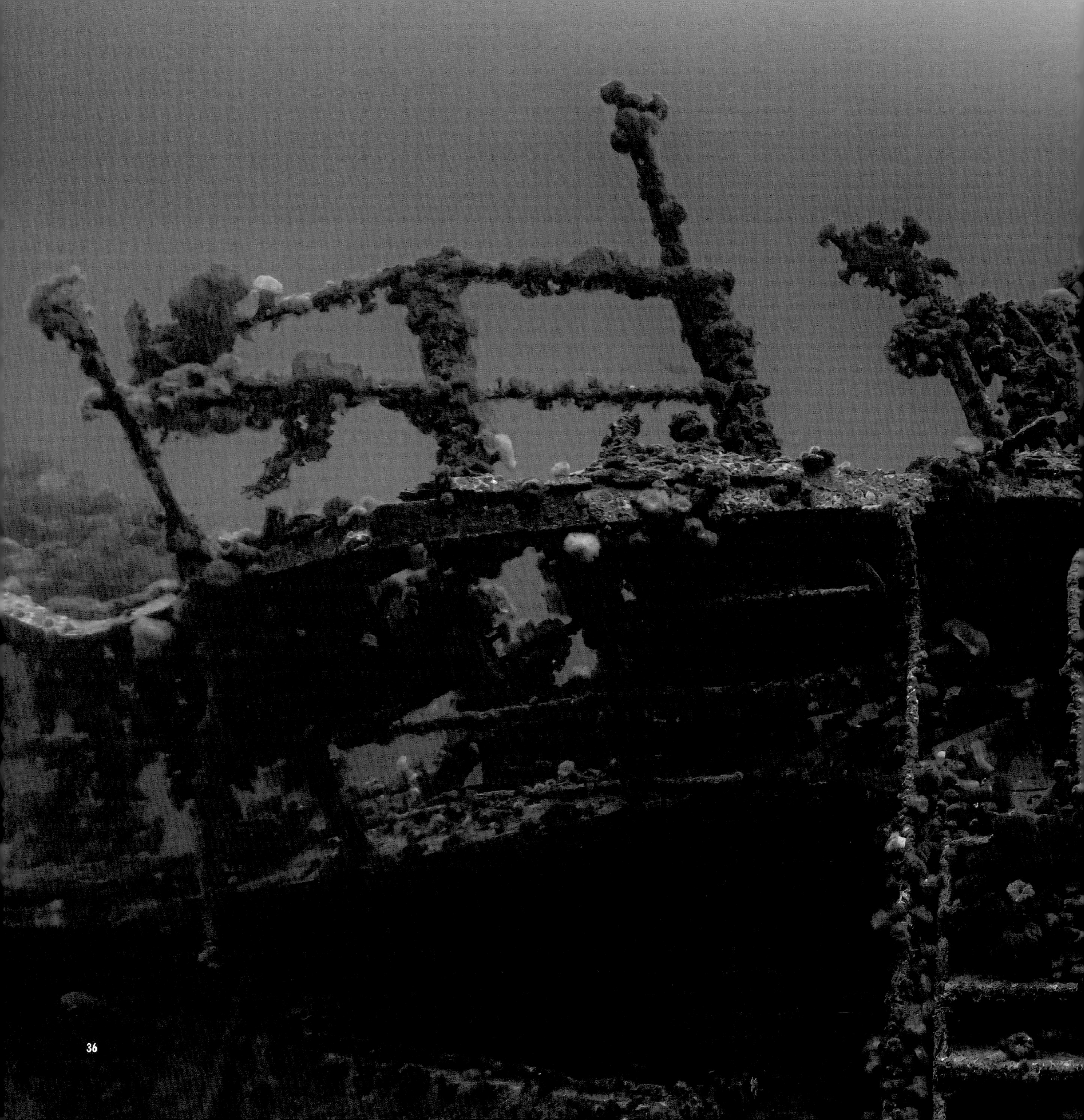

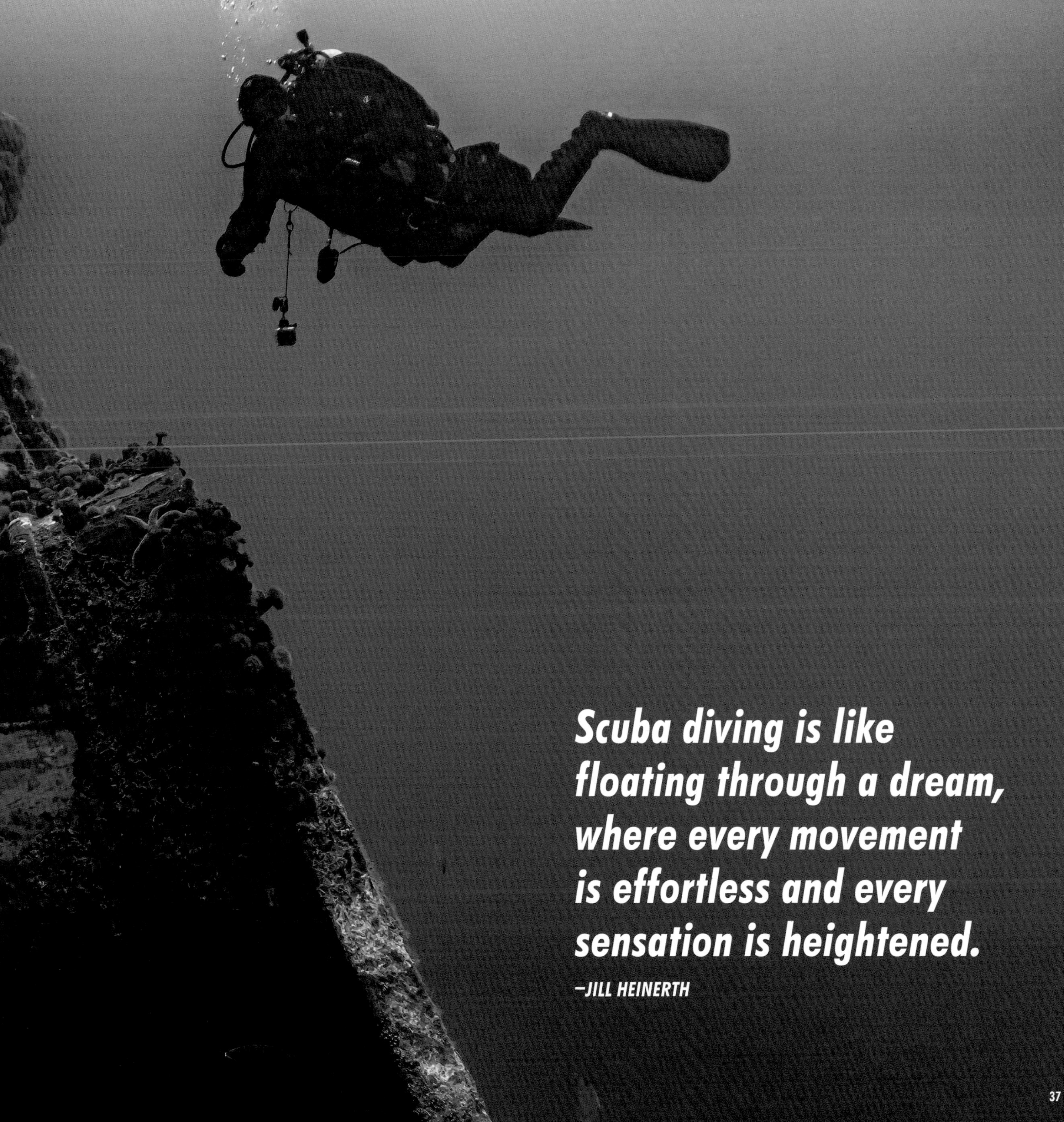

Scuba diving is like floating through a dream, where every movement is effortless and every sensation is heightened.

—JILL HEINERTH

and propeller is large enough to swim through; those who have the opportunity to do so feel incredibly fortunate.

Moving along the midship brings divers to the torpedo impact site. The twisted metal heap is a stark reminder of the impact of war on oceans. Iron ore from Bell Island was used to create the U-boats, which eventually returned to wreak this havoc and destruction. The abundance of artifacts exposed by the impact is a marvel for the diver with a keen eye.

At about this point, it's time to turn around. An air supply check shows about one-third of the tank's air has been used up. That allows another third to return to the mooring line and boat above, and a healthy third in reserve for

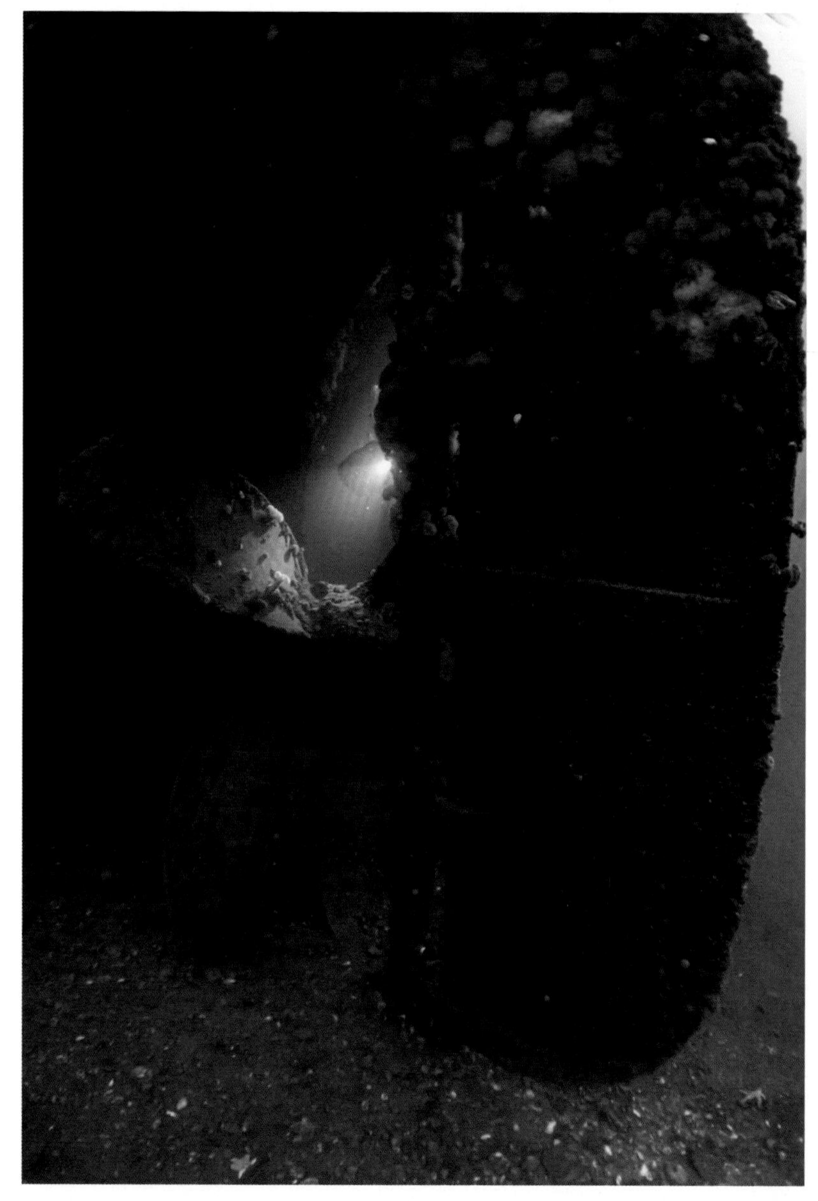

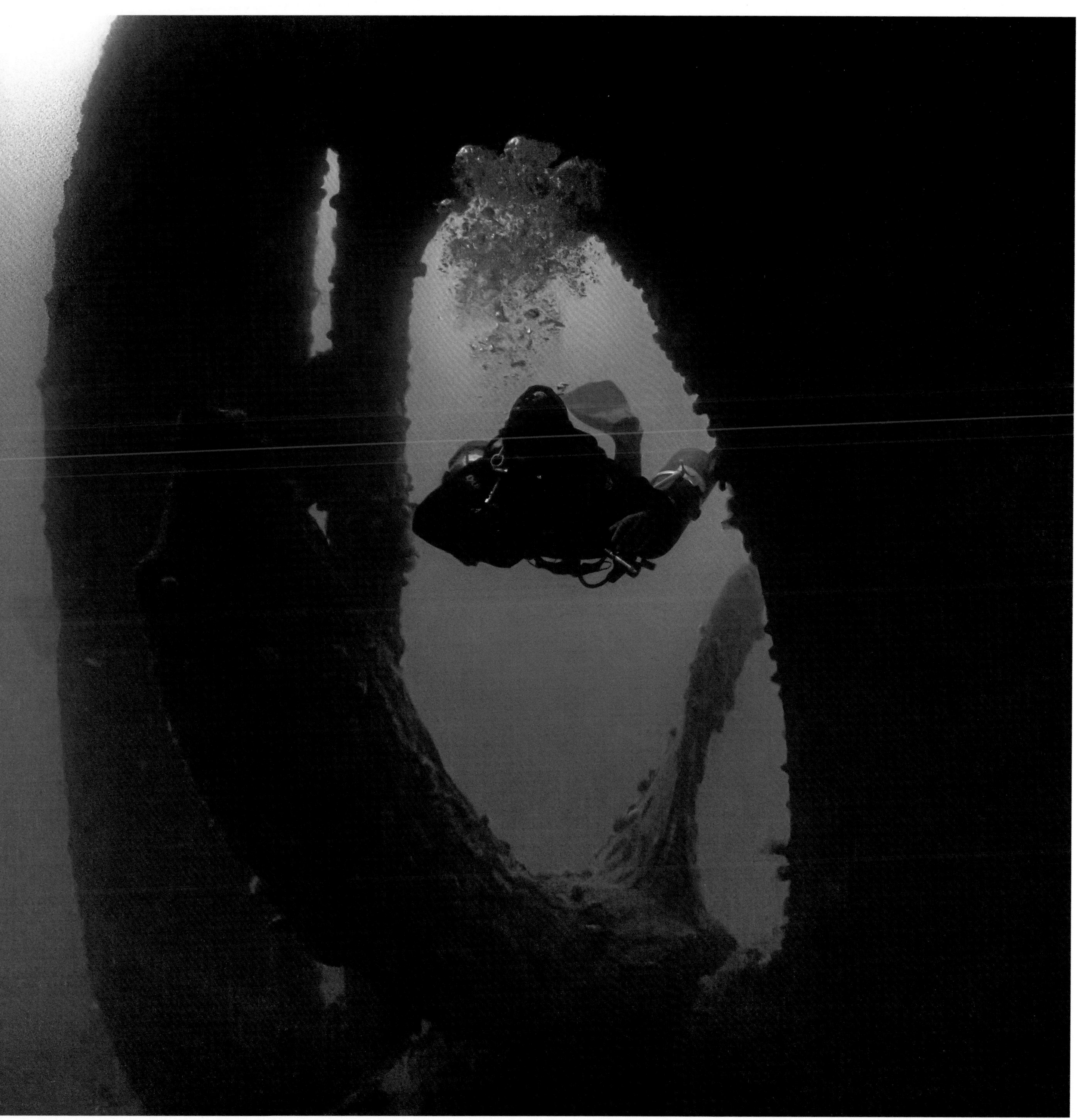

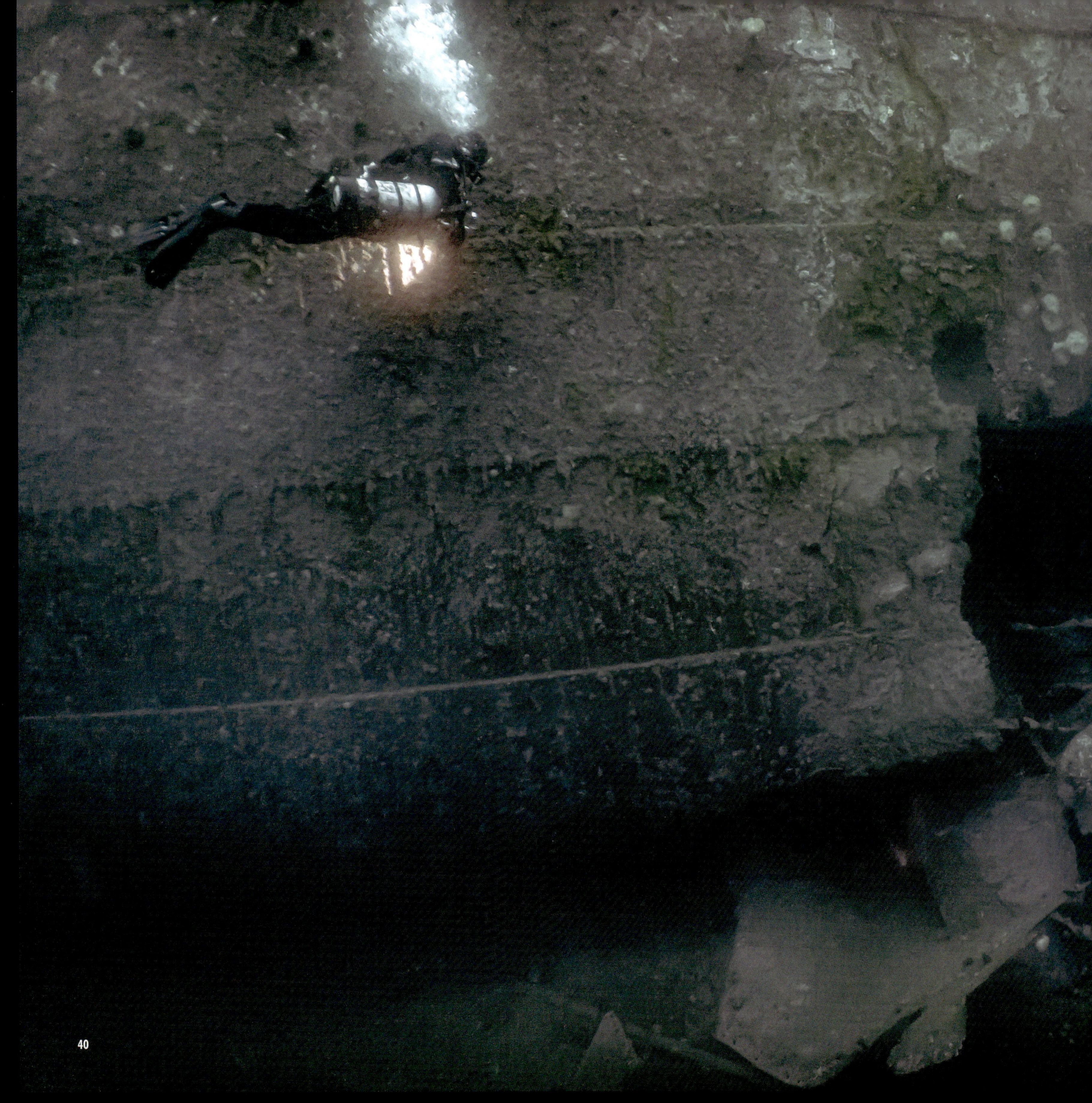

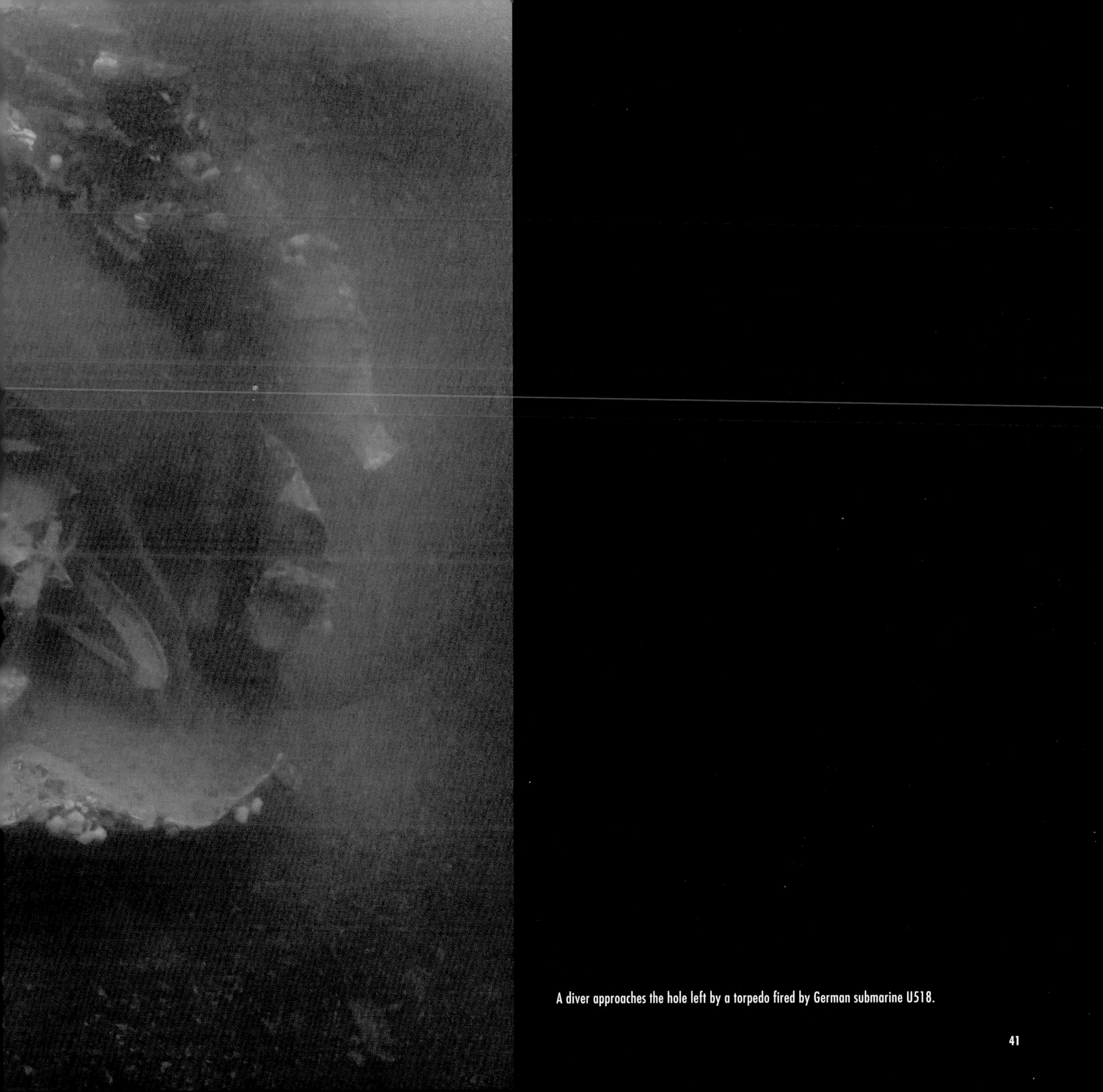

A diver approaches the hole left by a torpedo fired by German submarine U518.

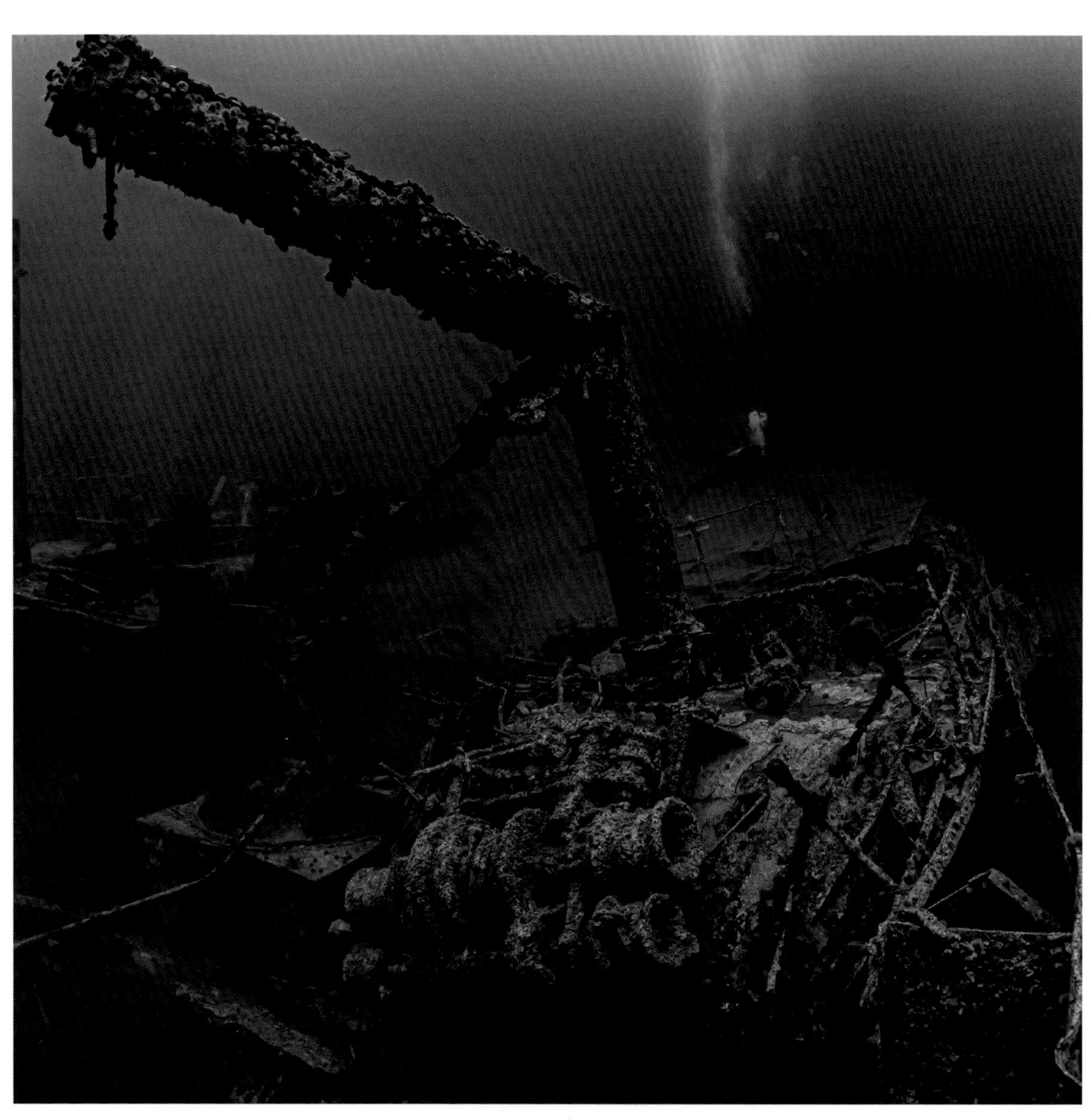

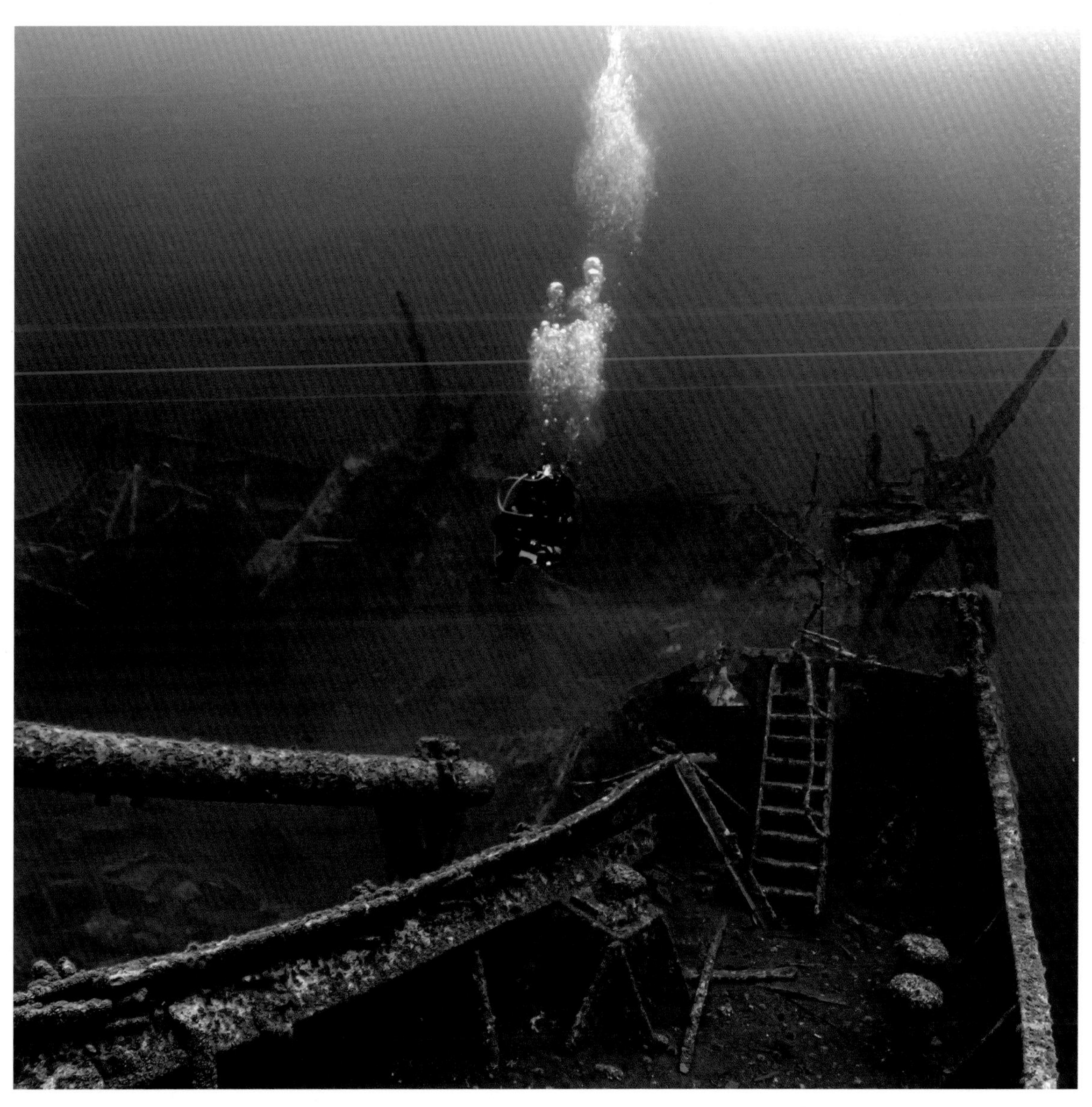

emergencies. With an exchange of hand signals, the divers turn and make their way back along the starboard side to the bow, taking in all the wonders the *PLM-27* has to offer.

Just past a windlass hovers a lumpfish about the size of a basketball. These odd but cute fish wobble through the water, swimming much less gracefully than many of the other fish divers encounter in the waters of Newfoundland. It poses for a picture before diver and lumpfish both continue on their way.

At the bow, dive buddies exchange signals indicating that it's time to return to the surface. After a long dive at these depths, the nitrogen in the divers' air, harmless at the surface, has dissolved into their body tissues.

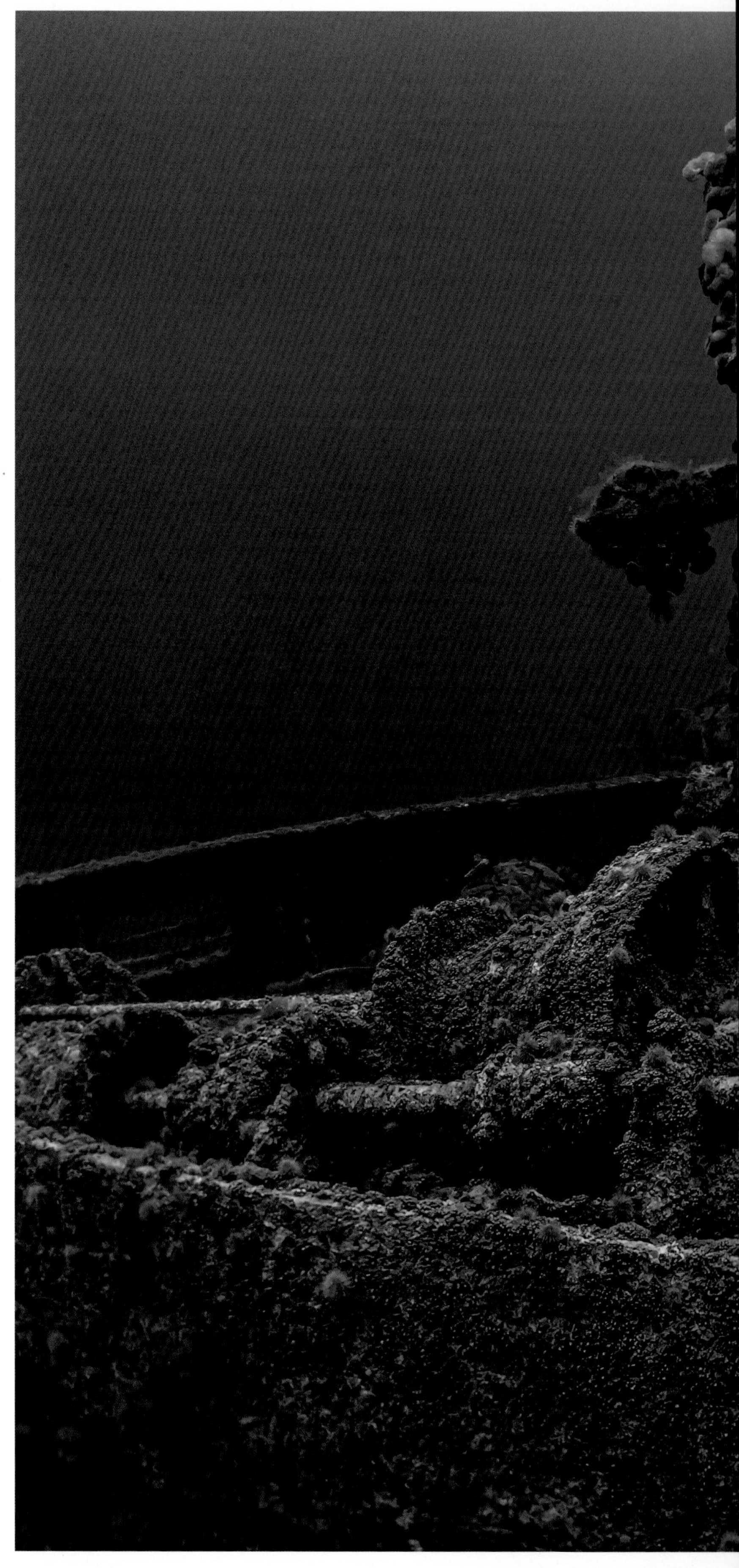

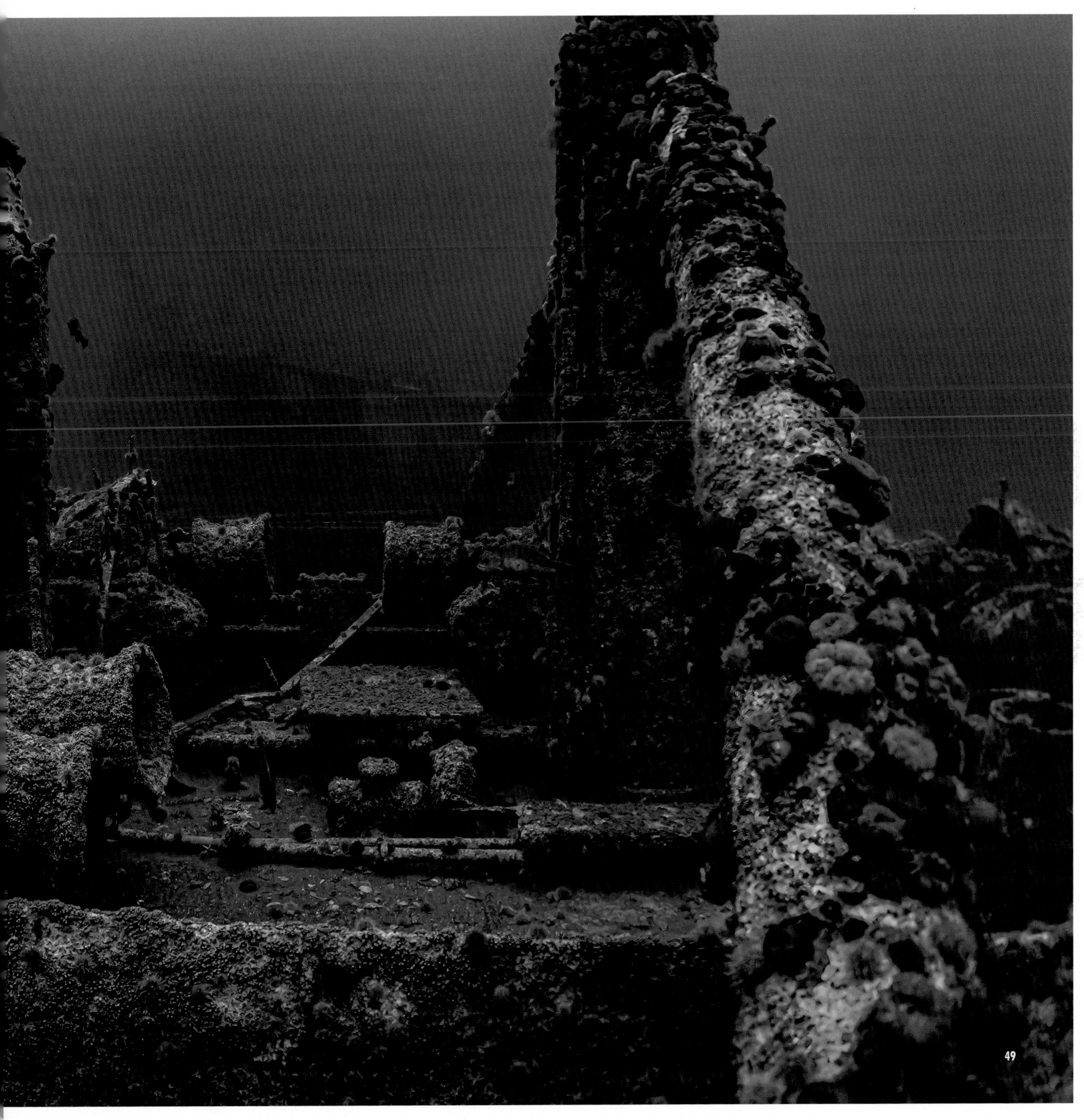

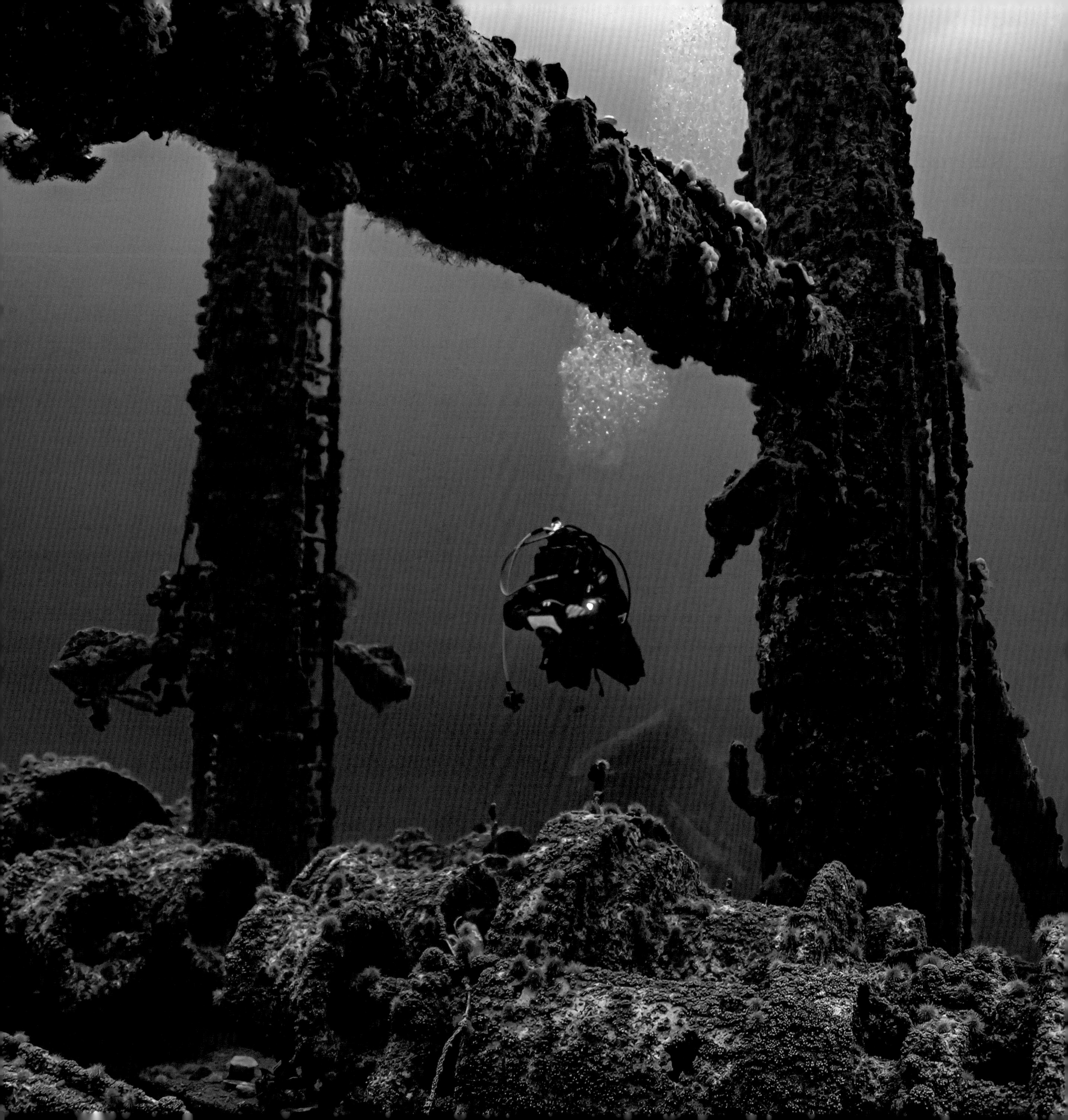

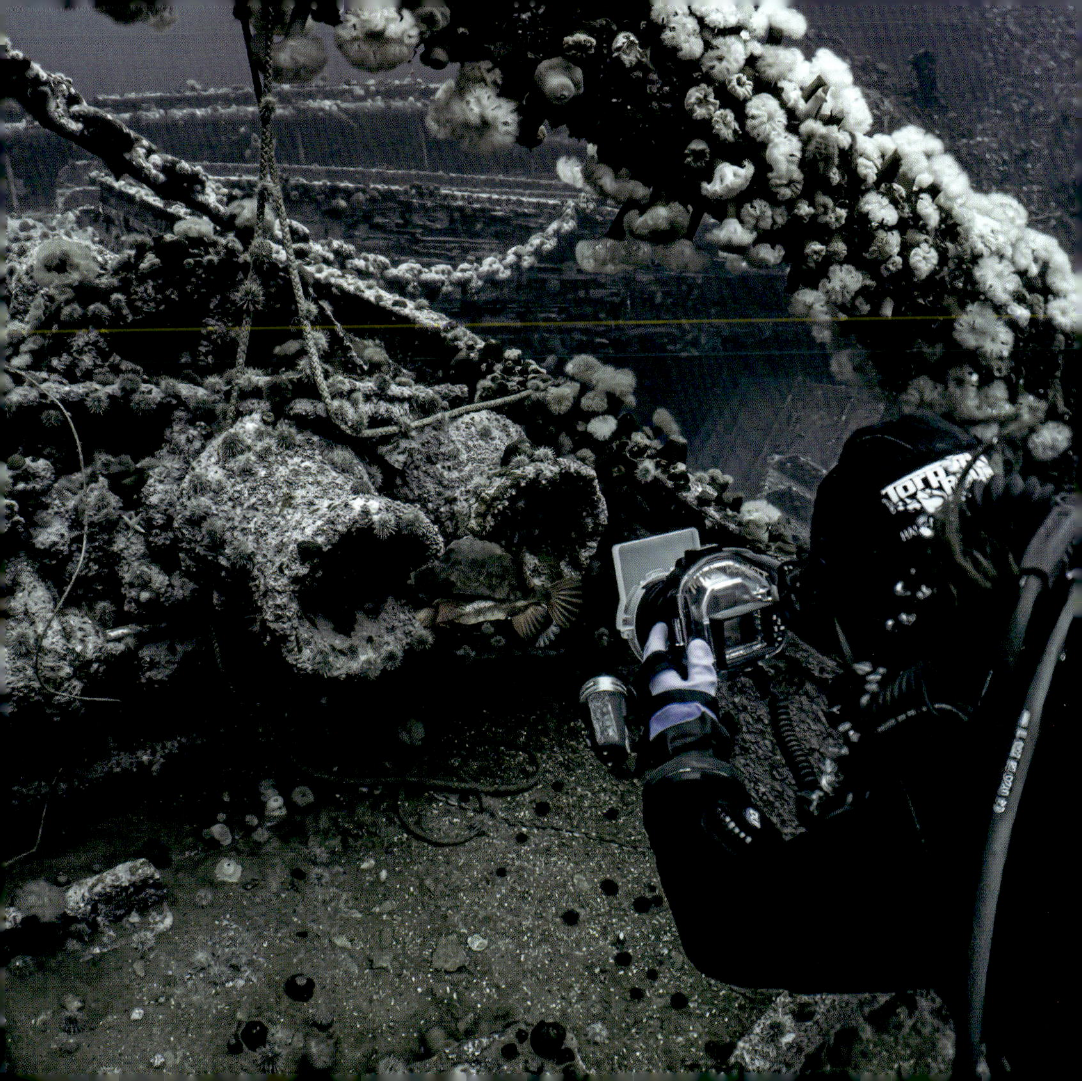

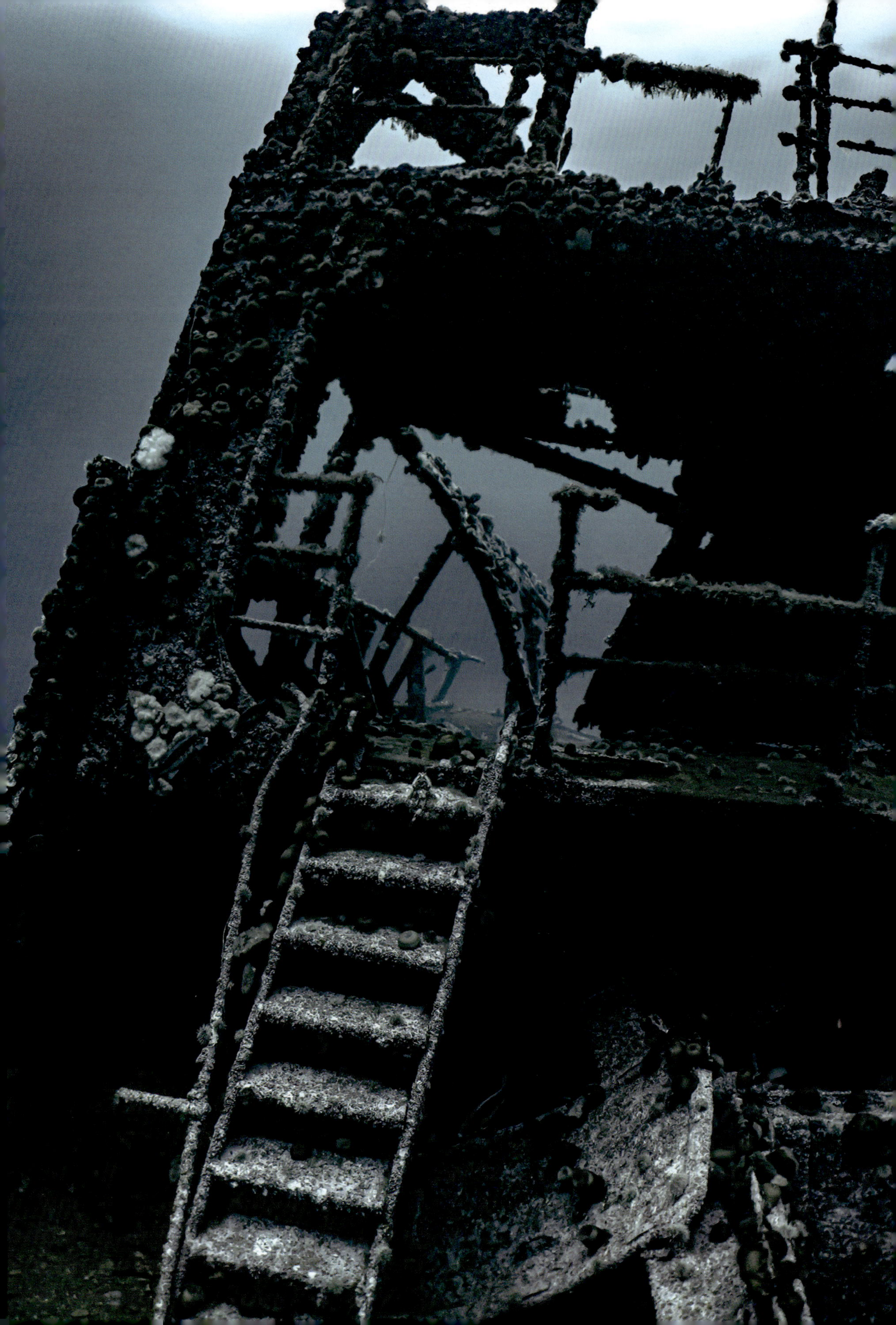

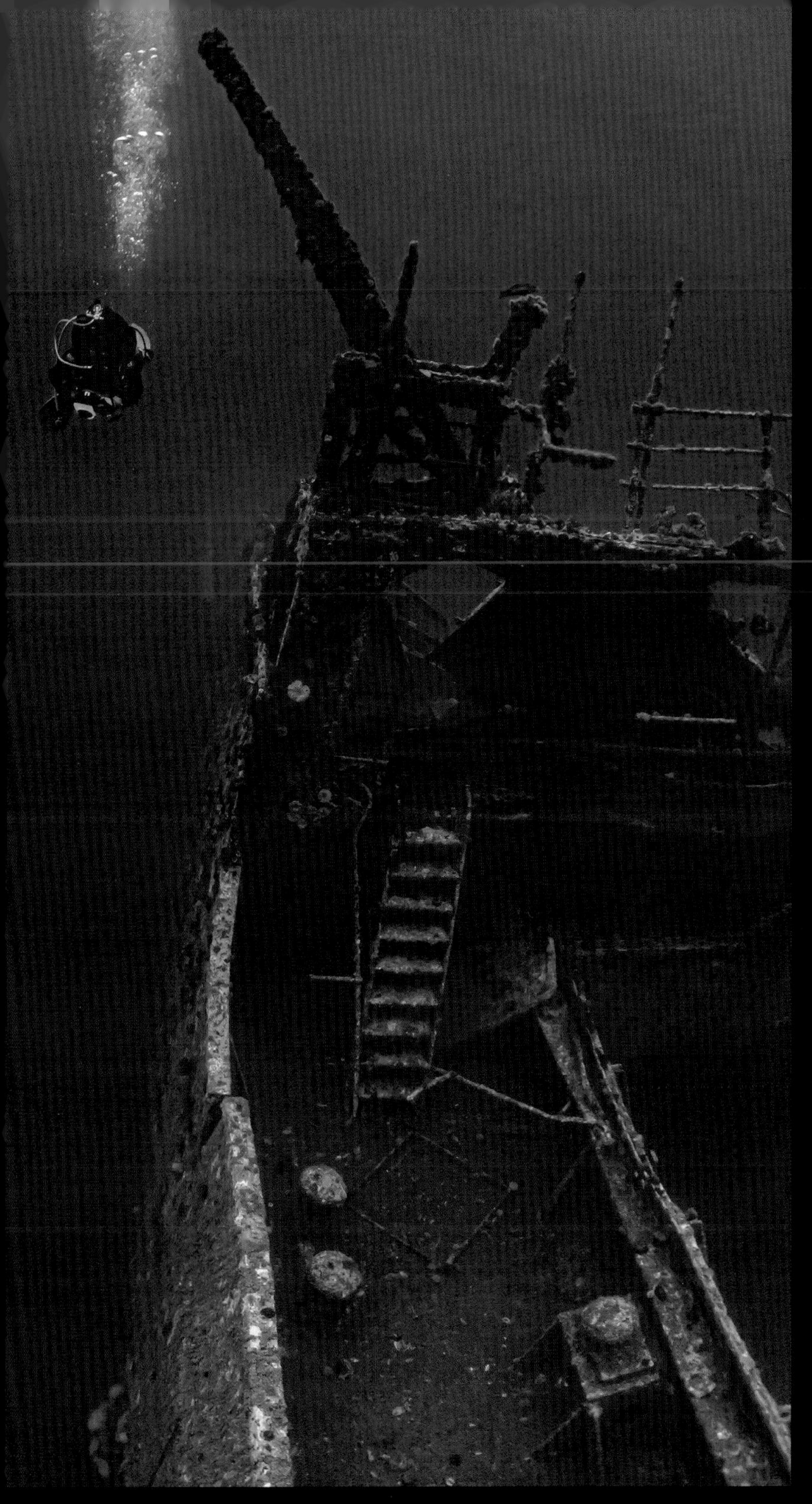

They approach the mooring line and start a slow ascent, allowing the nitrogen to leave their systems, a process often referred to as off-gassing. Hovering at 15 feet below the surface, divers pause for a safety stop—time at this depth allows accumulated nitrogen to dissipate safely, limiting the risks of decompression illness. The stop typically lasts three minutes but, on this day, because a thermocline has warmed the water, the divers stay for five minutes—a longer safety stop is always better—to soak in the environment and reflect on the shipwreck and the dive experience. Already there is an eagerness for the next dive, the next chance to explore the wonders of the deep.

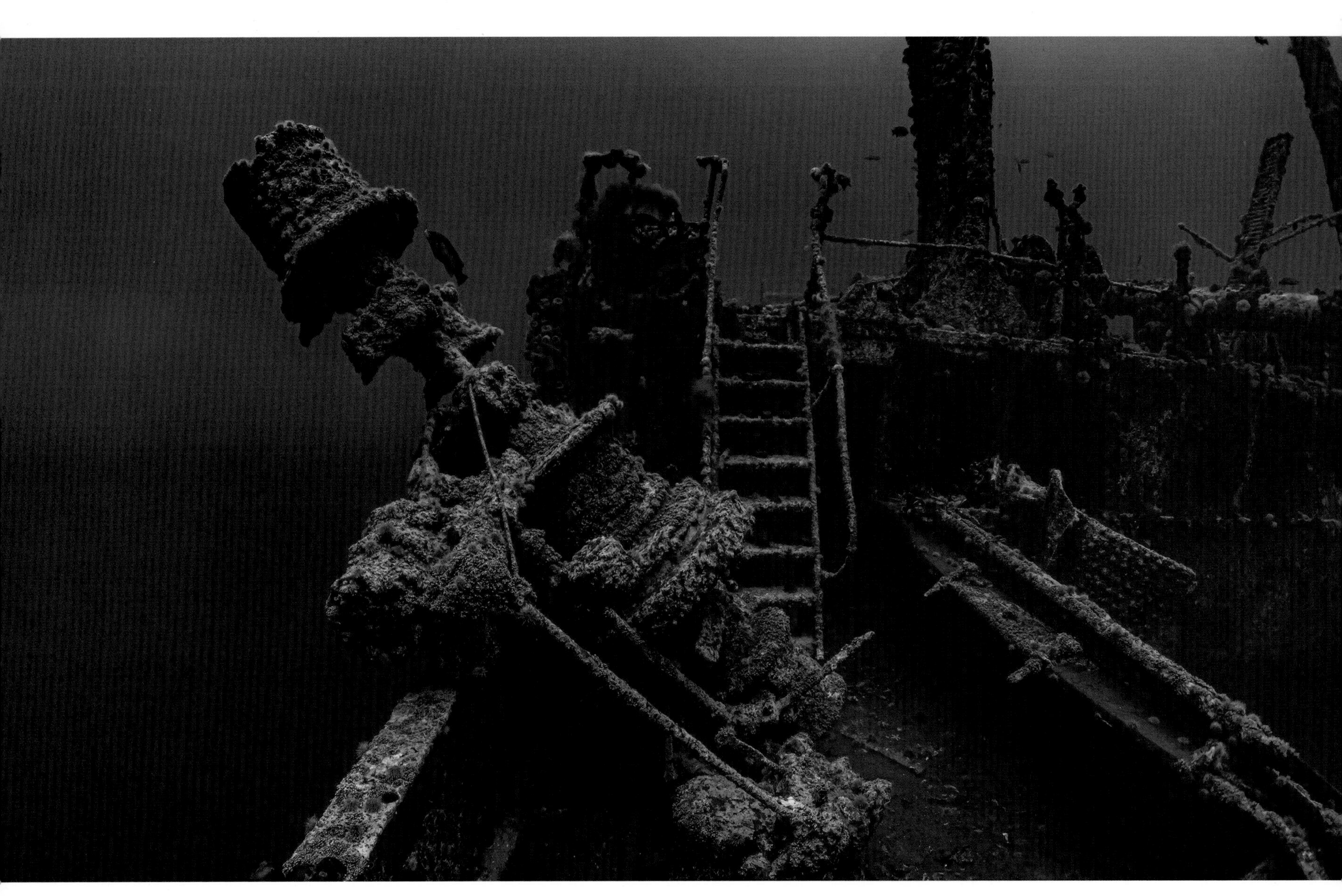

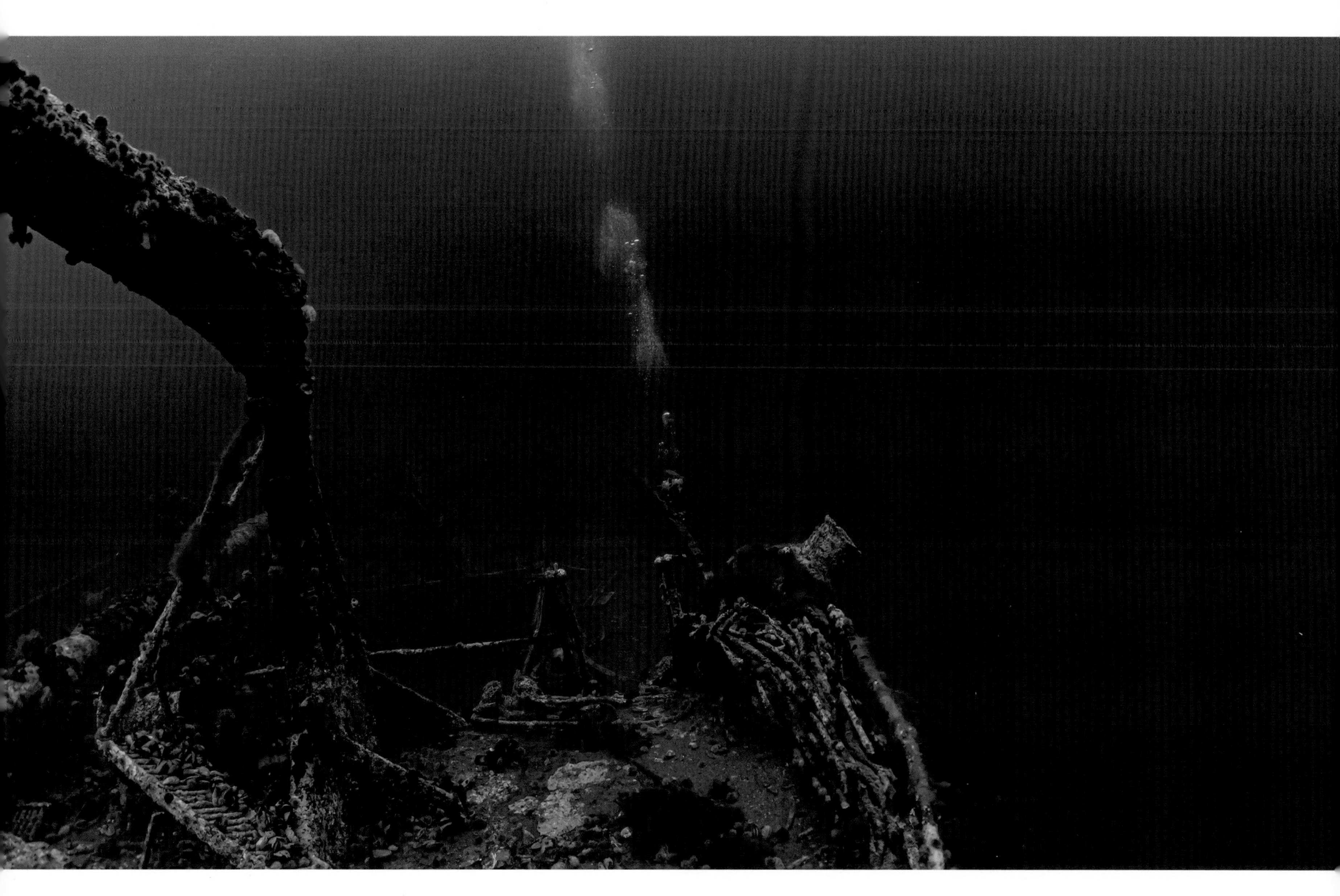

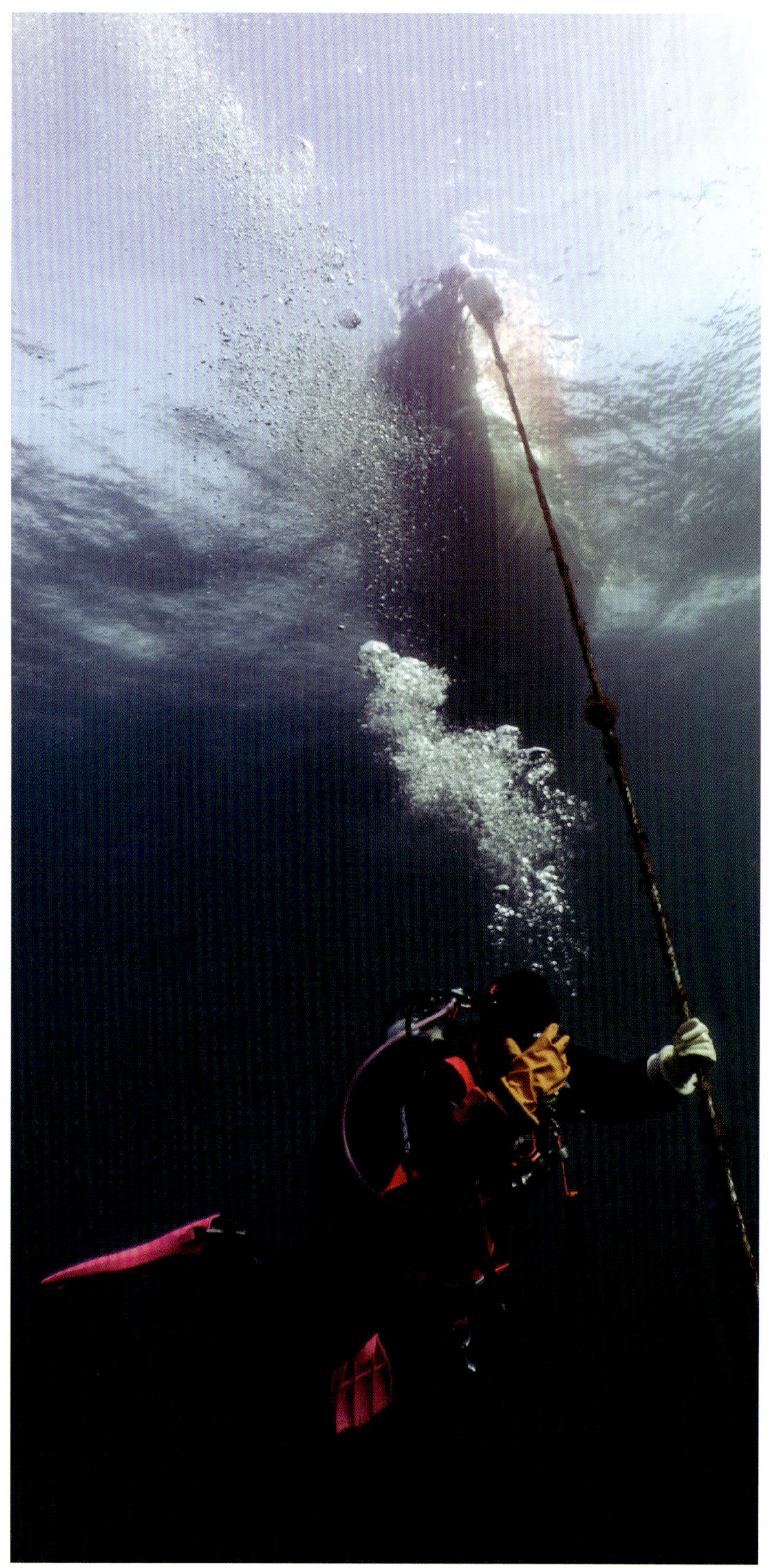

Returning to this boat is a treat. *The Mermaid* is equipped with an elevator that plucks divers out of the ocean with ease—much more pleasant than struggling up a ladder while wearing heavy equipment. Exploring the *PLM-27* requires more swimming than exploring smaller wrecks, and tired legs appreciate this luxury.

The smiles on divers' faces as they remove their gear speak volumes about the *PLM-27* adventure. The excitement is palpable as lively discussions about the dive continue for hours—no longer limited to just hand signals.

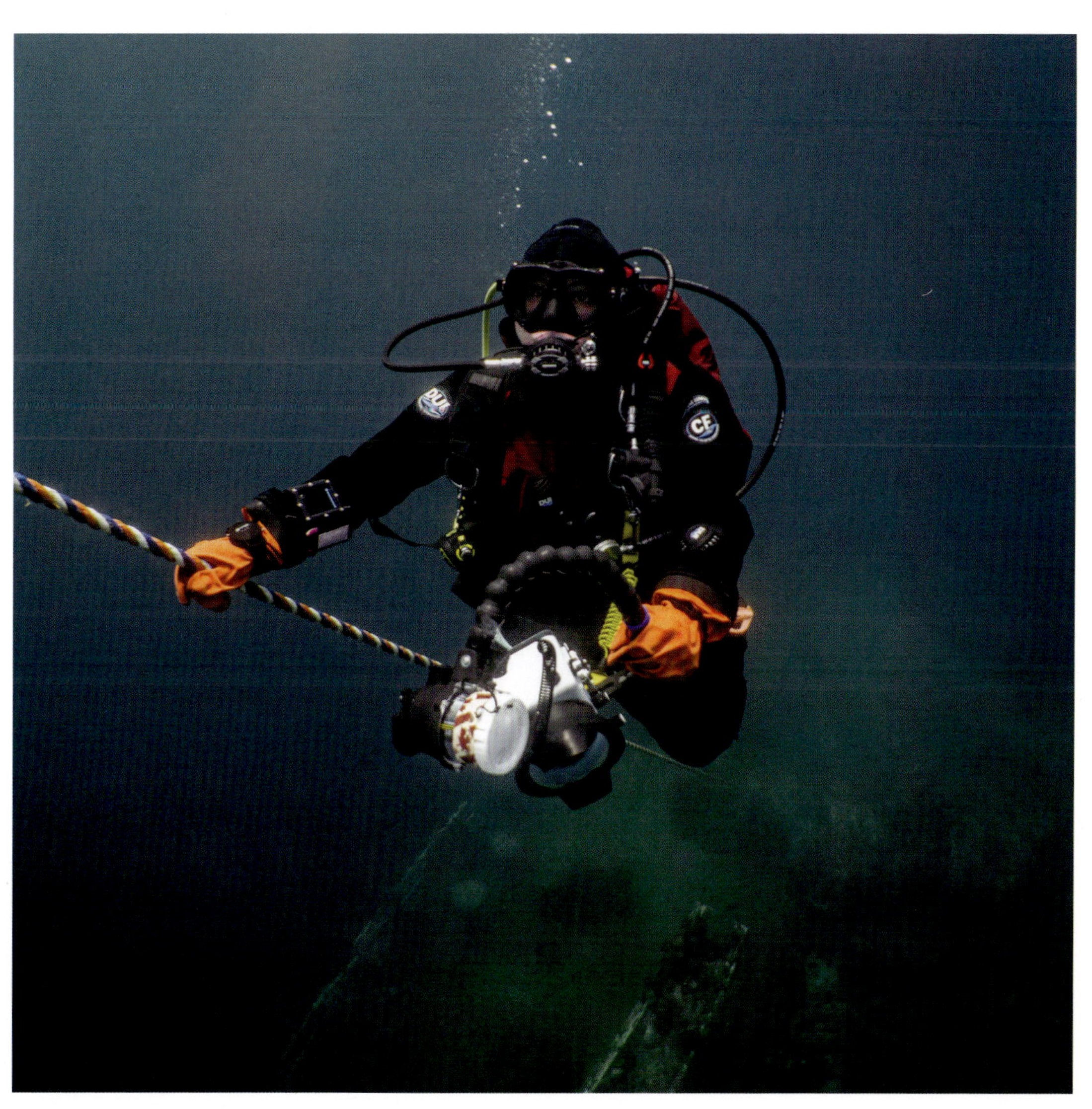

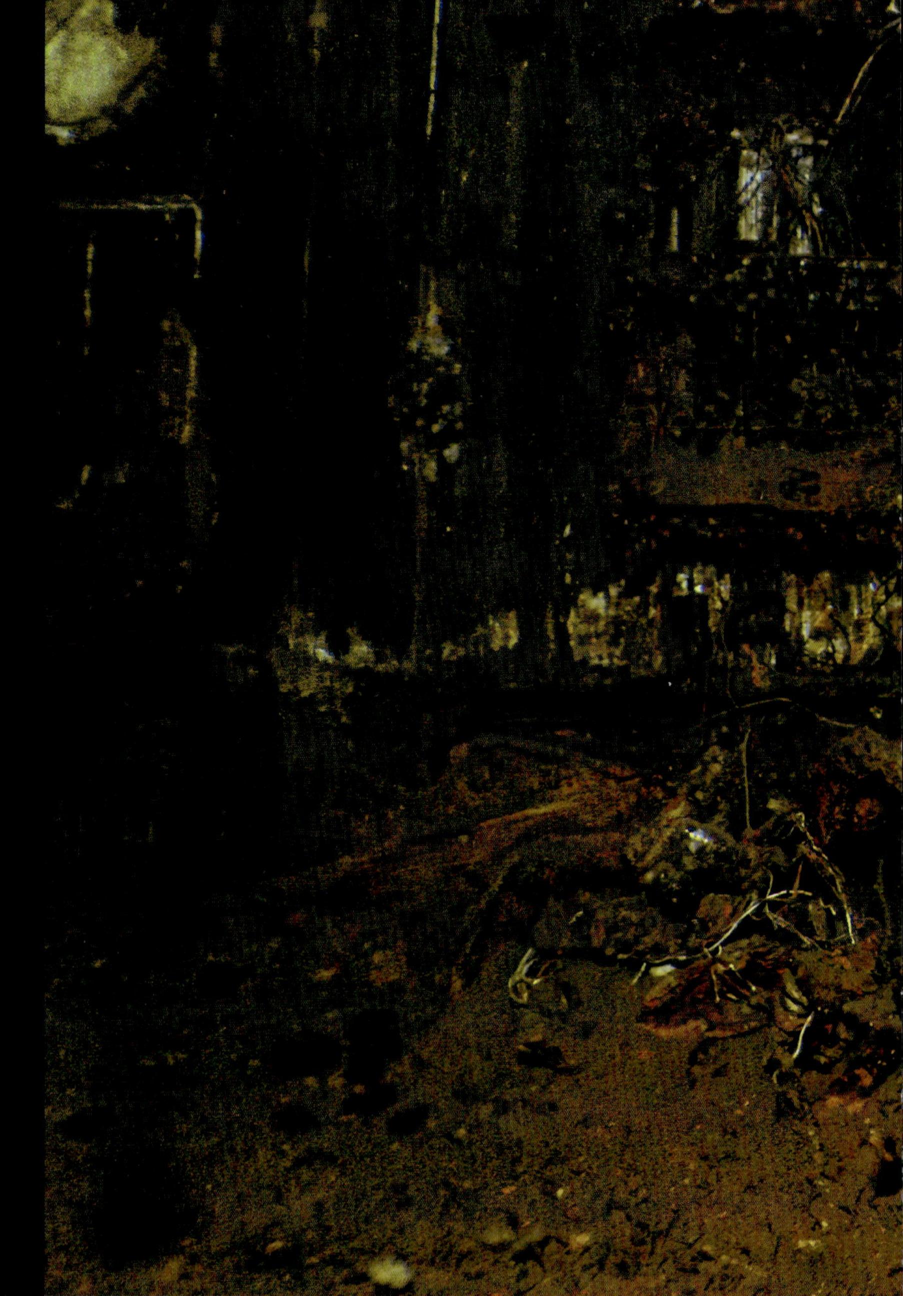

The *Rose Castle's* Marconi Room, found at the top of the ship at a depth of 95 feet. This depth has preserved the equipment so divers can still read radio gauges and plaque.

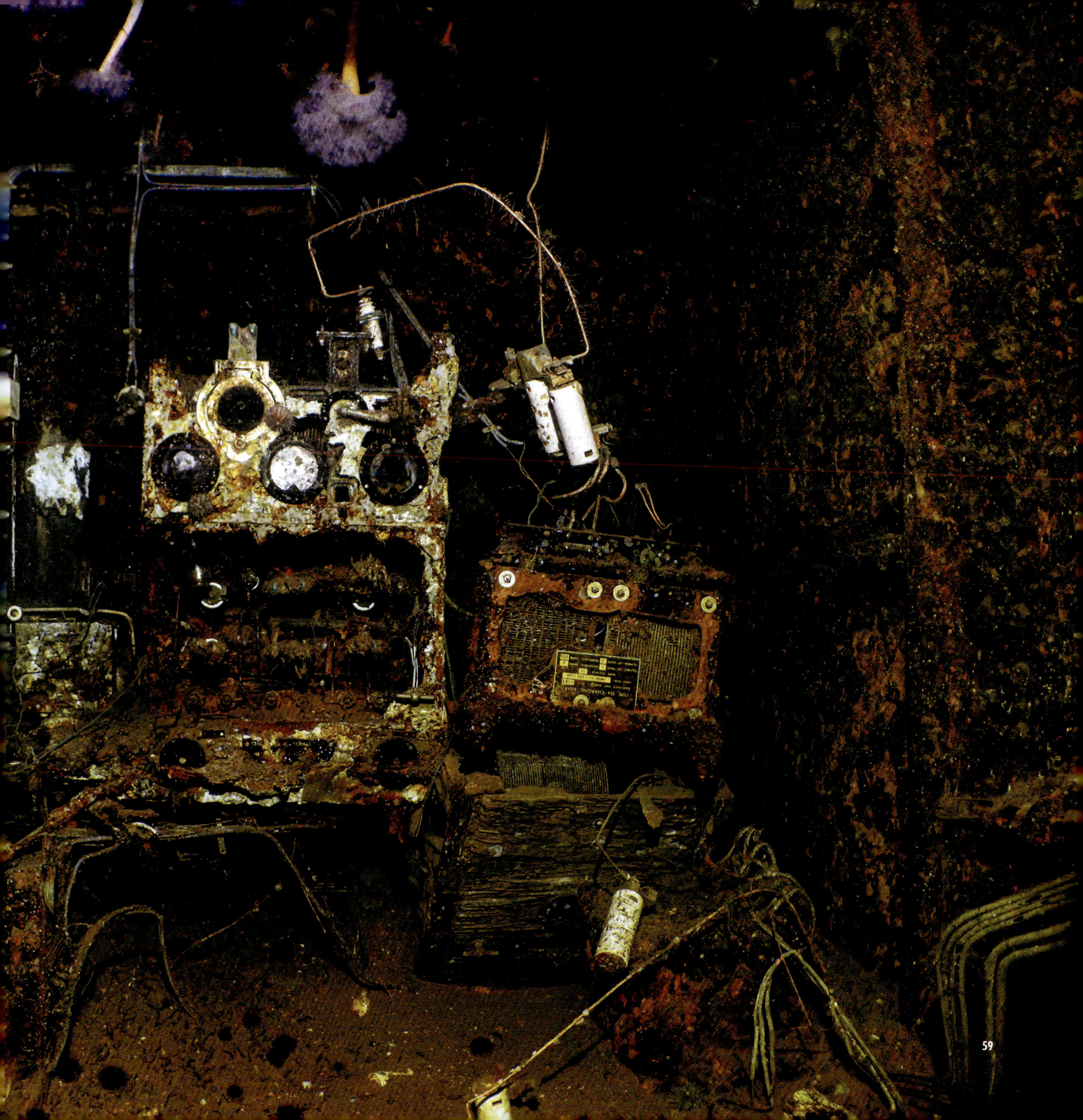

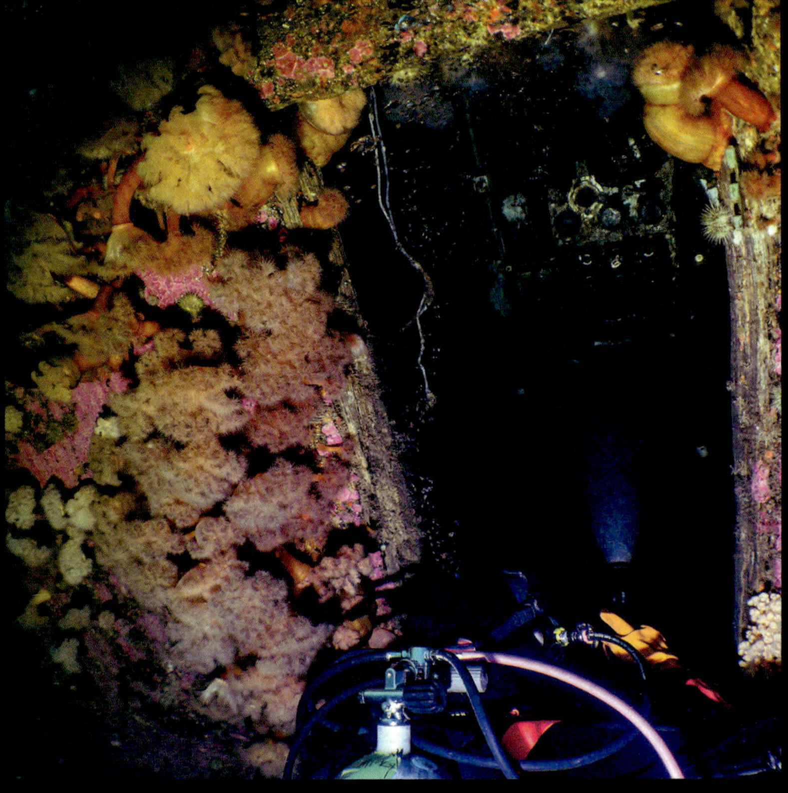

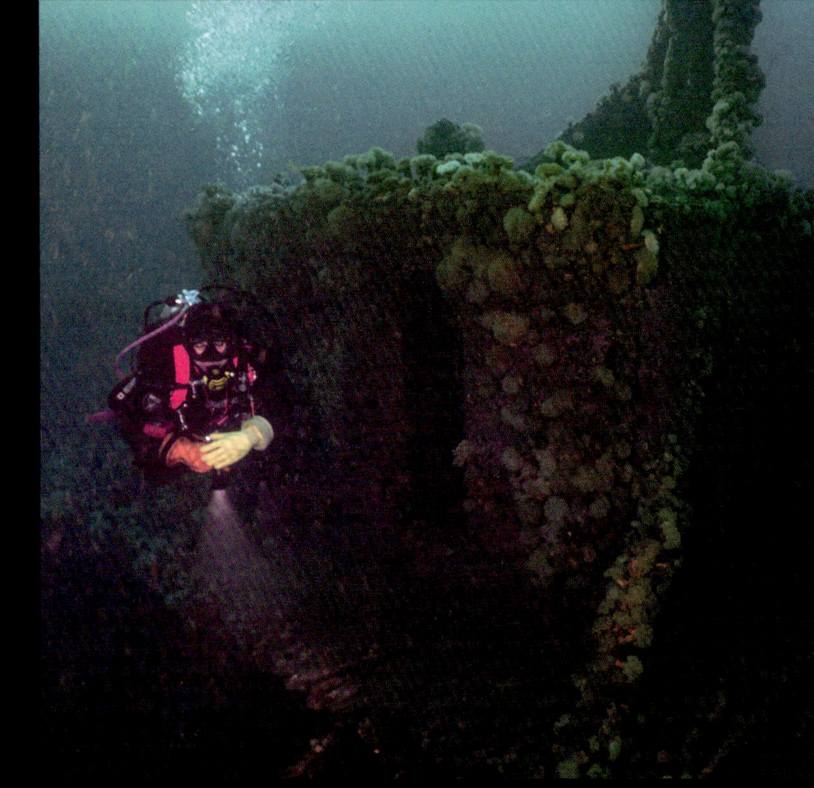

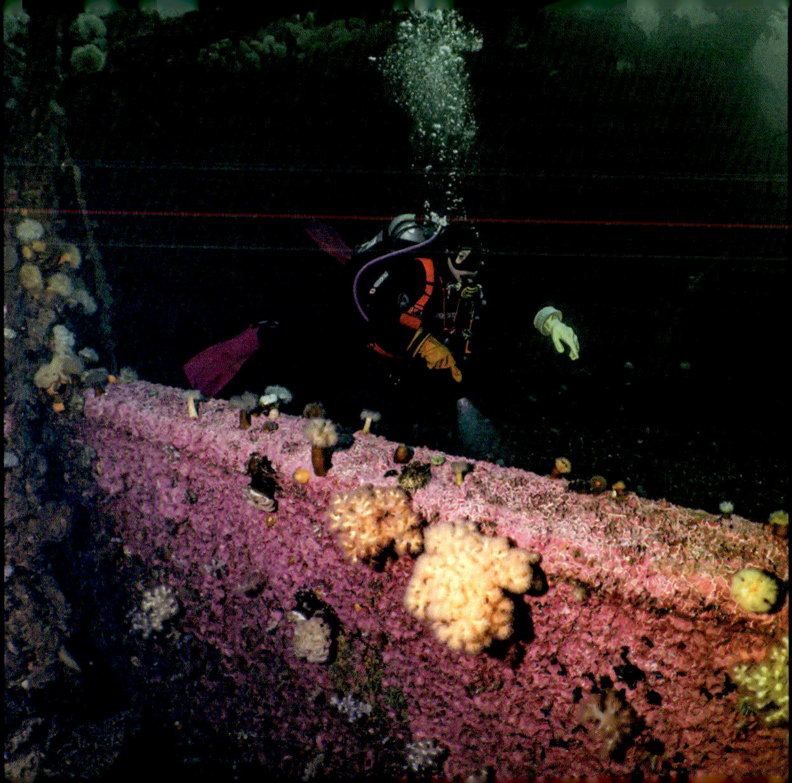

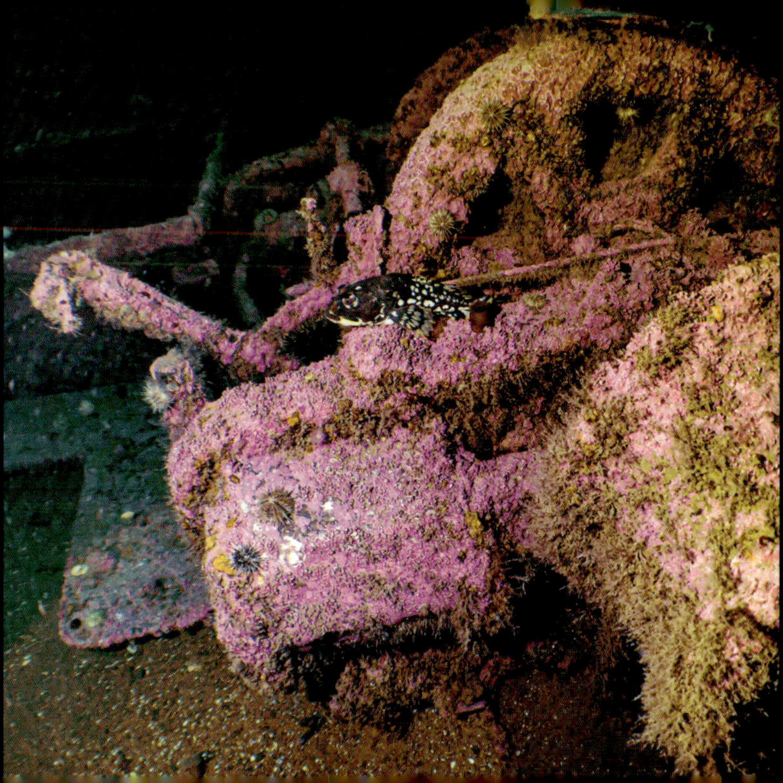

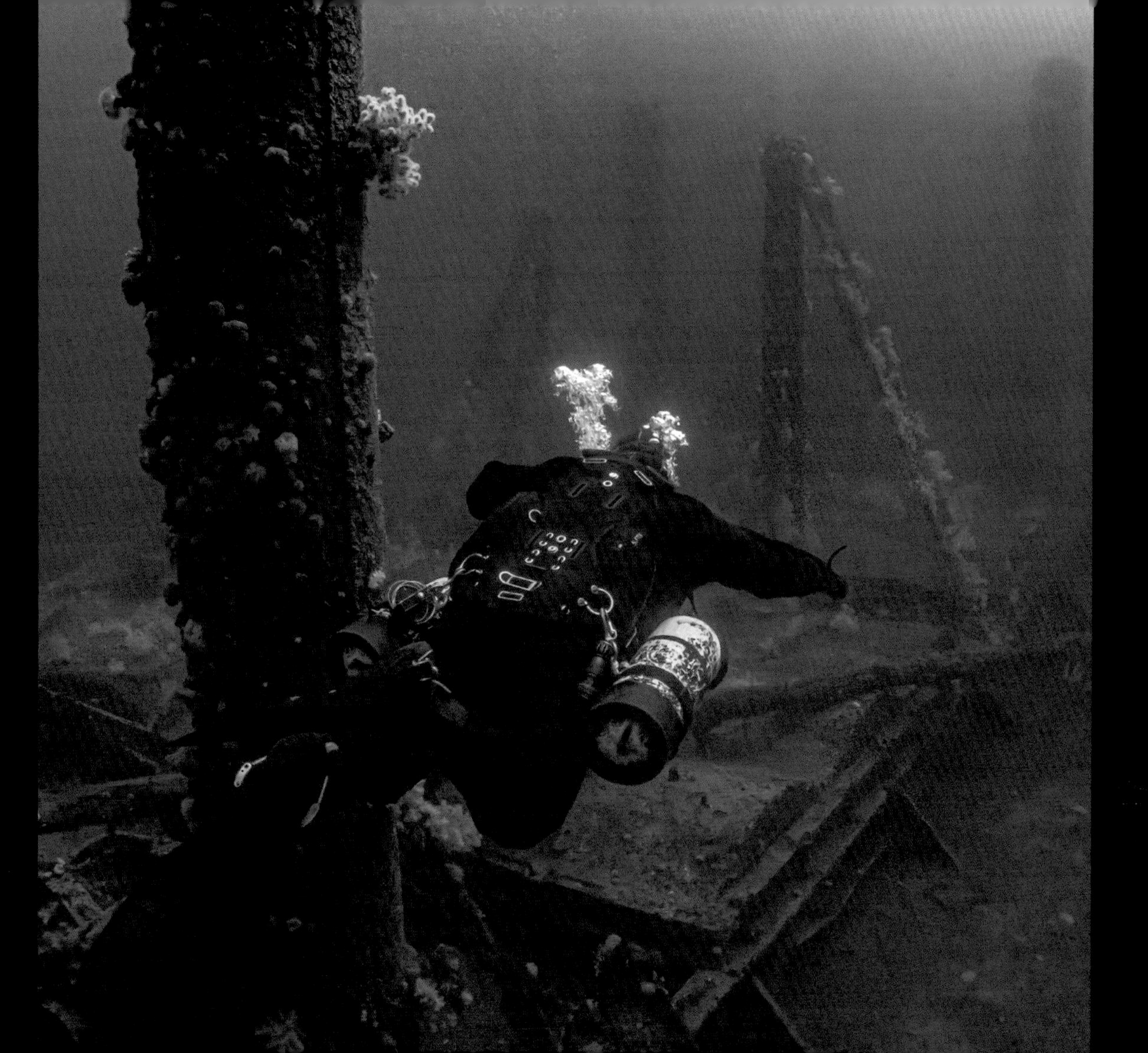

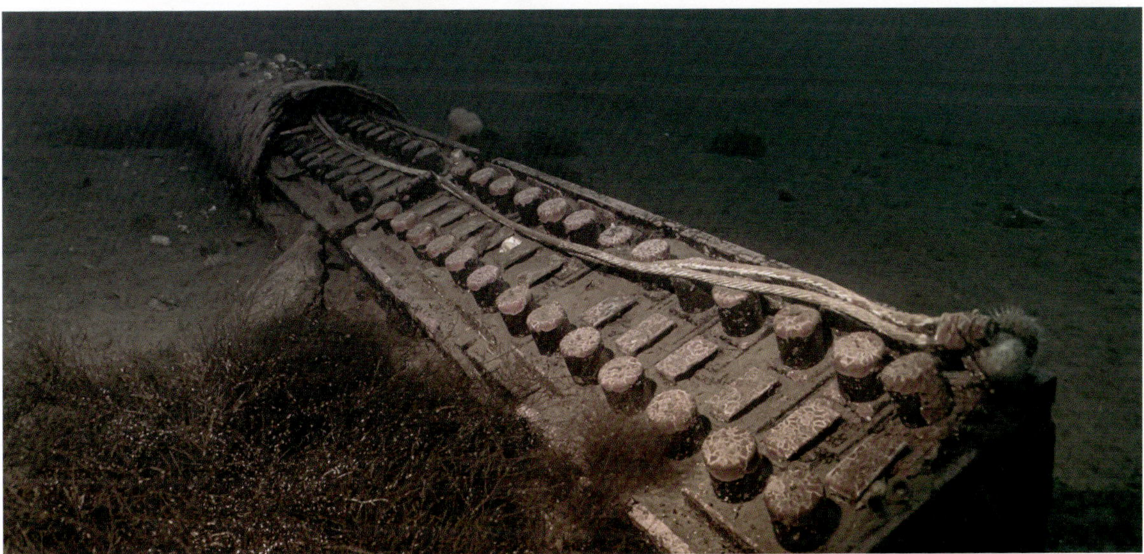

This undetonated German torpedo is located below recreational dive limits. The warhead was removed many years ago. The top of the battery bank, which once powered this artifact, is visible.

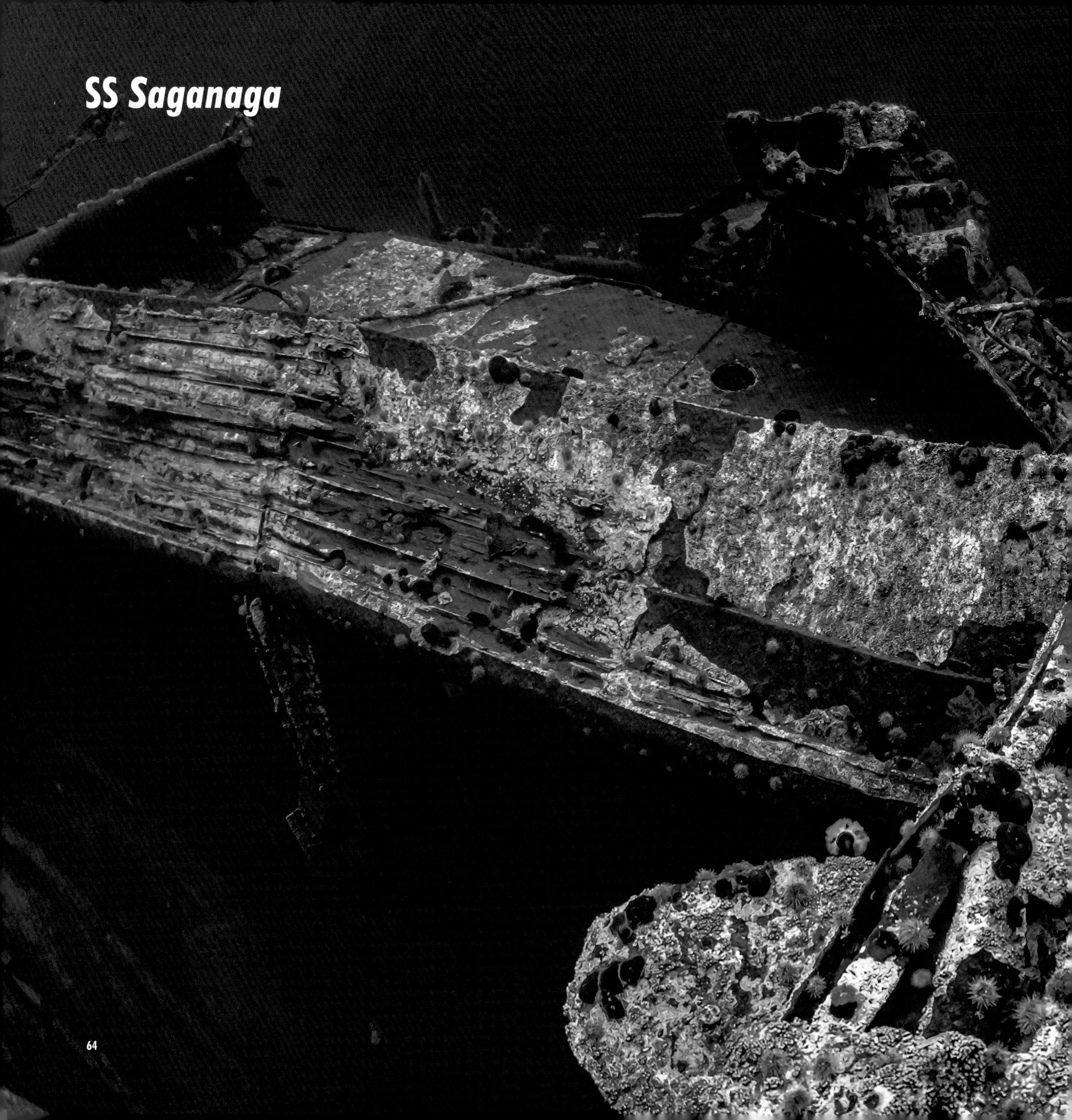

SS Saganaga

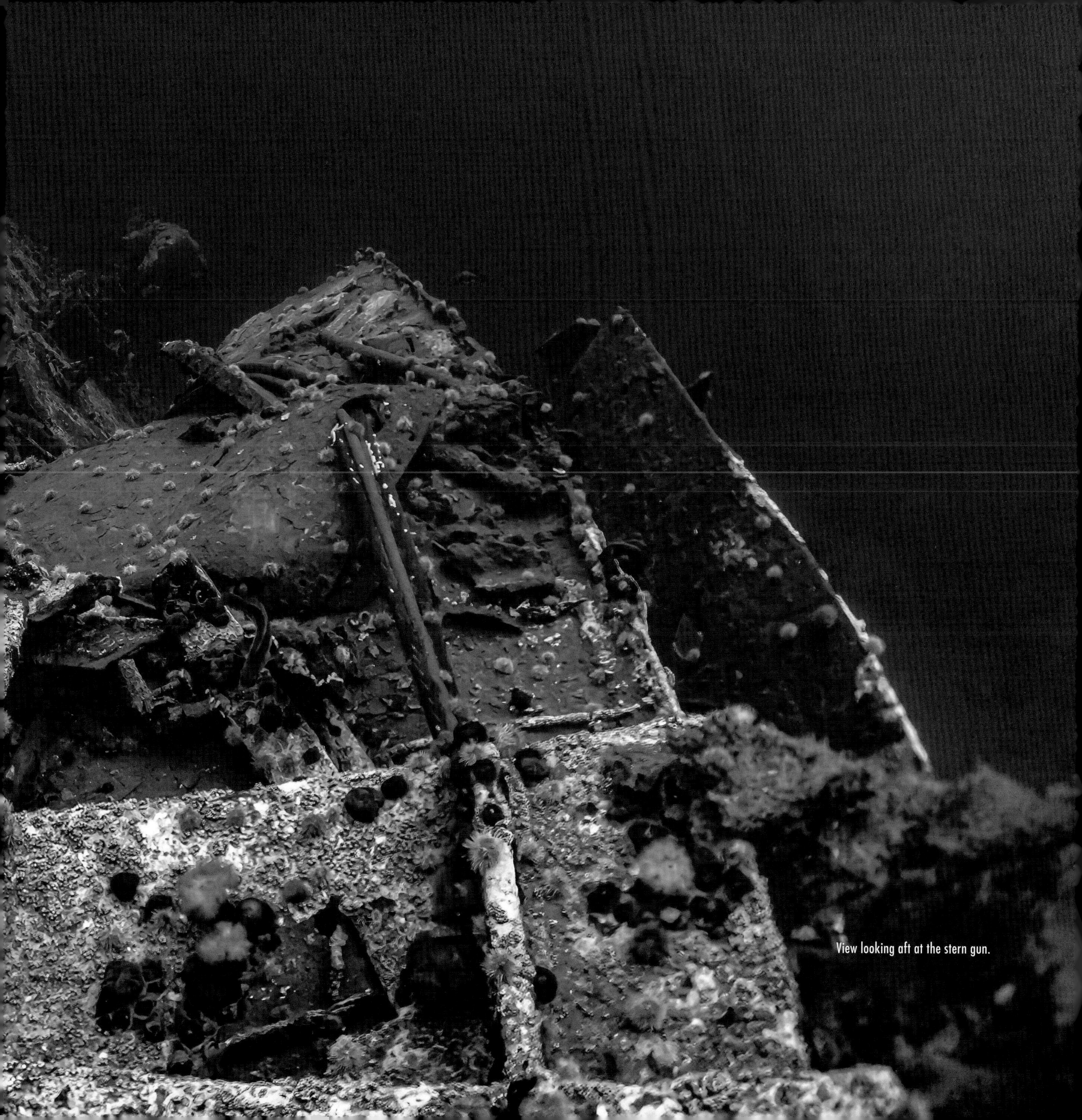

View looking aft at the stern gun.

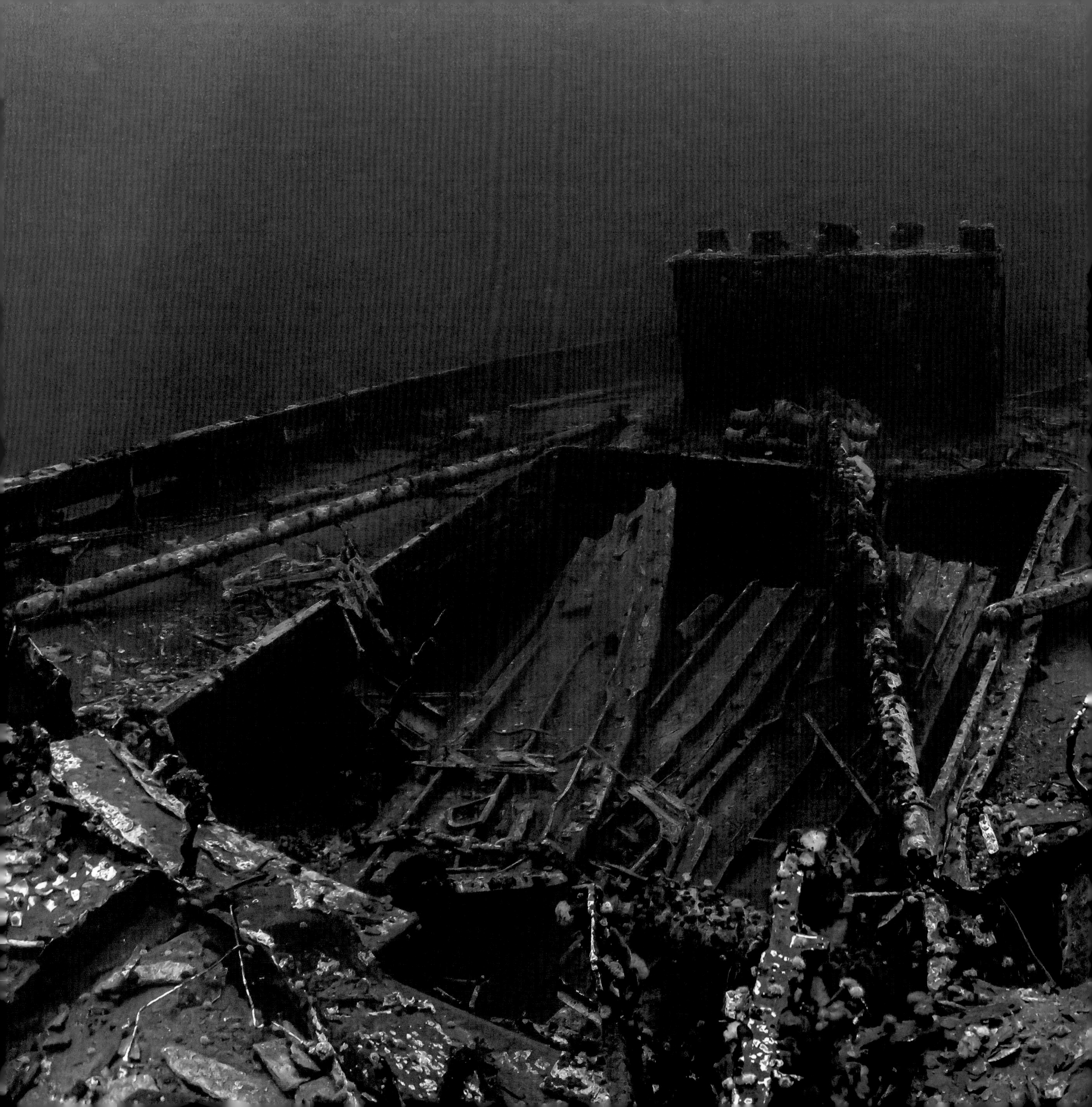

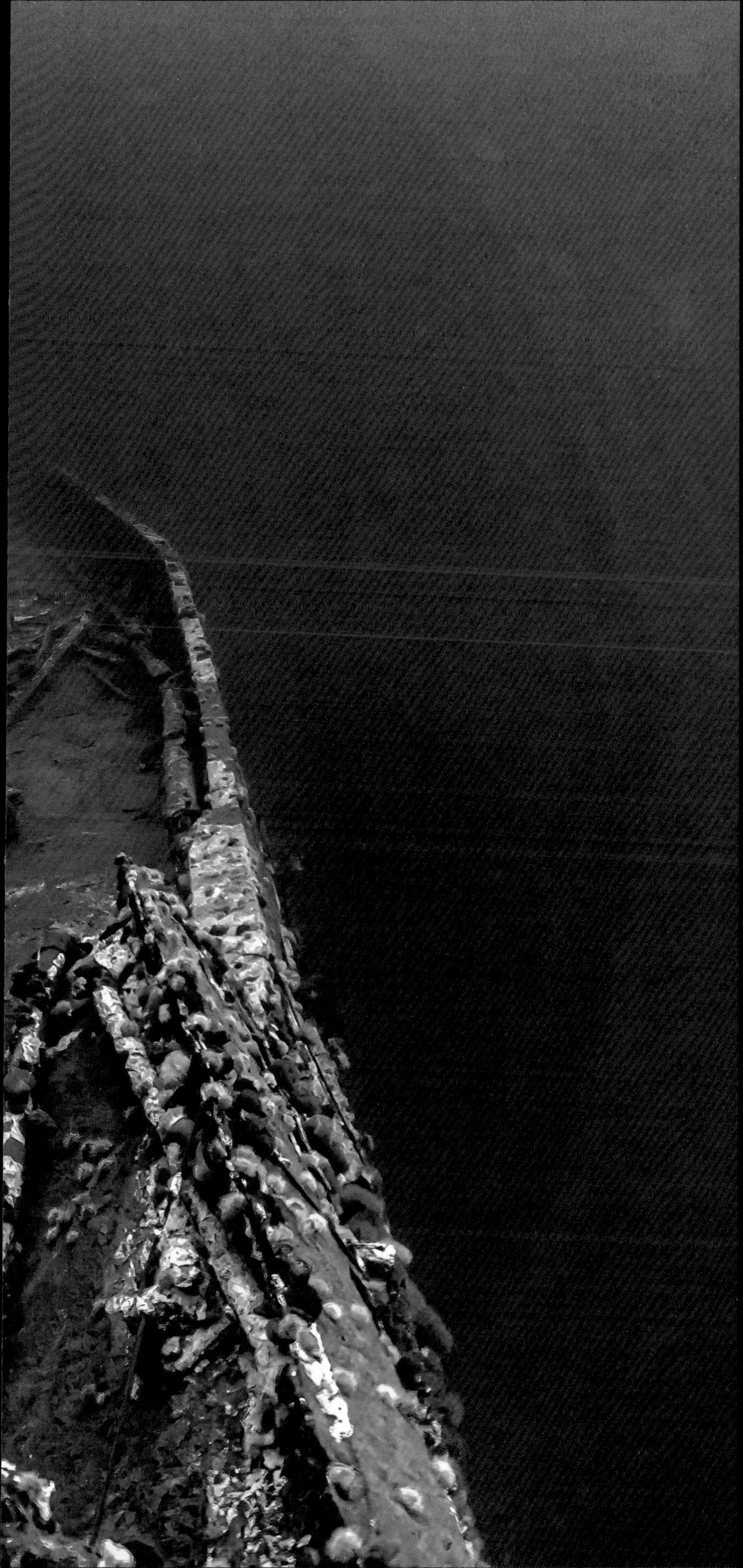

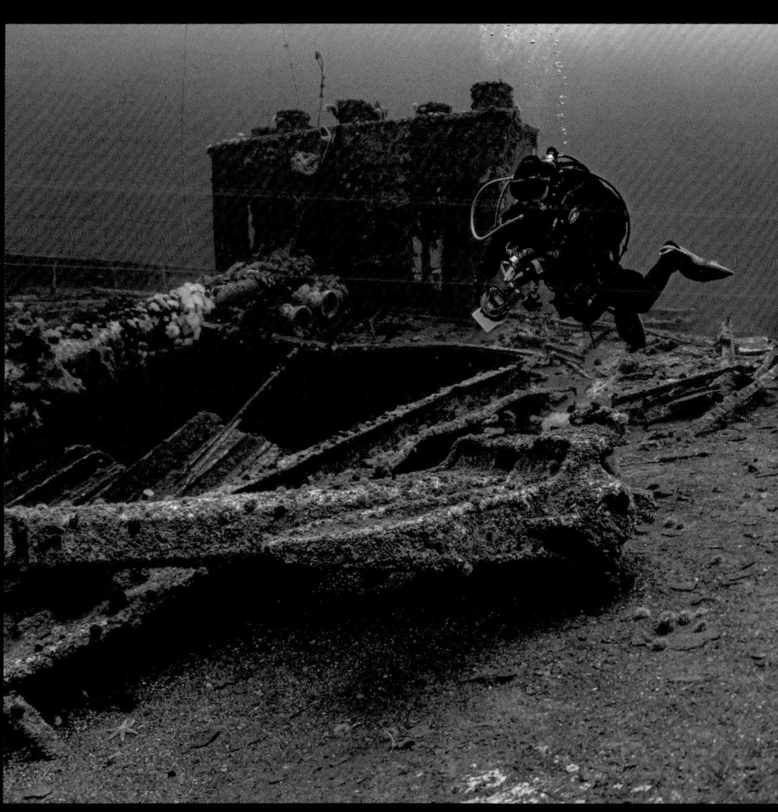

The *Saganaga*'s forward anchor was resting on the ocean floor when she was torpedoed. The anchor was violently torn from its position and launched across the deck during the explosion.

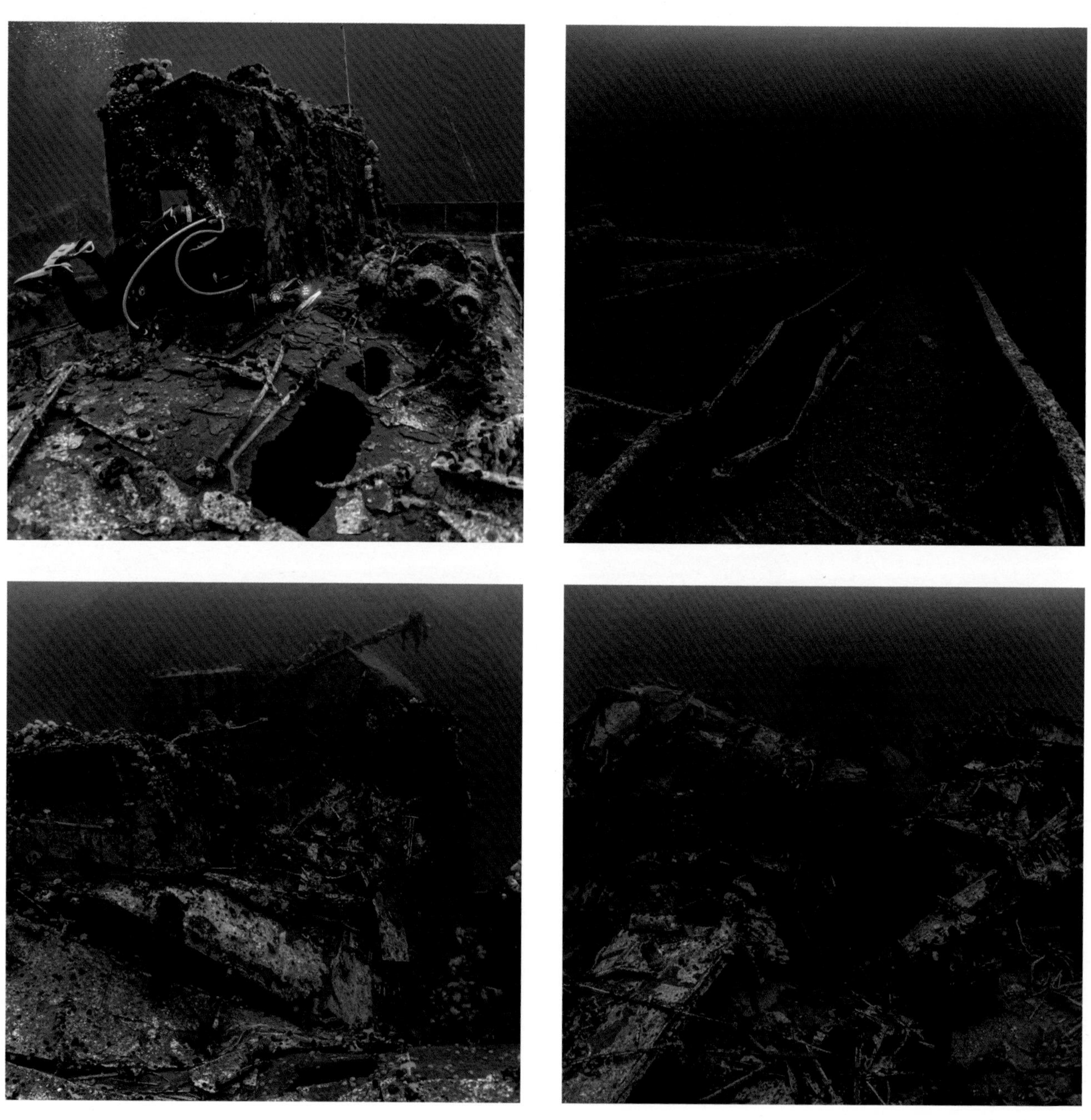

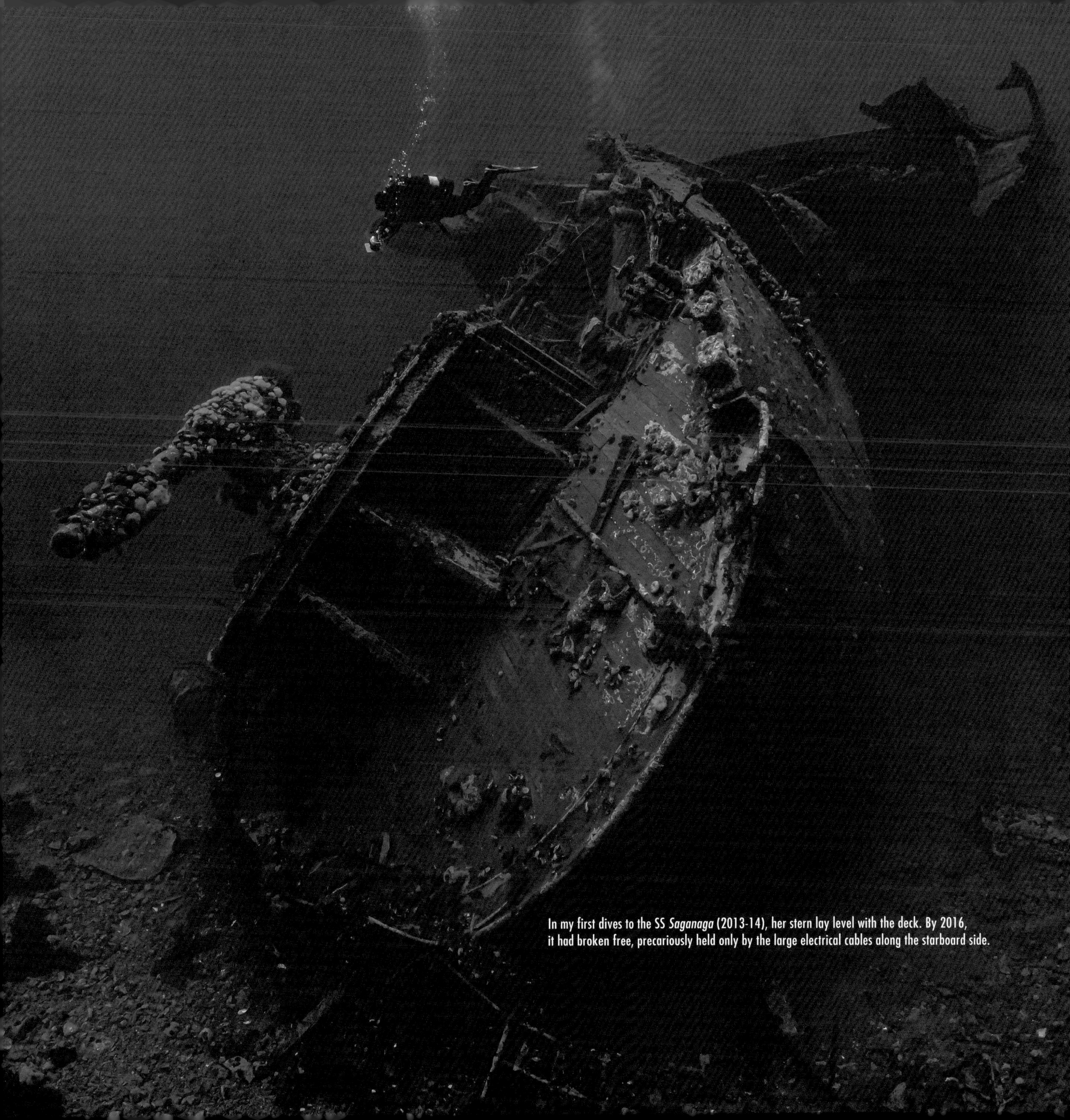

In my first dives to the SS *Saganaga* (2013-14), her stern lay level with the deck. By 2016, it had broken free, precariously held only by the large electrical cables along the starboard side.

SS *Lord Strathcona*

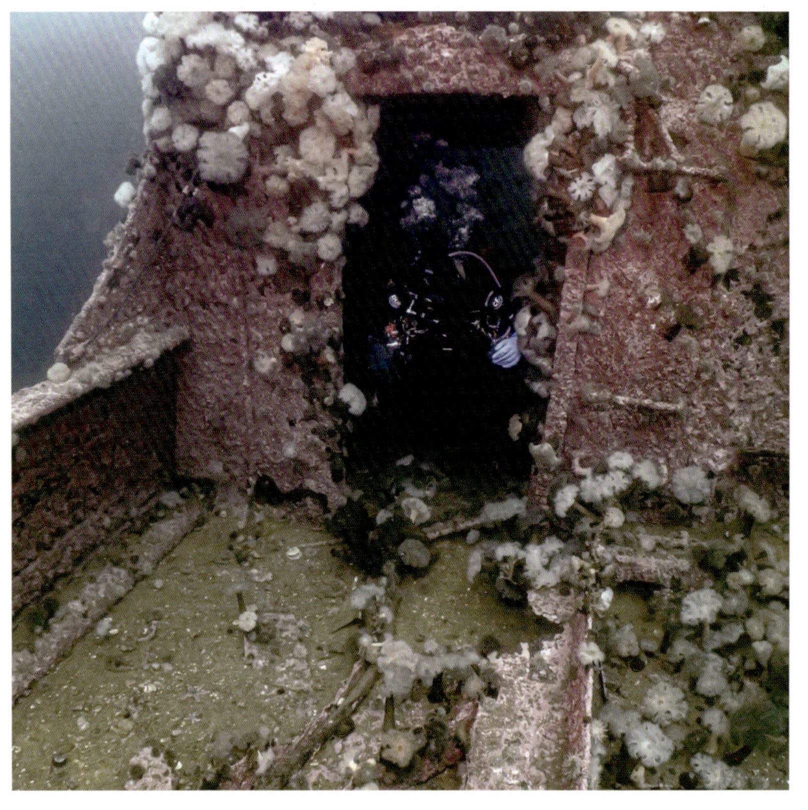

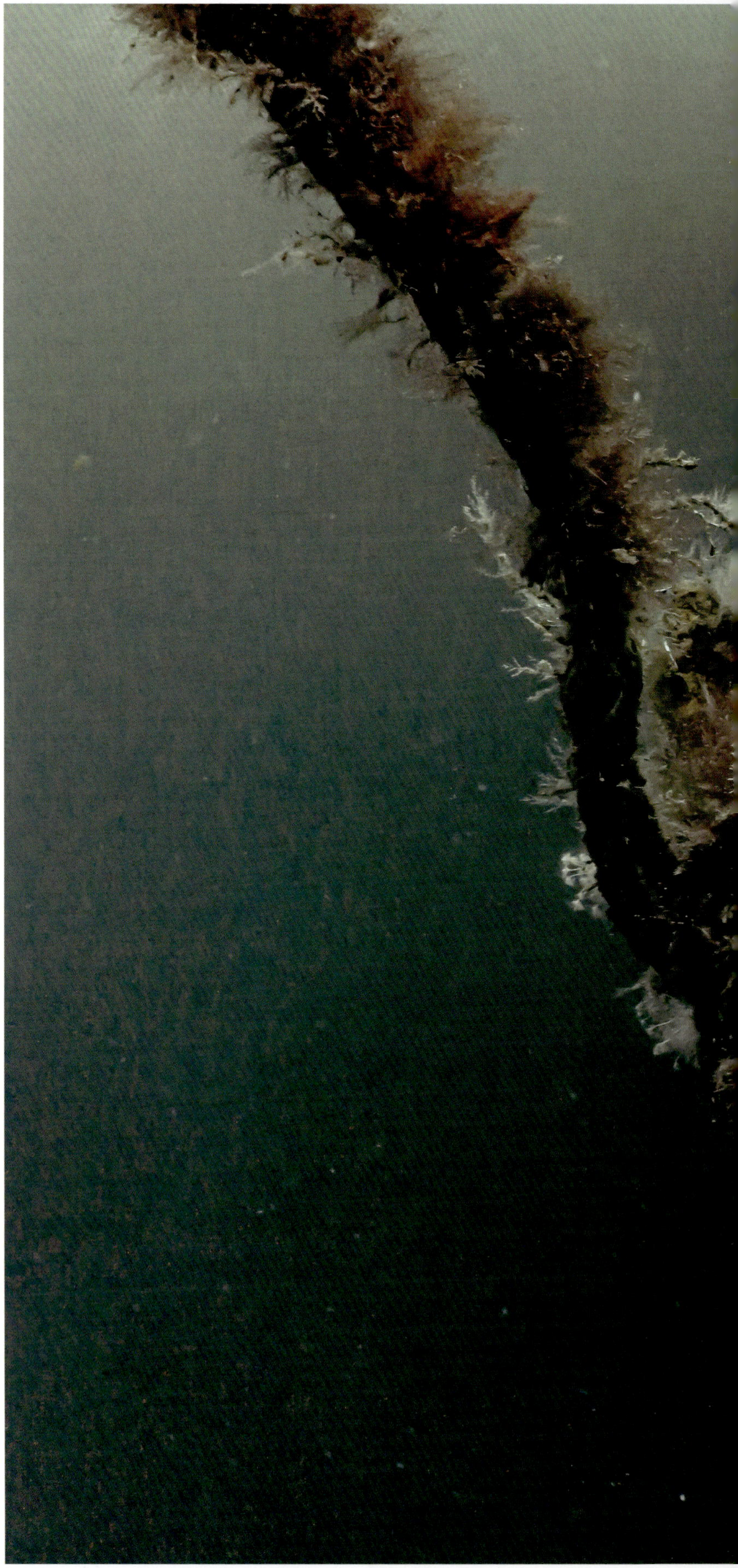

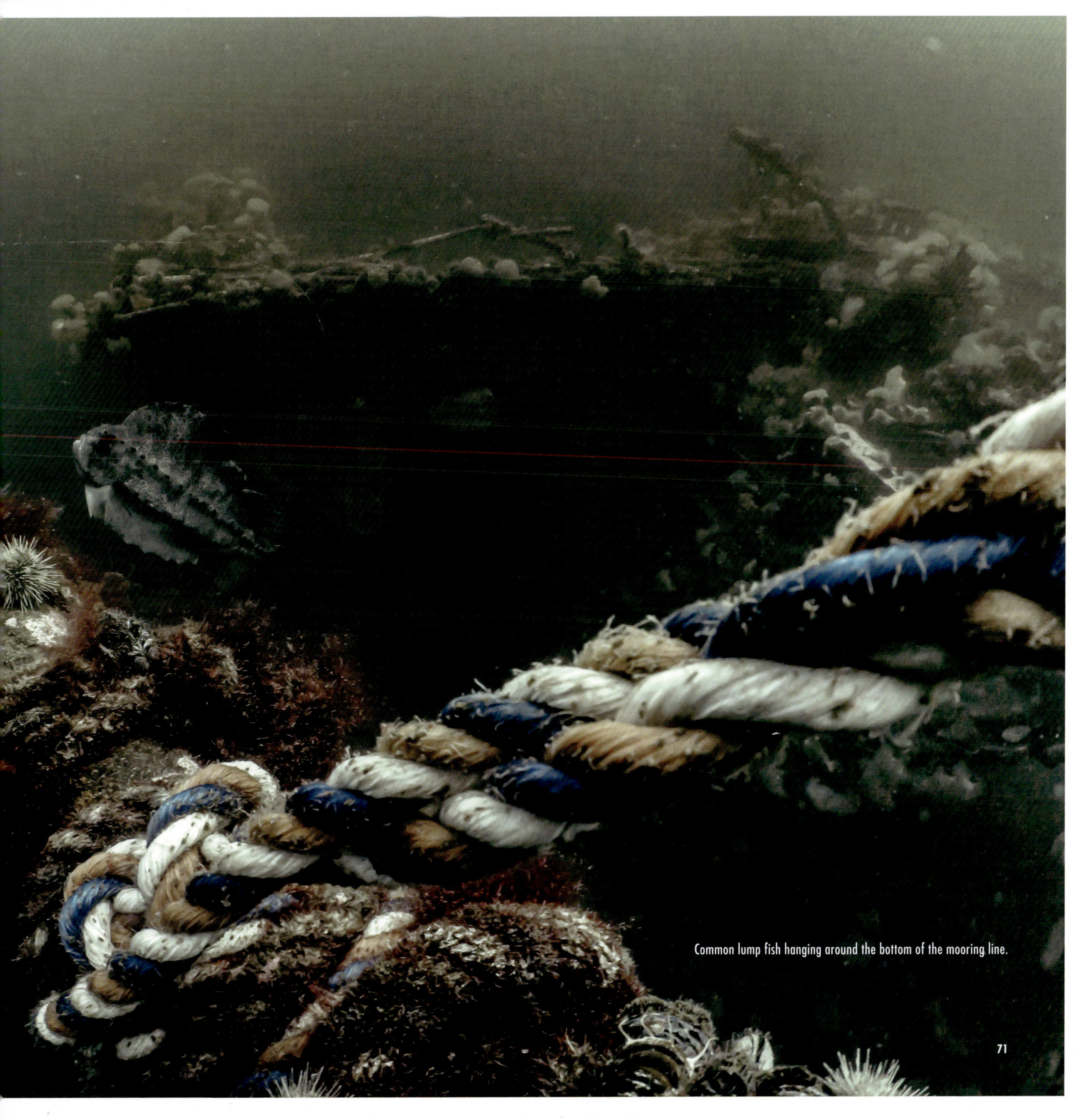

Common lump fish hanging around the bottom of the mooring line.

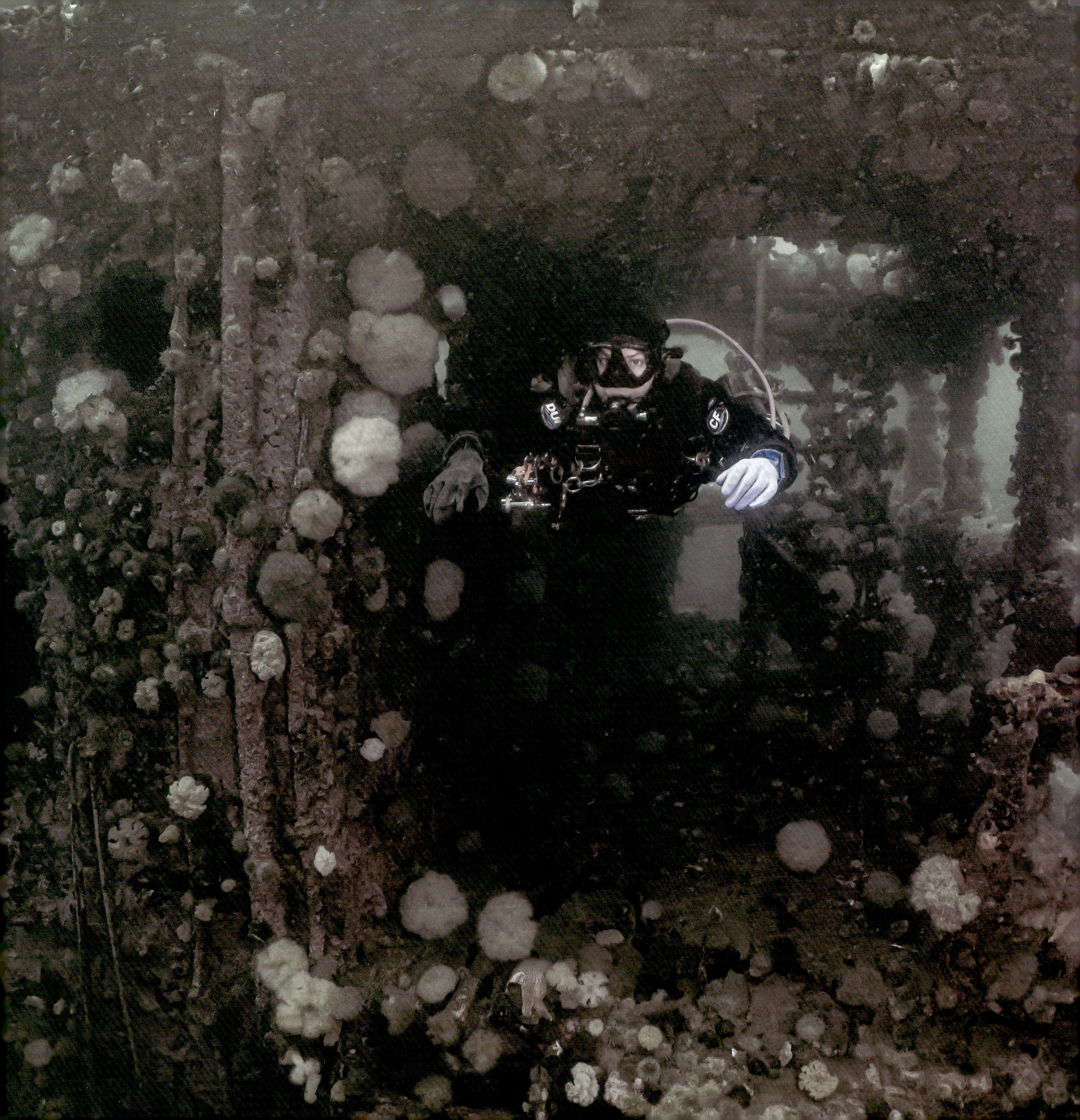

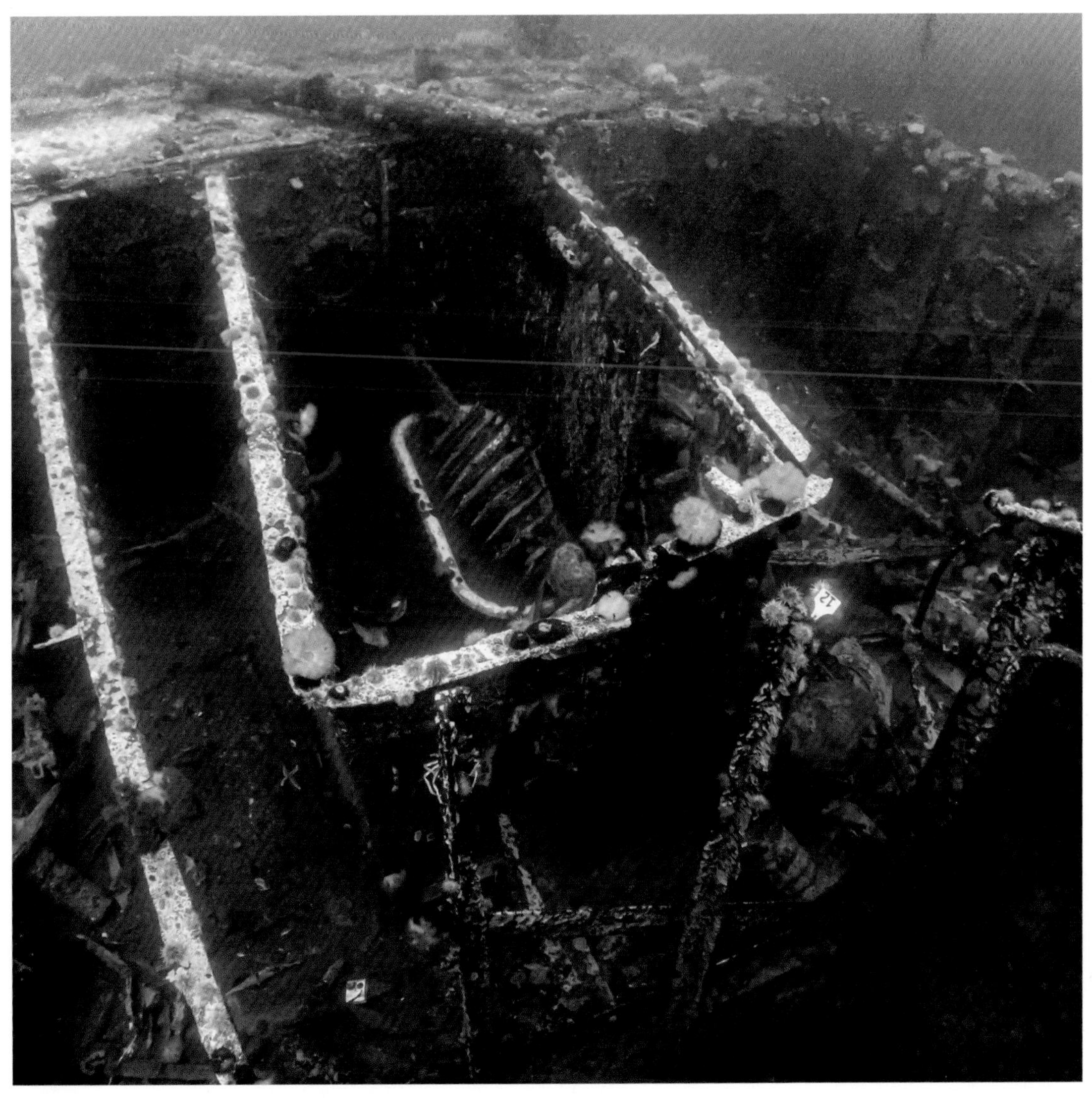

Bathroom found just aft of the wheelhouse, complete with bathtub.

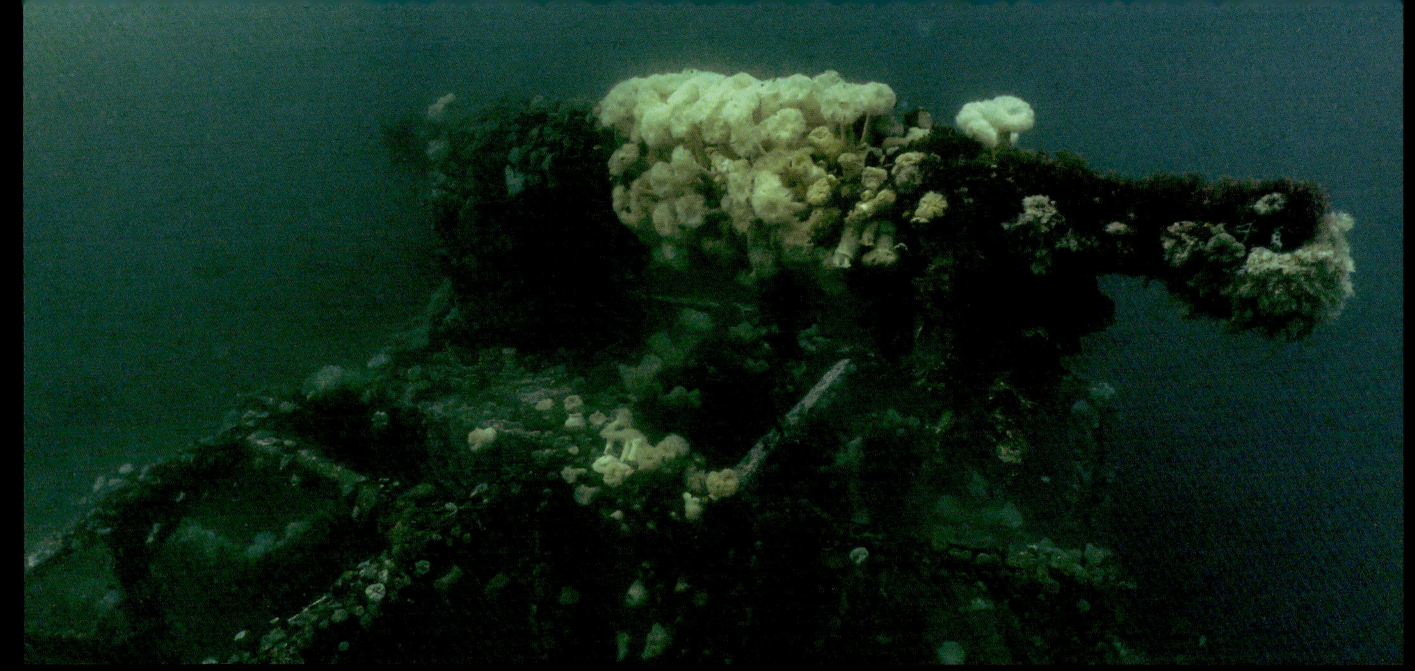

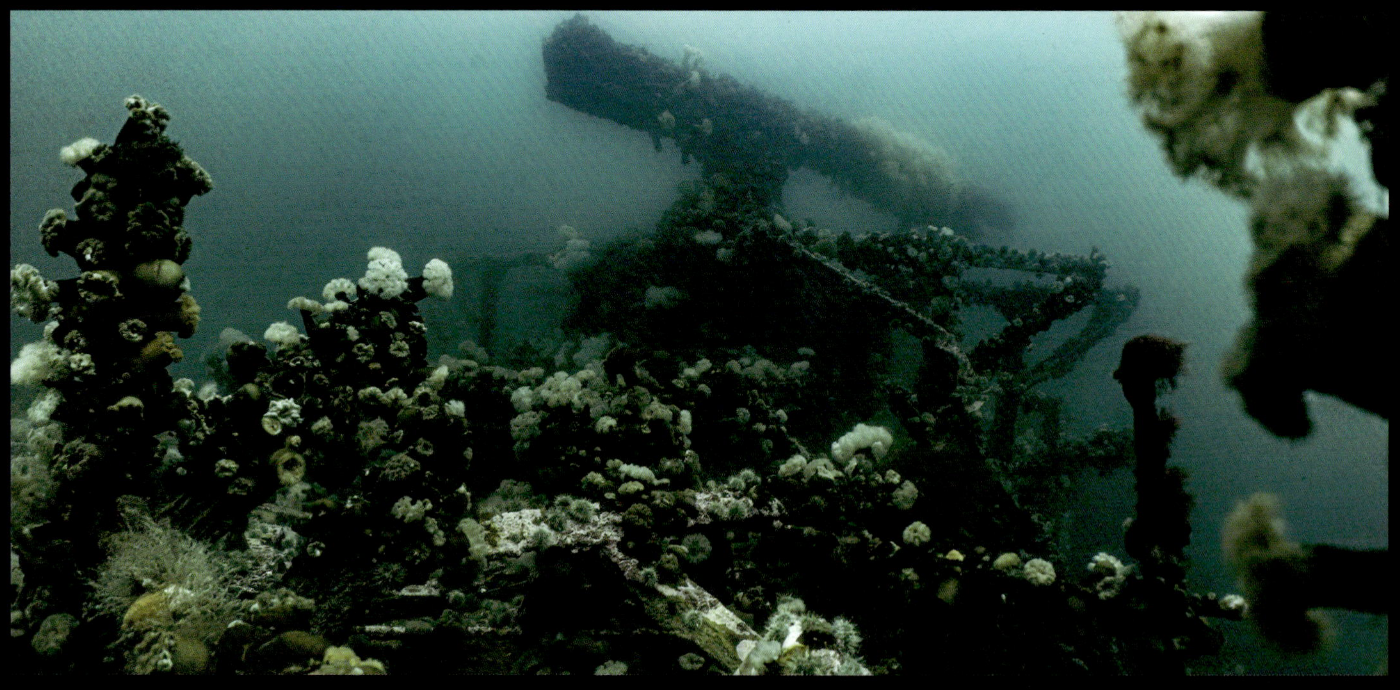

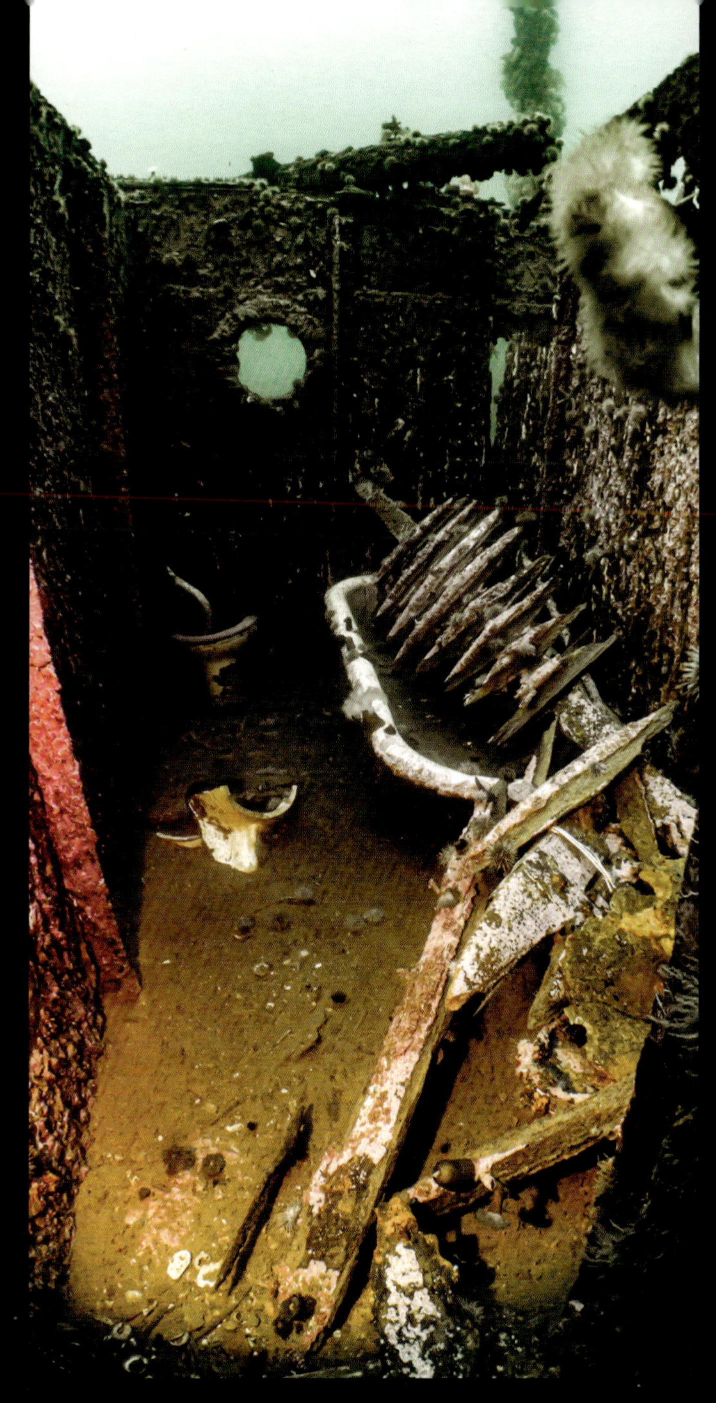

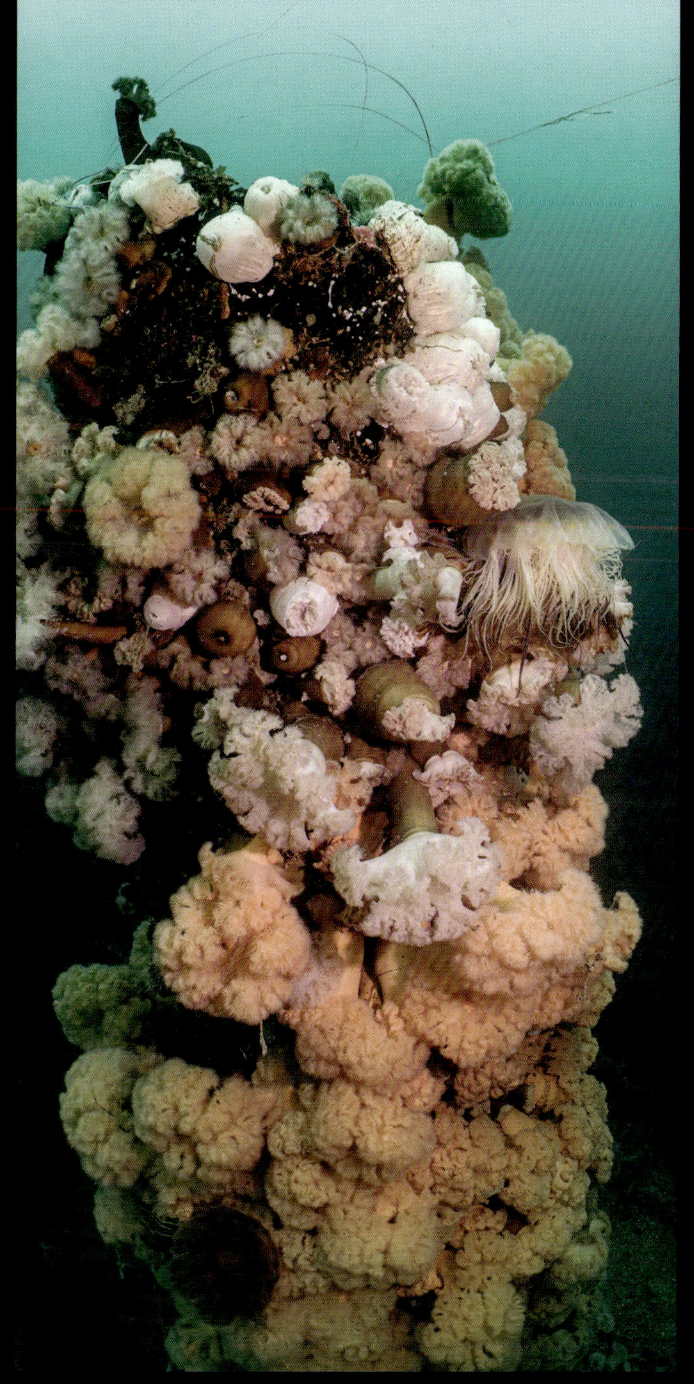

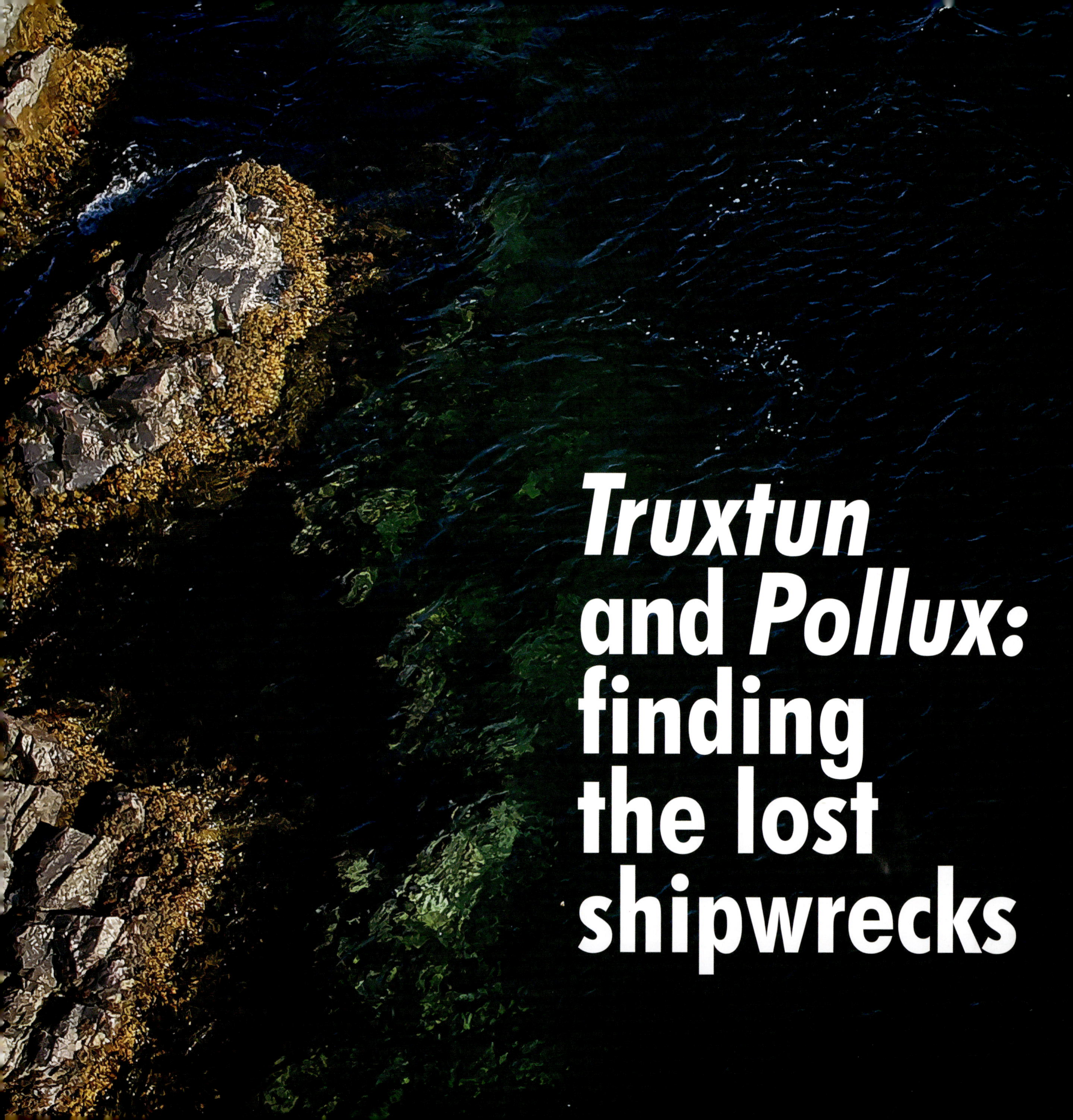

Truxtun and *Pollux*: finding the lost shipwrecks

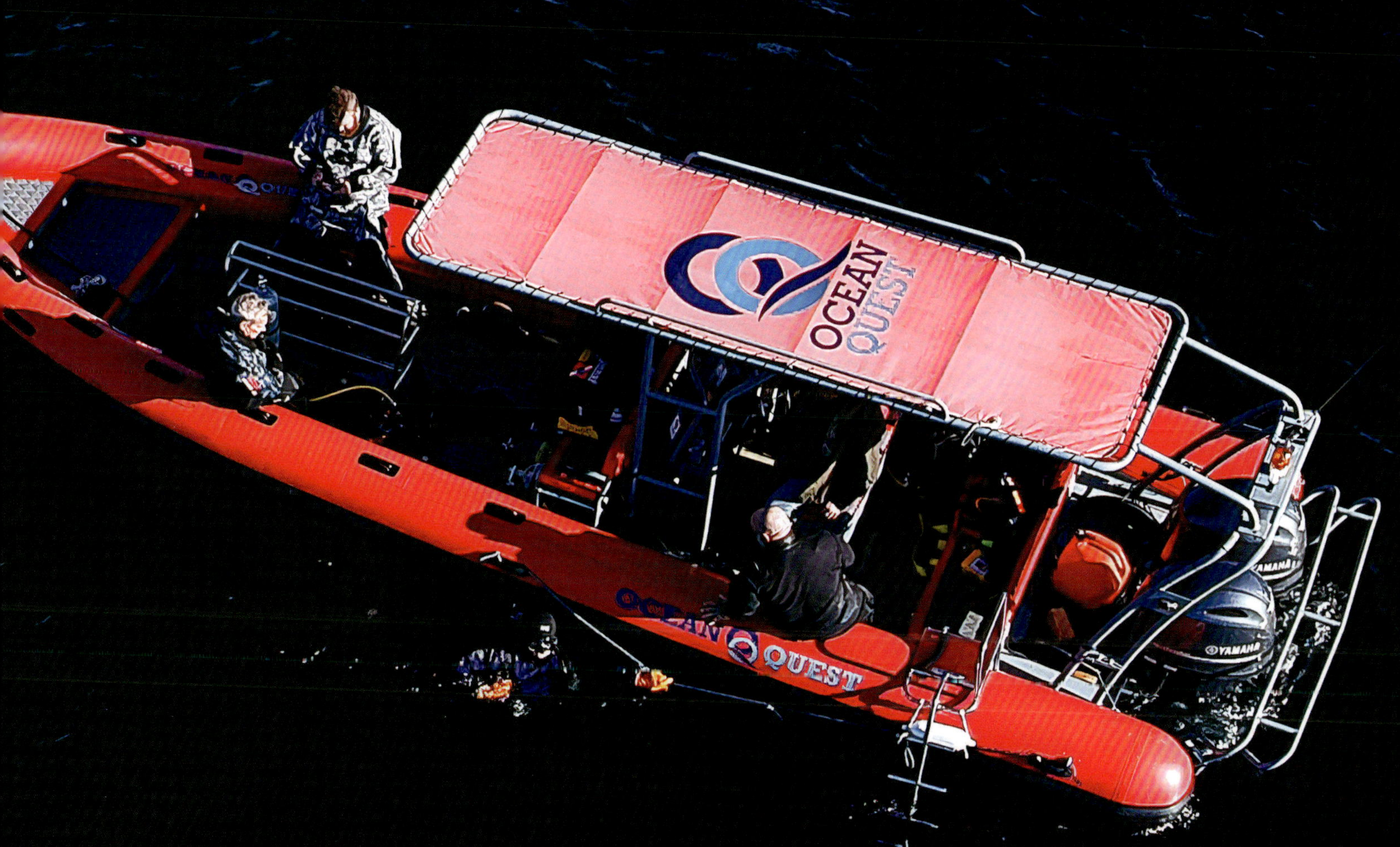

The wrecks of the USS *Truxtun* and USS *Pollux*, two military vessels that ran aground during the winter of 1942, long remained unexplored. The story of the sailors' perseverance and their heroic rescue by the residents of St. Lawrence and Lawn deserves to be remembered and celebrated. Their legacies live on through the documentary *As If They Were Angels* and the book *Hard Aground.*

The sailors aboard these ships found themselves off course due to errors in the still-developing technology of radar. In total, three ships ran aground. The USS *Wilkes* was able to get off the rocks; the *Truxtun* and the *Pollux* were beyond help. The sailors aboard had to brave the frigid temperatures and winter storm conditions to reach the shore. Eventually, workers at a nearby mine were alerted to the disaster. Residents from the surrounding communities coordinated a massive rescue effort; 189 passengers survived—many of whom were stranded below the cliffs, looking up, hoping for help. Another 203 souls were lost at sea, but the tragedy would have been so much worse if not for the heroic efforts of the local residents.

As a participant in two expeditions led by Ocean Quest, in search of these lost vessels, I have been fortunate to experience the thrill of discovering a part of history. Our first expedition, in 2013, was ultimately a success, as we located the USS *Truxtun* and made new friendships with residents of the area. The USS *Pollux*, however, was a

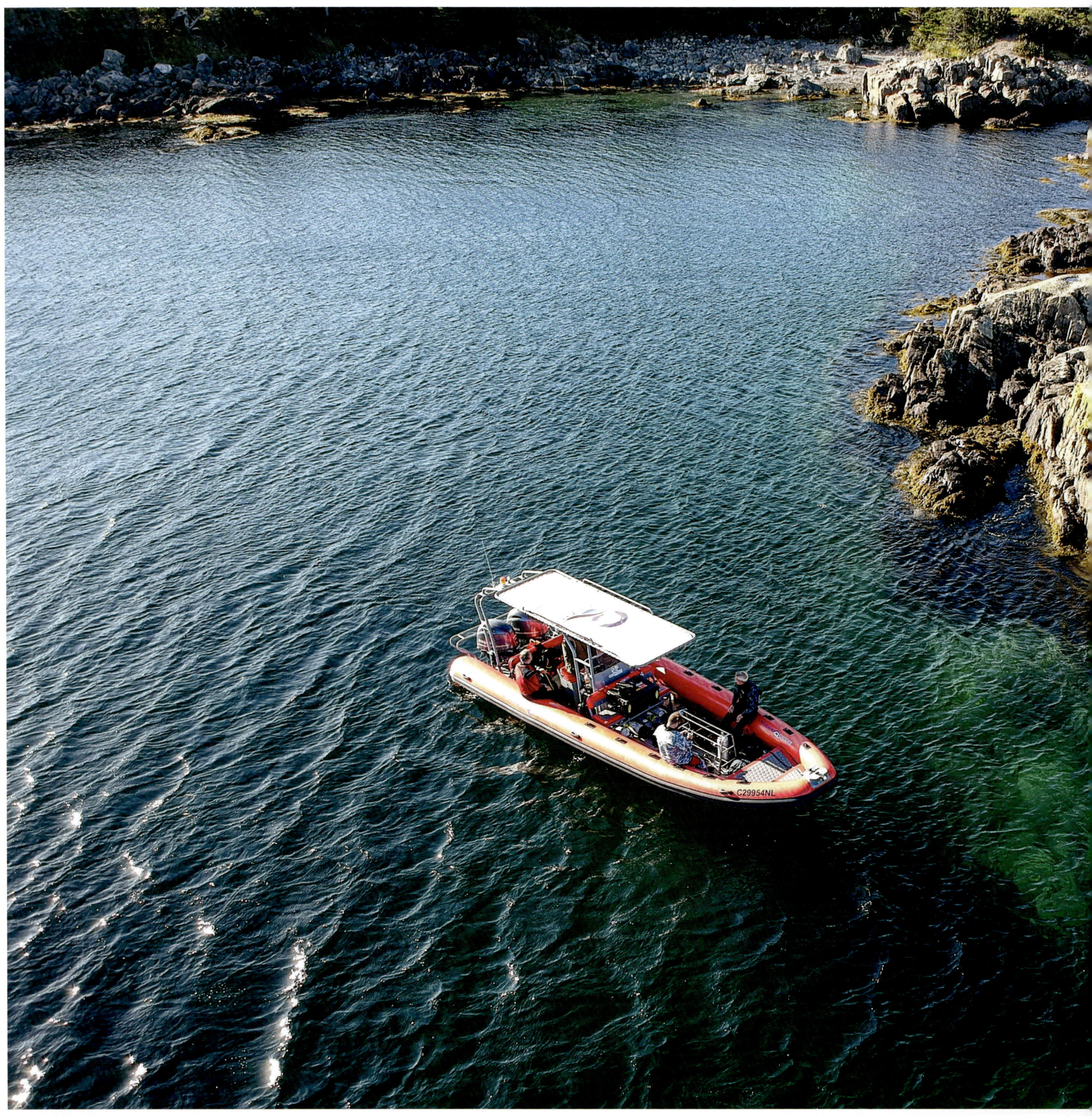
C29954NL

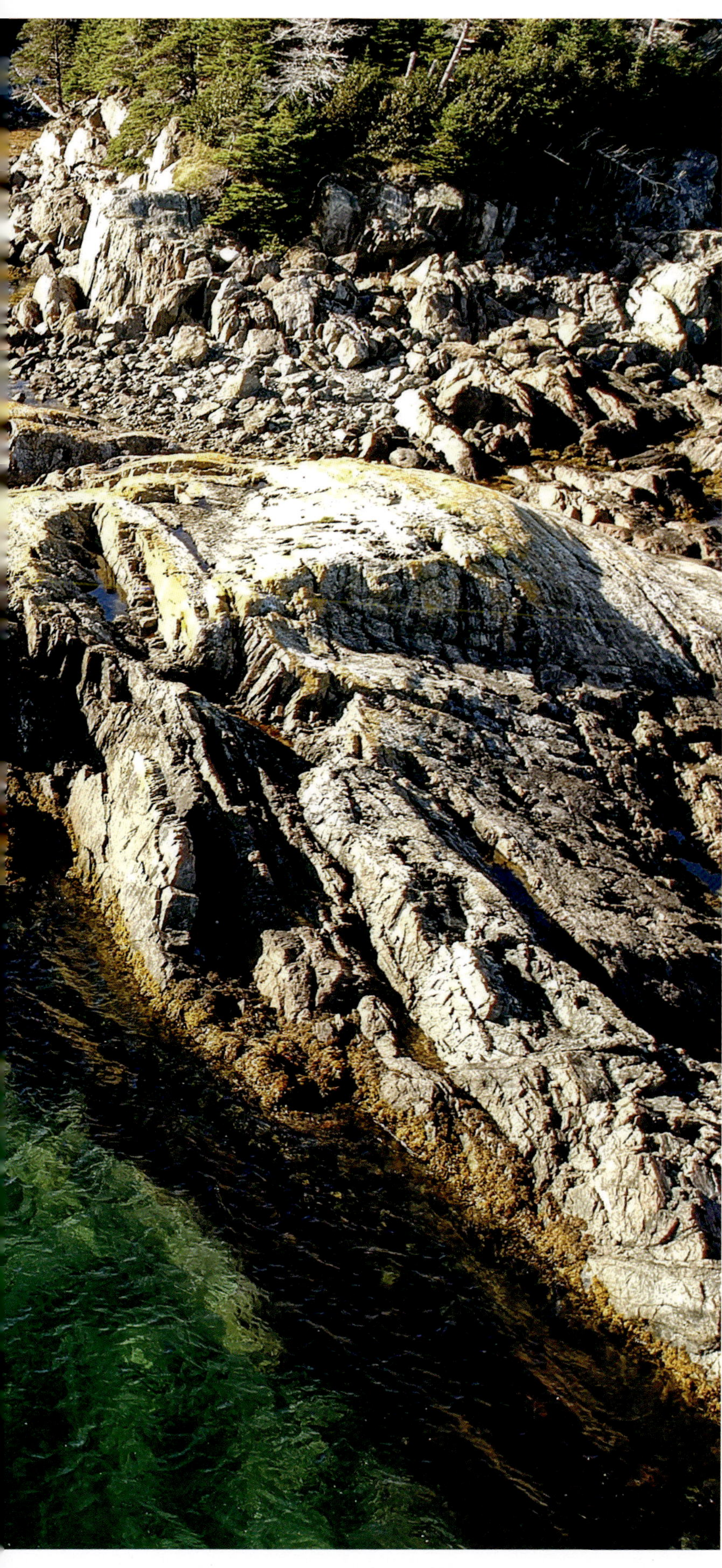

flirt—showing us just enough to know that we were close, but her final resting place remained elusive.

Our second expedition, in 2020, is where this telling starts, for two reasons. First, that initial trip was a decade ago, and the clarity of more recent memory aids in the telling of a good story. But more importantly, I did not have my camera on the first trip.

Being part of an expedition, not just to a new dive site but one with a target and goal, is not an opportunity all divers have. I'm grateful to leaders Rick Stanley, Johnny Olivero, and fellow divers Alain Langlais, Neil Burgess, and Tony Merkle for the experience.

Our expedition began with an easy check-out dive near

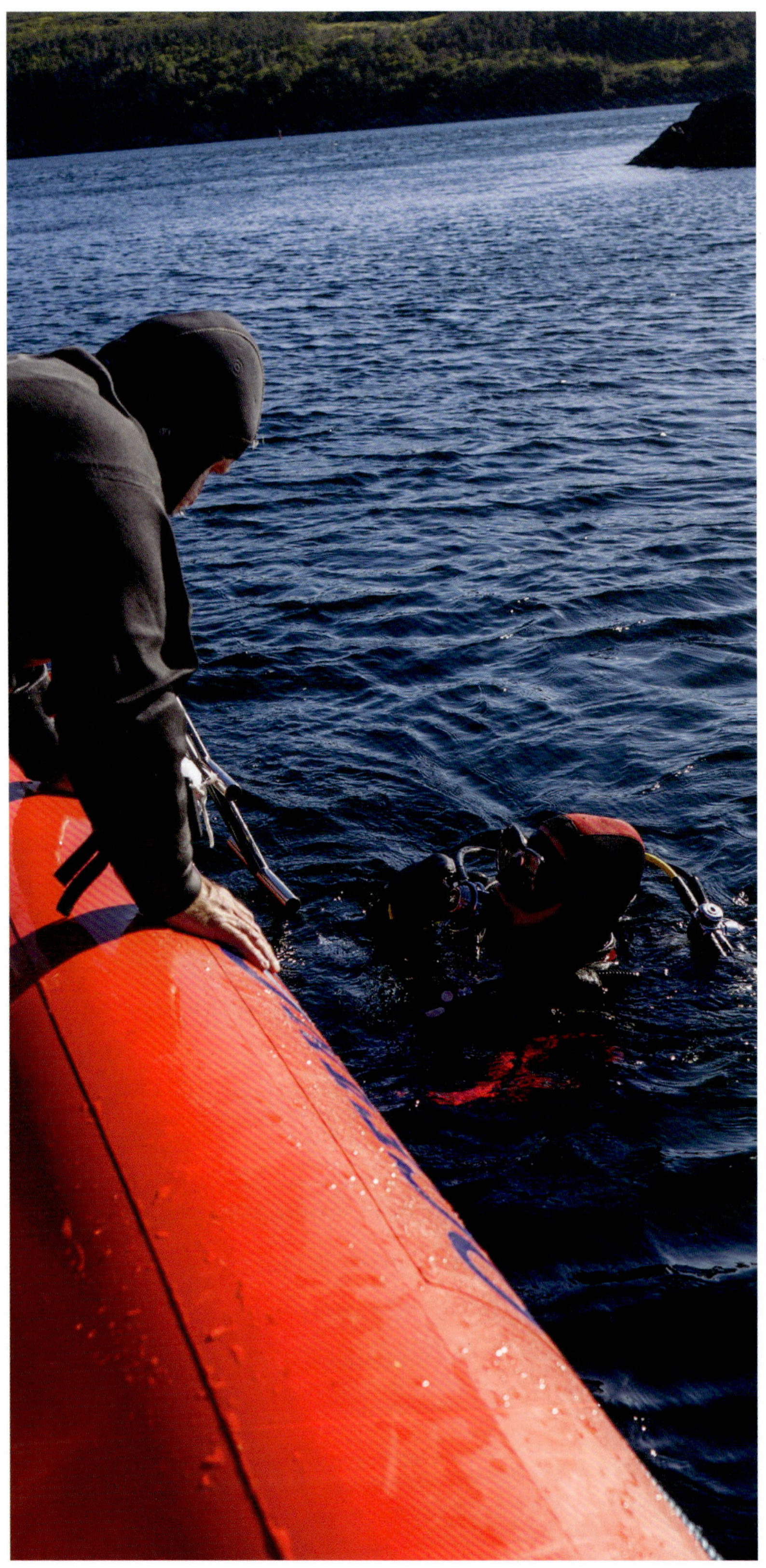

the harbour of St. Lawrence, in search of lost cannons. We had been told that cannons may have been lost to the depths there. The ocean is relatively shallow in the area, making it a great location to check gear and ensure that it's all in working condition. Although we were treated to beautiful rocky terrain covered in green urchins, we found no signs of the cannons.

The next day, the real journey began.

Anticipation was high as we set out on the rigid-hulled inflatable boat (RHIB), geared in our drysuits. Our destination was Chambers Cove, the final resting place of the USS *Truxtun*. Memories of my first visit flooded back as I geared up. The wreck sits between several rocks protruding above the water. On this calm day, the waters below the cliffs encompassing the cove resembled a shimmering pool, a stark contrast to the washing machine of waves that often rage in this area.

Visitors who venture up to the scenic lookout on the cliffs can view the waves from the safety of a memorial to those lost during the disaster. We perform our final checks as the captain declares "pool is open," letting us know that it's safe to proceed. We lean back, tanks first, and plunge off the side on the RHIB. (Some people ask why divers roll off backwards. The simple answer is, if we sit on the edge and roll forward, we remain in the boat.)

As the tank hits the water, there is a little jolt and then

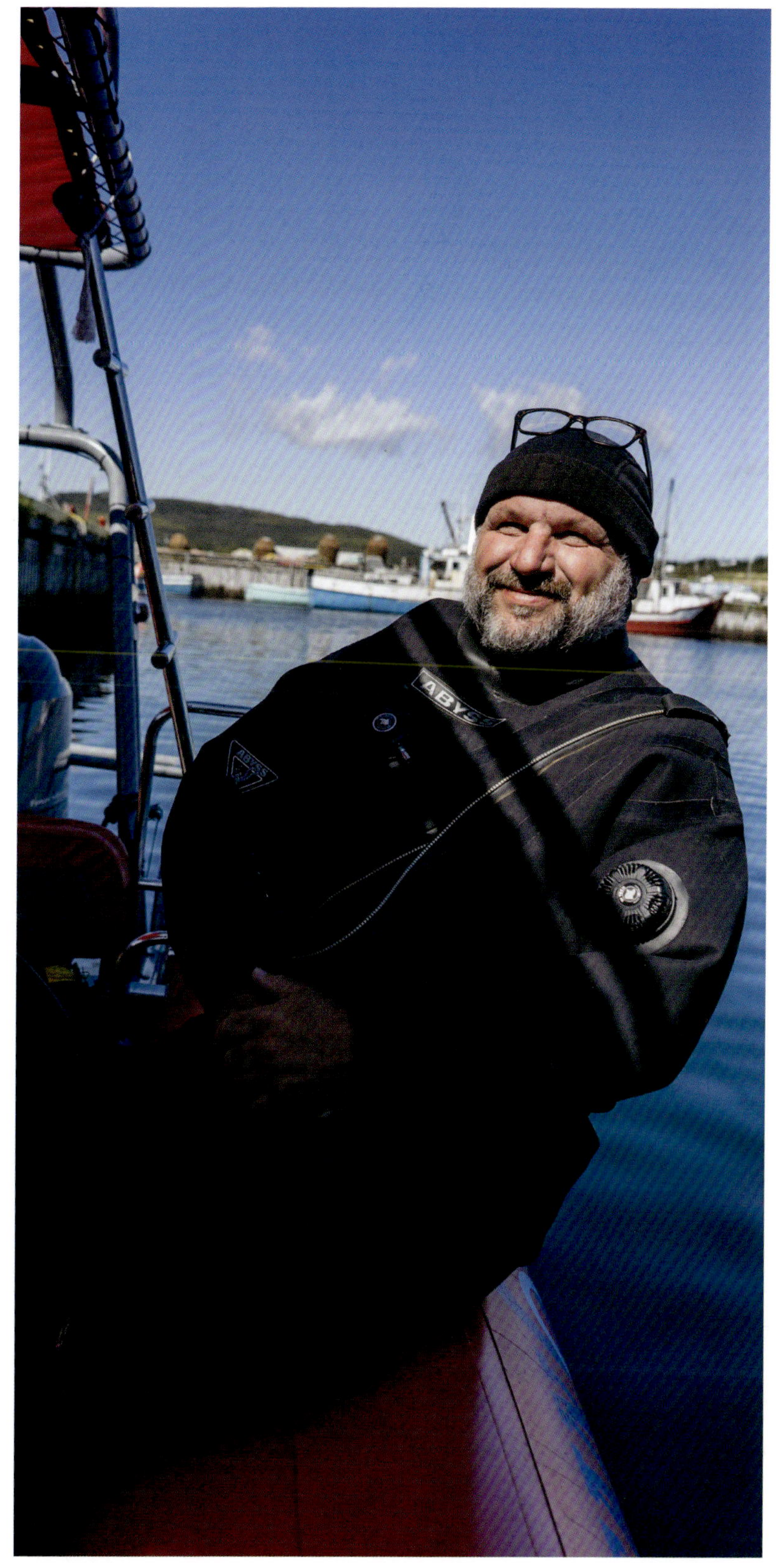

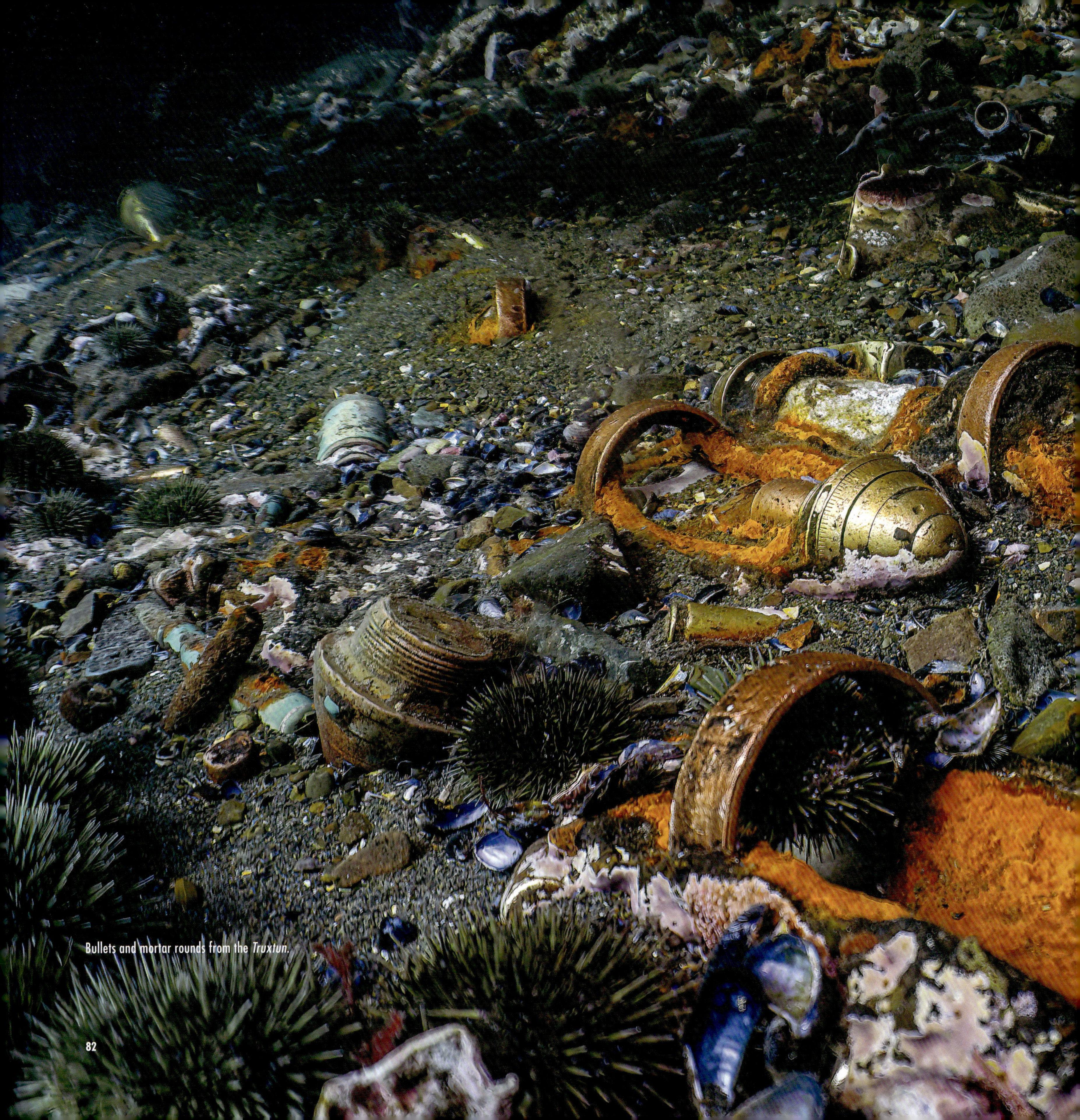

Bullets and mortar rounds from the *Truxtun*.

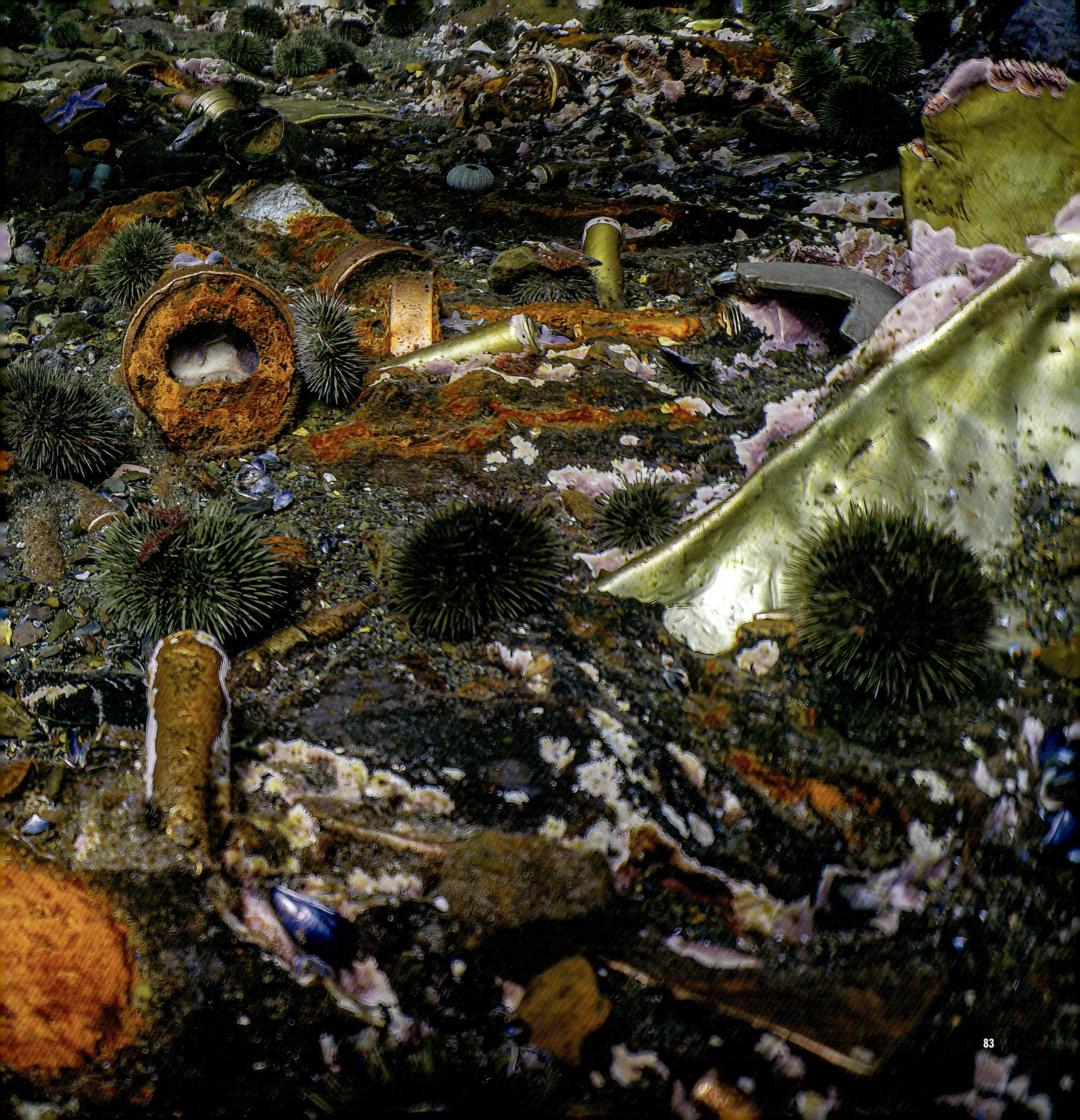

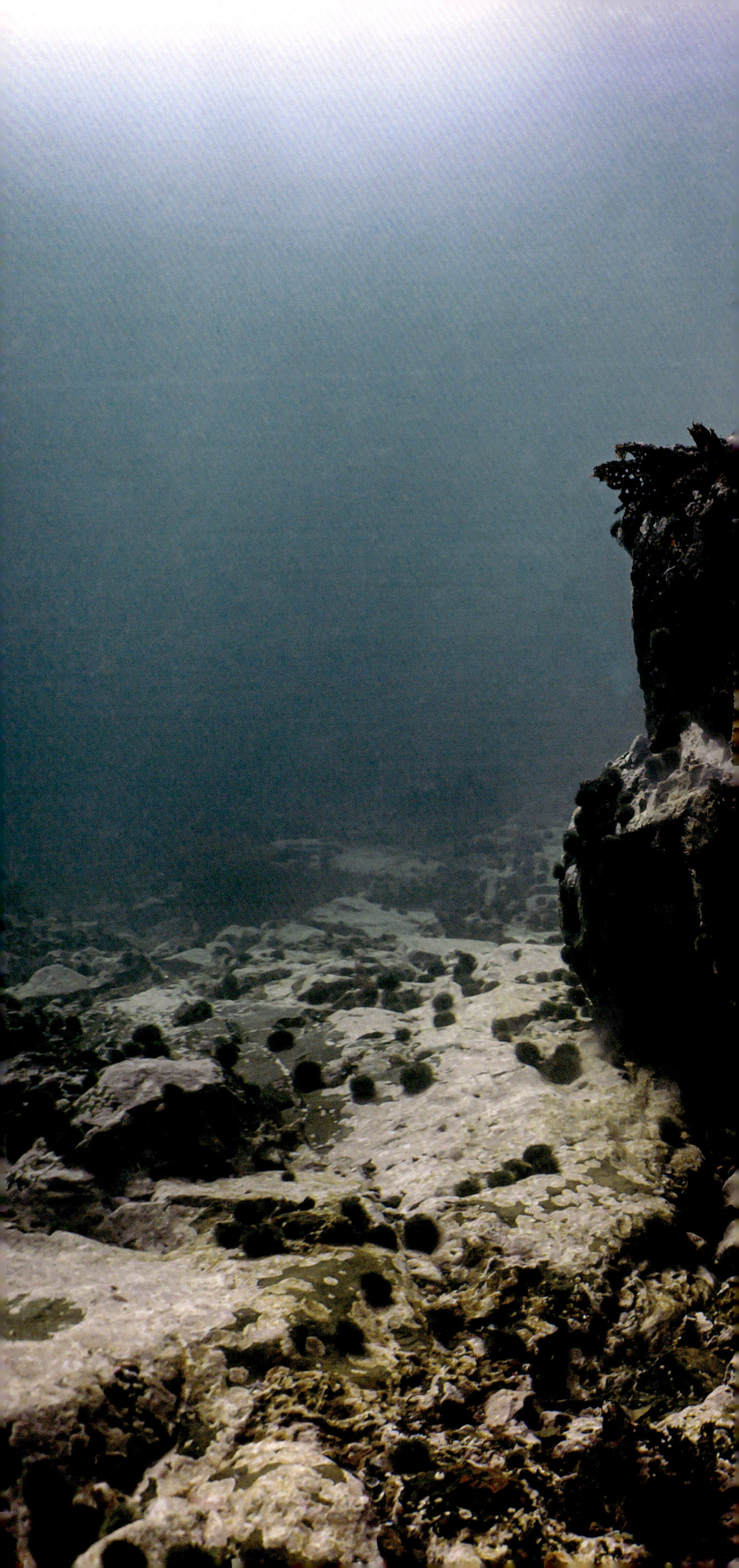

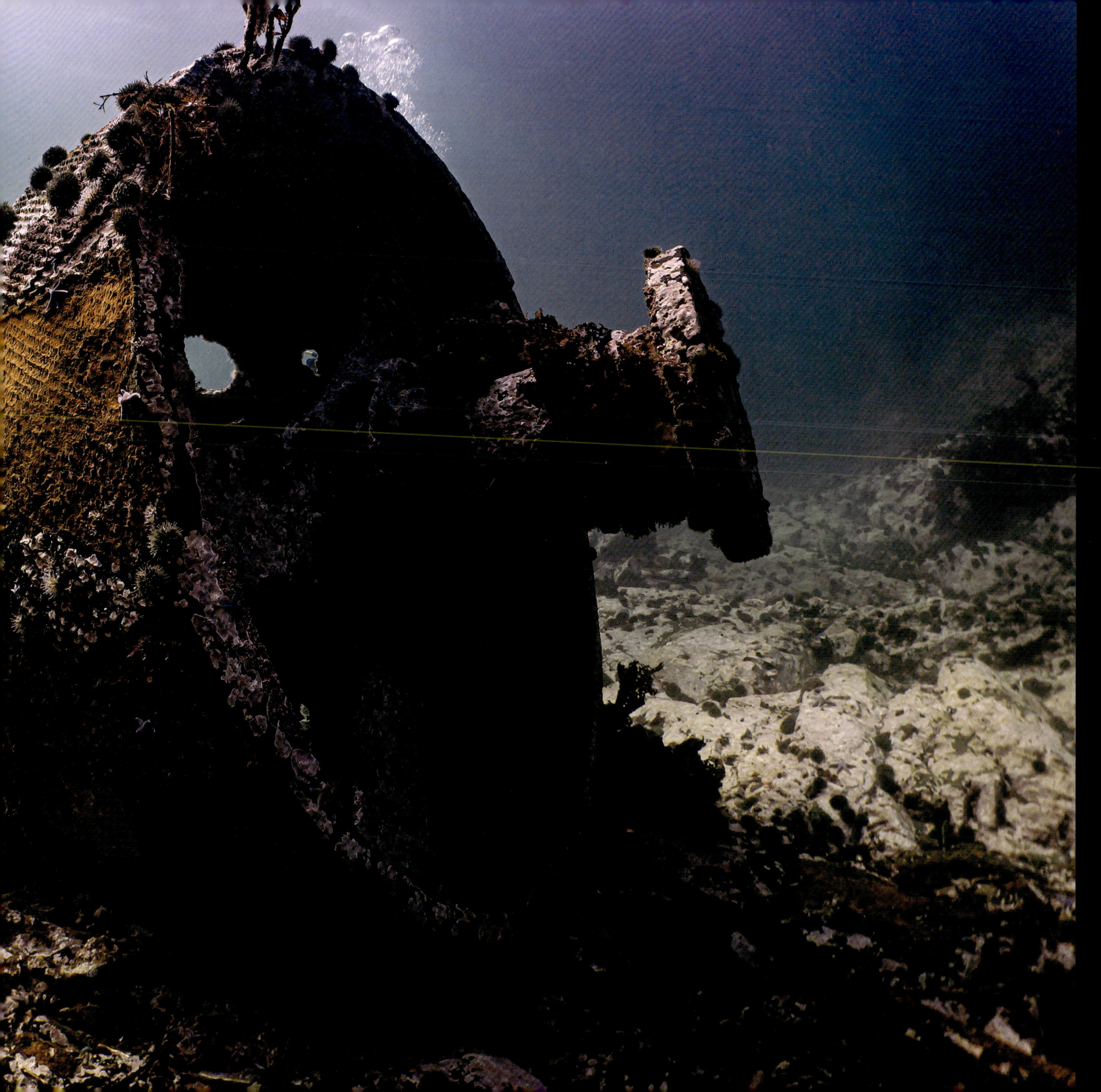

each diver floats back to the surface. We give the boat an OK signal and locate the team. Unlike at the Bell Island shipwrecks, the ocean floor here is clearly visible; this dive will reach a maximum of 25 feet—and only that deep if a diver chose to lie down on the bottom. Although the water was calm, the surge near the surface was relentless, swaying us back and forth, but we learned to embrace it, allowing it to rock us to its rhythm. The USS *Truxtun* lay before us, a field of debris. Many, if not most, other shipwrecks around Newfoundland are in this condition—the Bell Island shipwrecks are a notable exception.

On the fourth and final day of our expedition, we embarked to dive to the USS *Pollux*. We had explored the

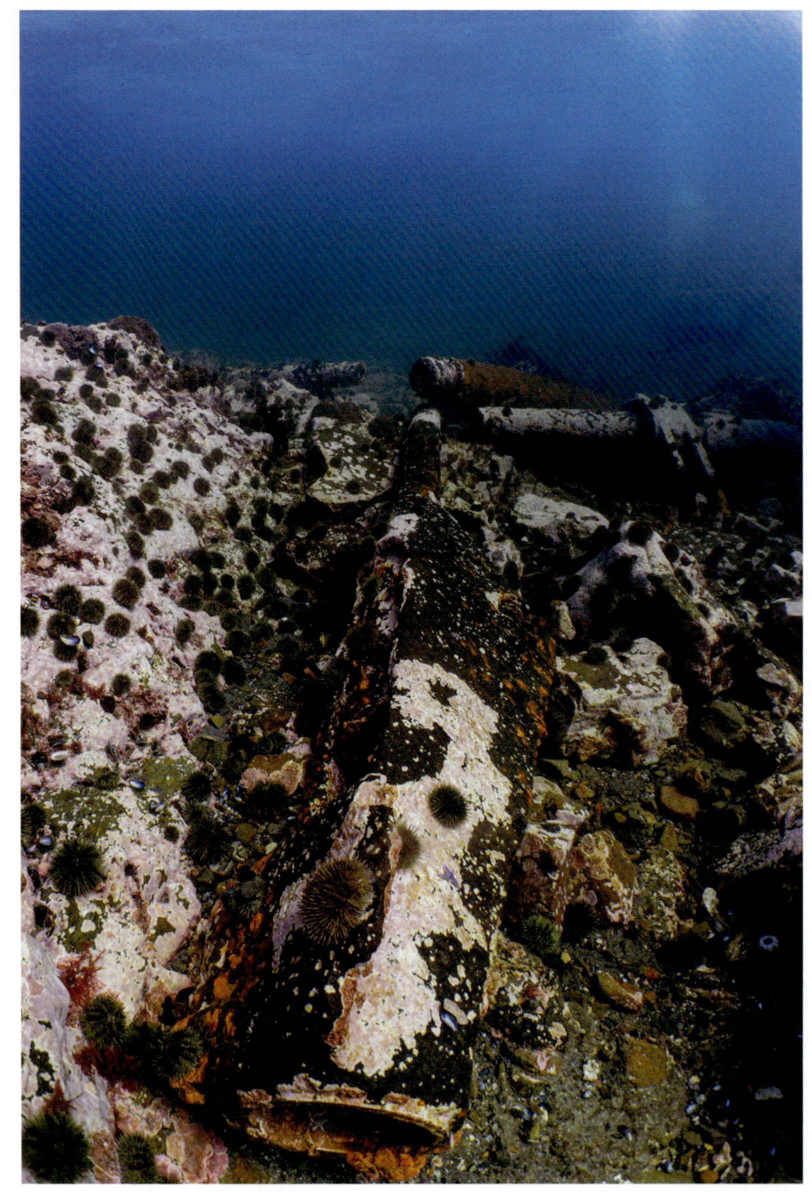

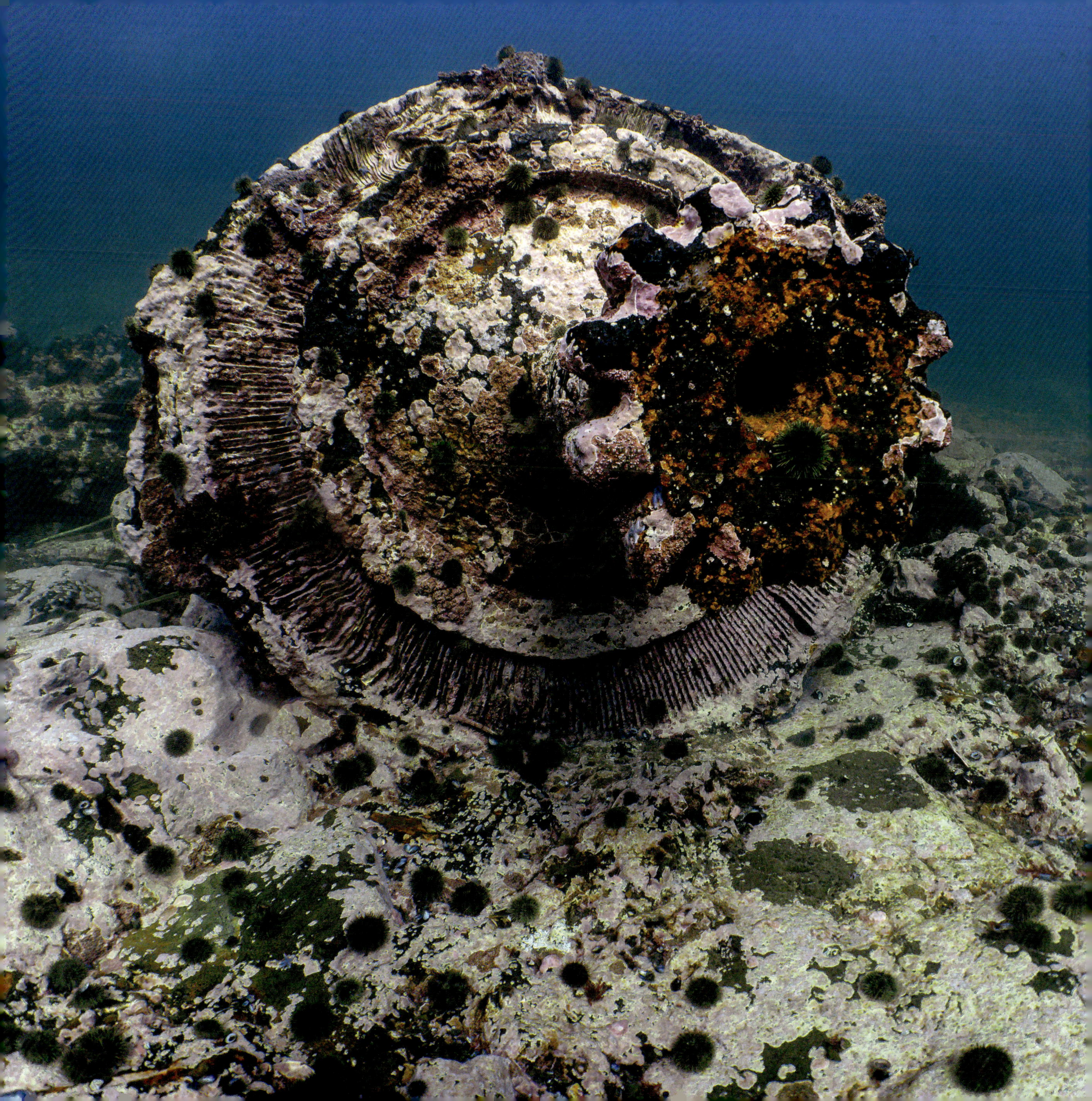

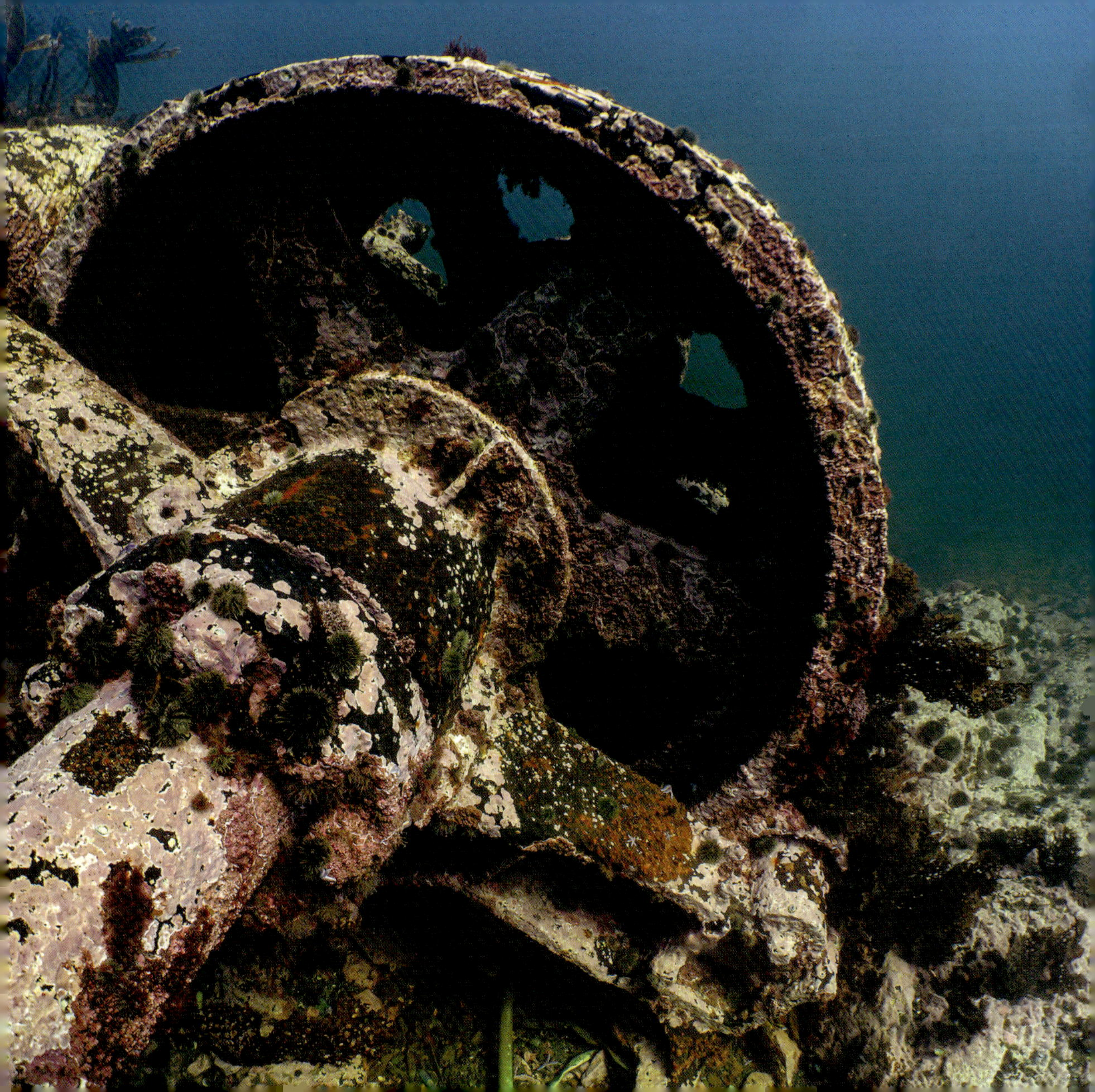

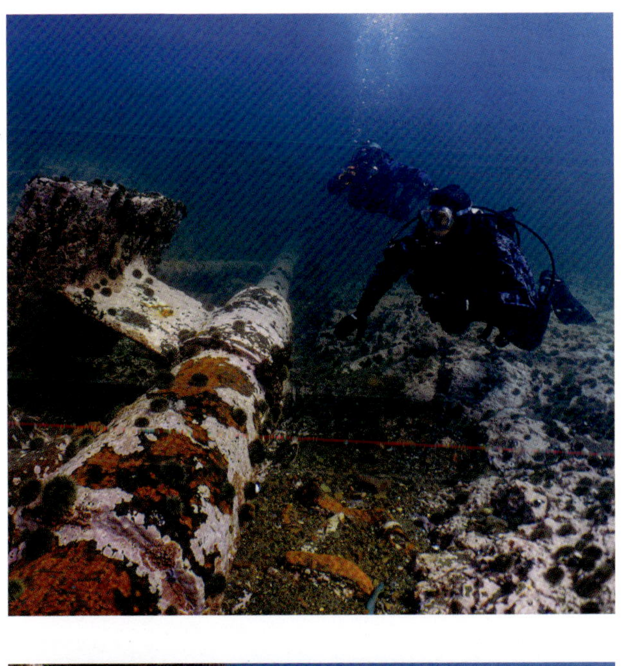
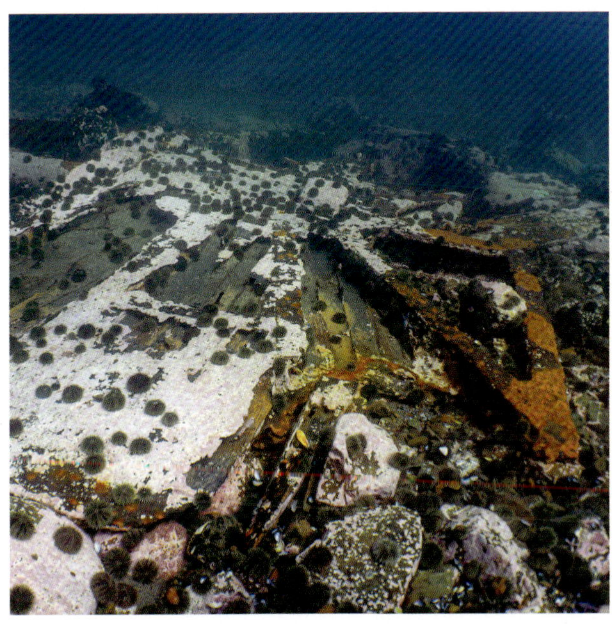
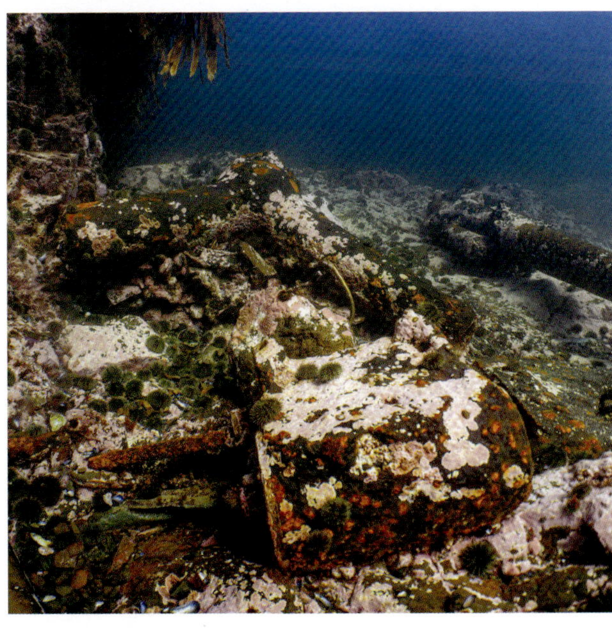
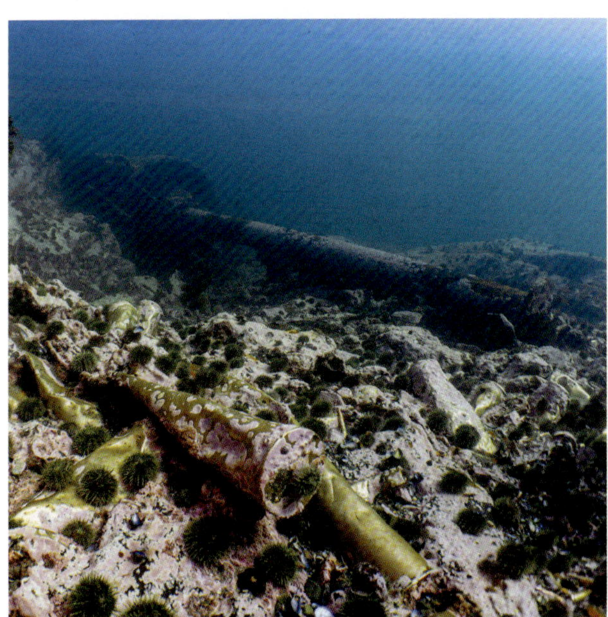

USS *Pollux*

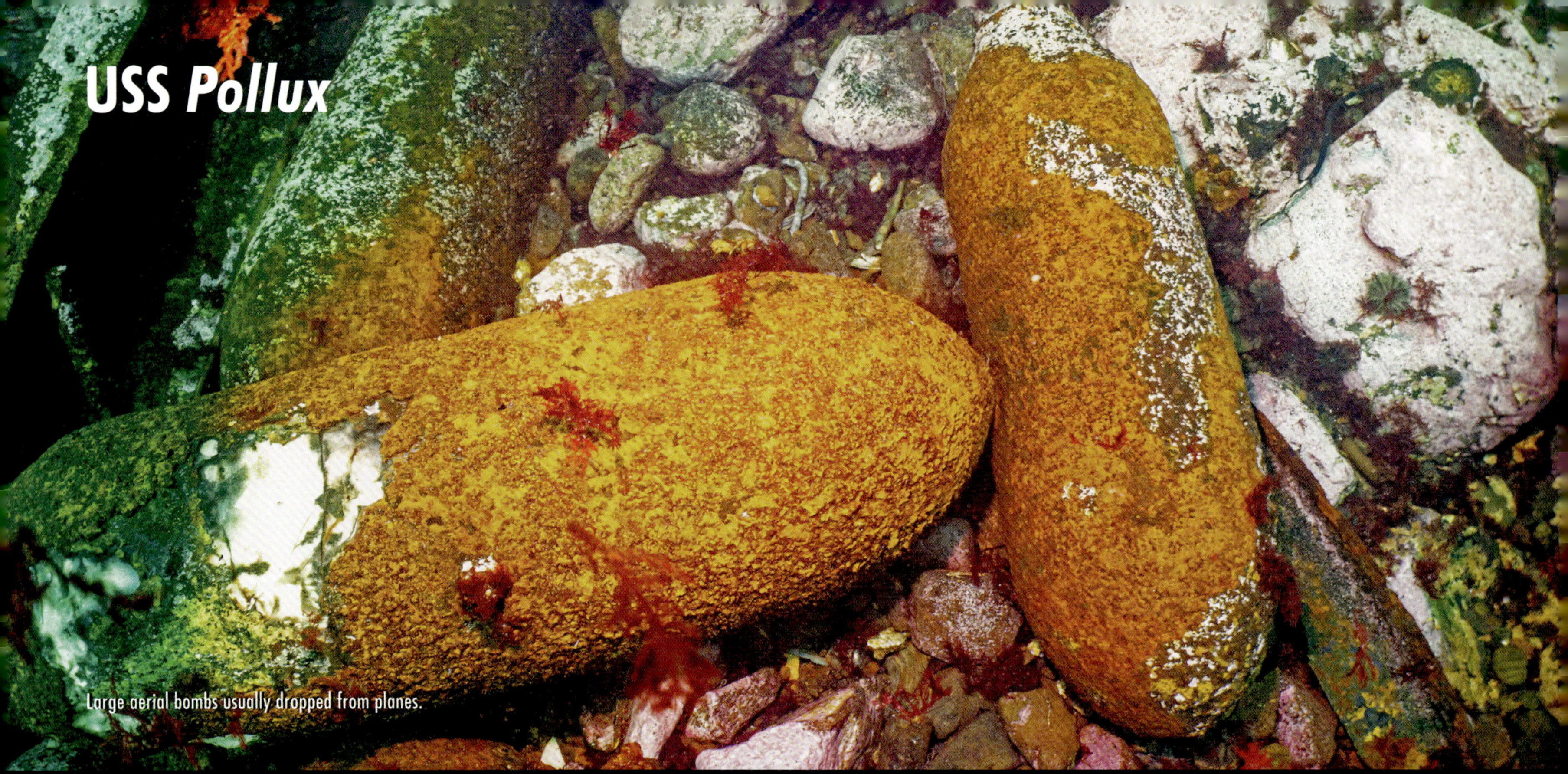

Large aerial bombs usually dropped from planes.

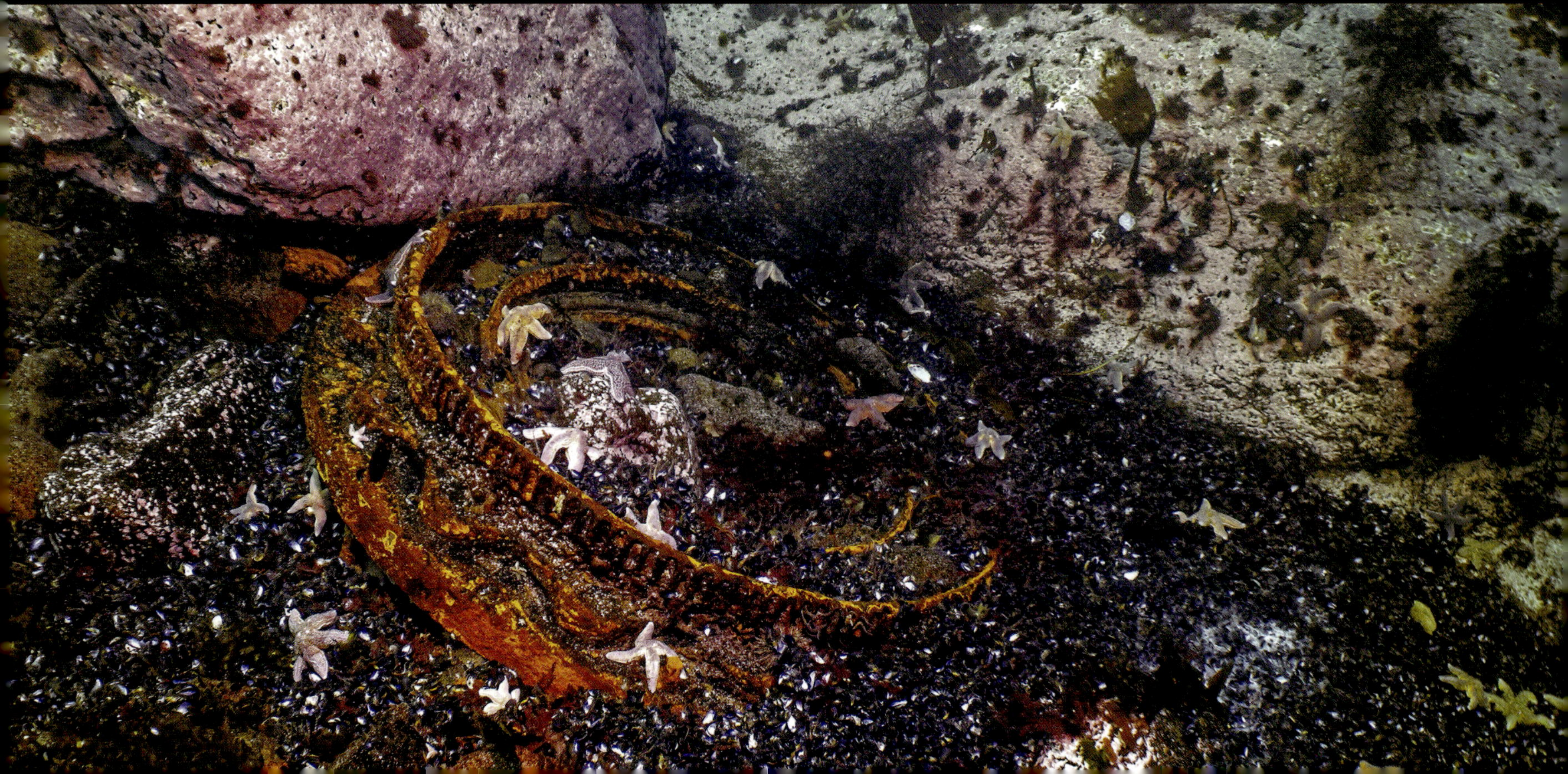

surrounding waters, but the main wreckage eluded us. We were excited and determined to explore farther west. The first pair of divers splashed down on a site that we had heard could be a location for the wreck. They returned, exhilarated—but, alas, they had not found the wreck. They reported a high surge which made navigating through an underwater canyon thrilling, as they were pushed between the canyon walls; they felt like fighter jets in a movie, dodging between the rocks. Once everyone was back on board, it was my team's turn to take the plunge.

We move to the next site. As the engine slowed, we jumped into action, putting on our gear and dropping into the deep. Linking up with my buddy, we made a blue water descent—we had no rope to follow or rocks or cliffs to use as reference; we relied solely on each other and our dive computers for reference. At 70 feet, we marvelled at the rocky bottom 20 to 30 feet below us, but as it offered no clues, we hovered at that depth, using our compass to guide us toward the shore.

Soon the sea floor began to rise, meeting us at 70 feet. We spotted the brass propeller of a lifeboat, the first sign of the *Pollux*. We eagerly followed the bottom toward shore as it led us into shallower water and hopefully the wreckage. As we approached the shore, we felt the surge the first team had described. Dodging between the rocks, we rounded a bend and were greeted by the stunning sight

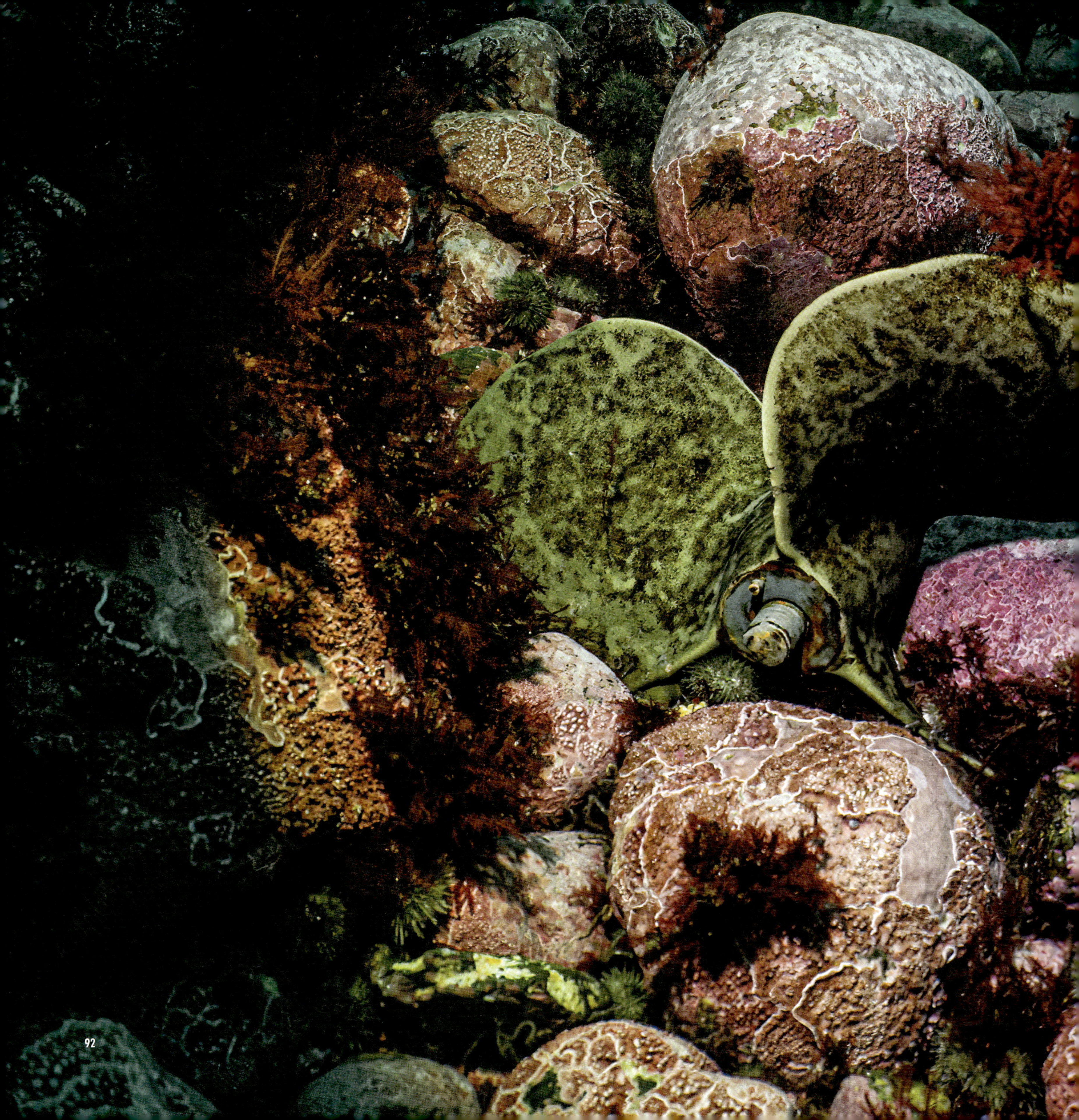

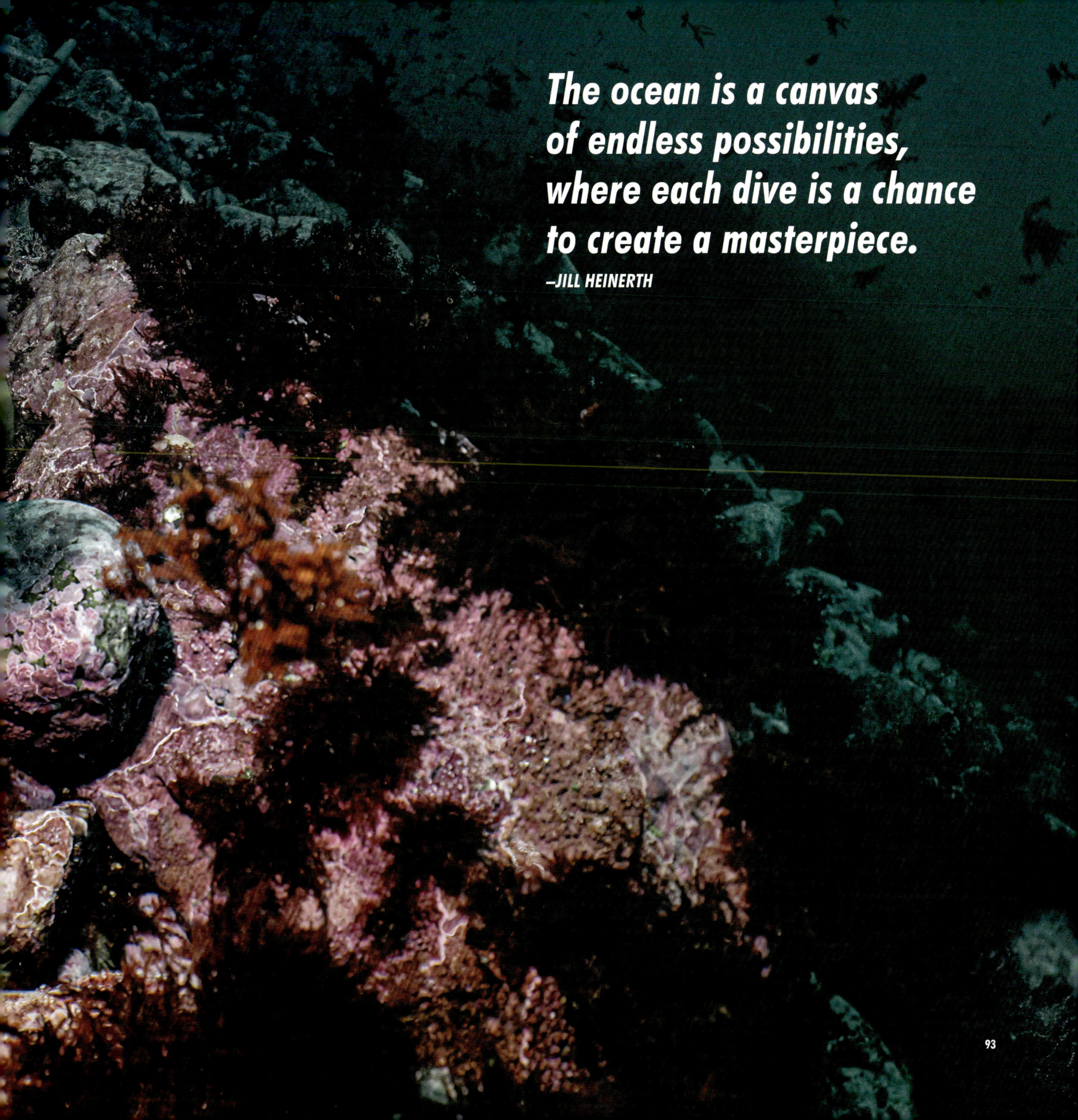

The ocean is a canvas of endless possibilities, where each dive is a chance to create a masterpiece.

–JILL HEINERTH

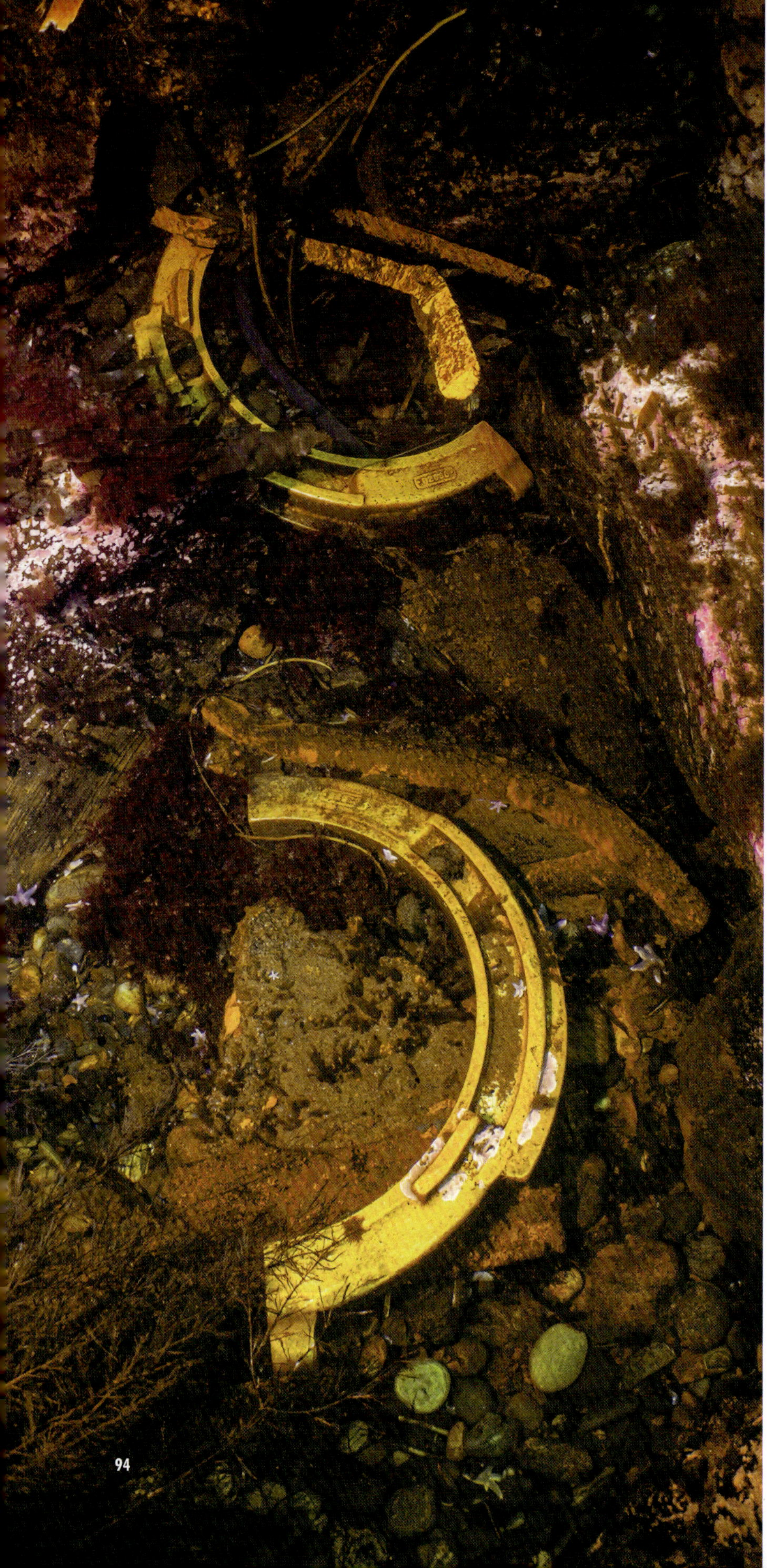

of heat exchangers and a brass porthole still attached to a section of hull lying flat on the sea floor. These artifacts were nestled in a small valley that offered a break from the surge—it formed a calm spot, like turning a corner in a strong wind. We paused to mark our location with a surface marker buoy, to indicate where the first dive team would continue their search. We couldn't resist the urge to venture a little closer to shore. In doing so, we caught a glimpse of what lay beyond, an engine shaft stretching into the distance.

We returned to the exchangers and surface marker buoy to ascend to the surface and share our discovery. I informed the boat how to get there. We hoped the engine

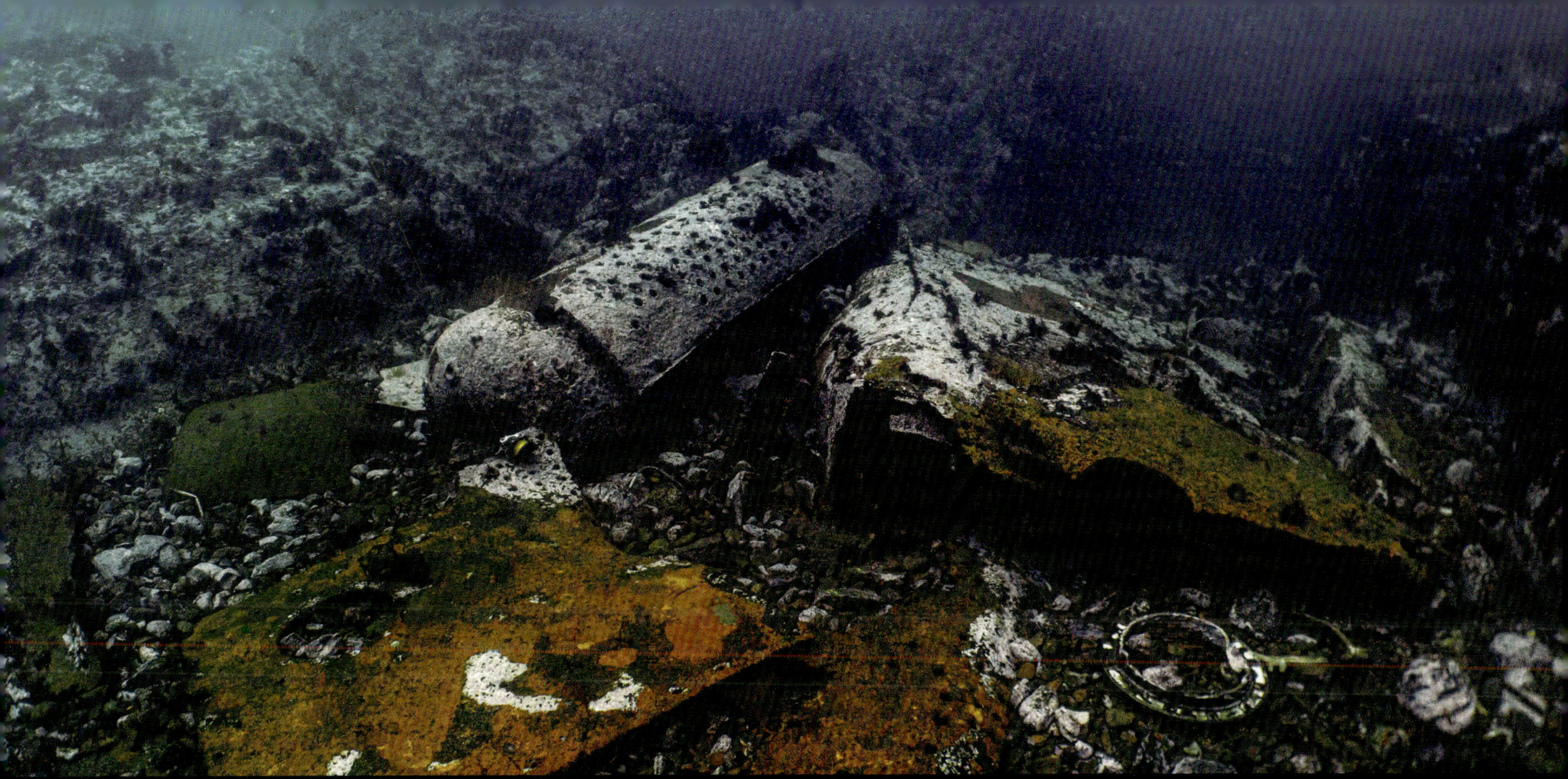

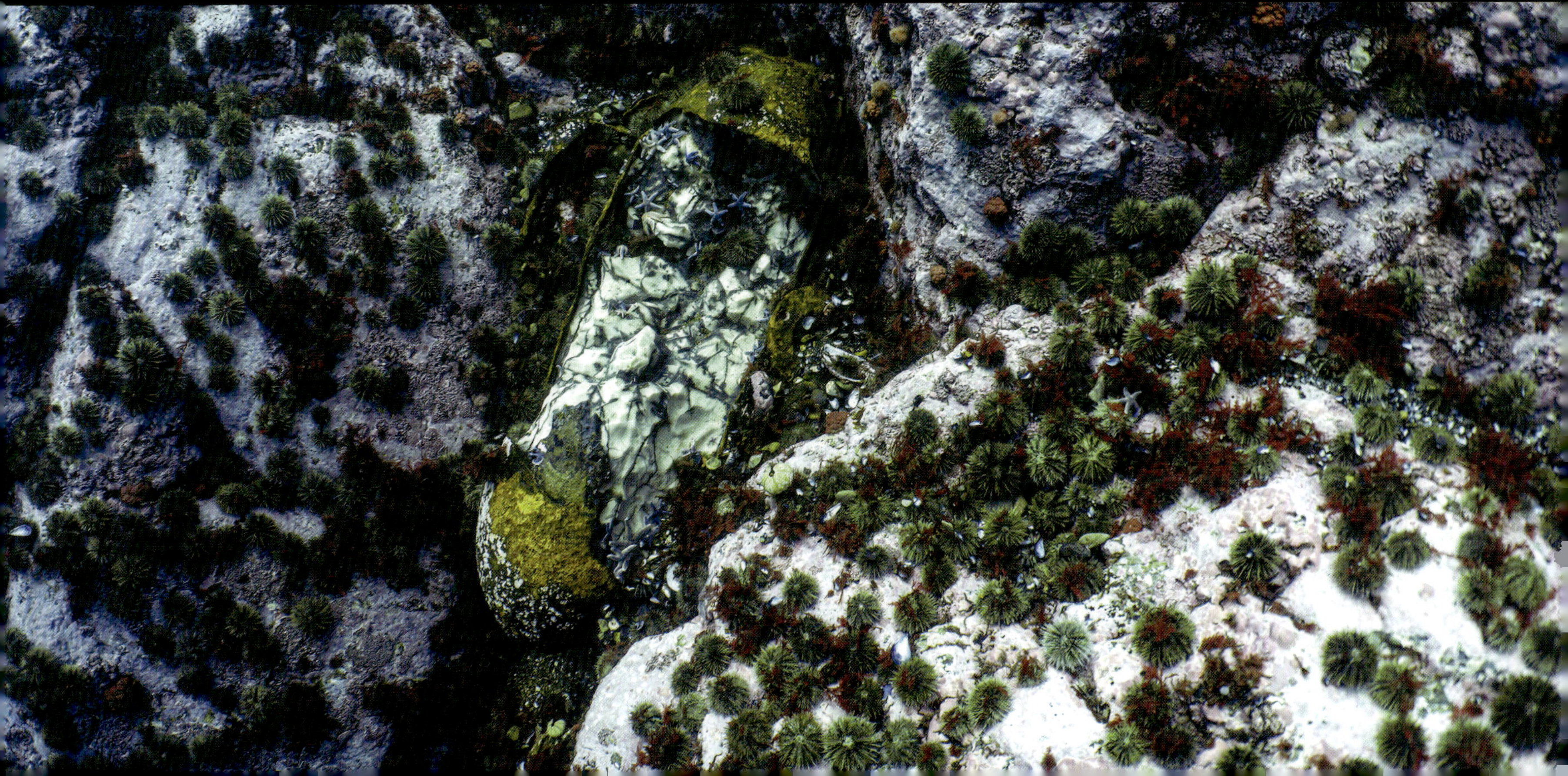

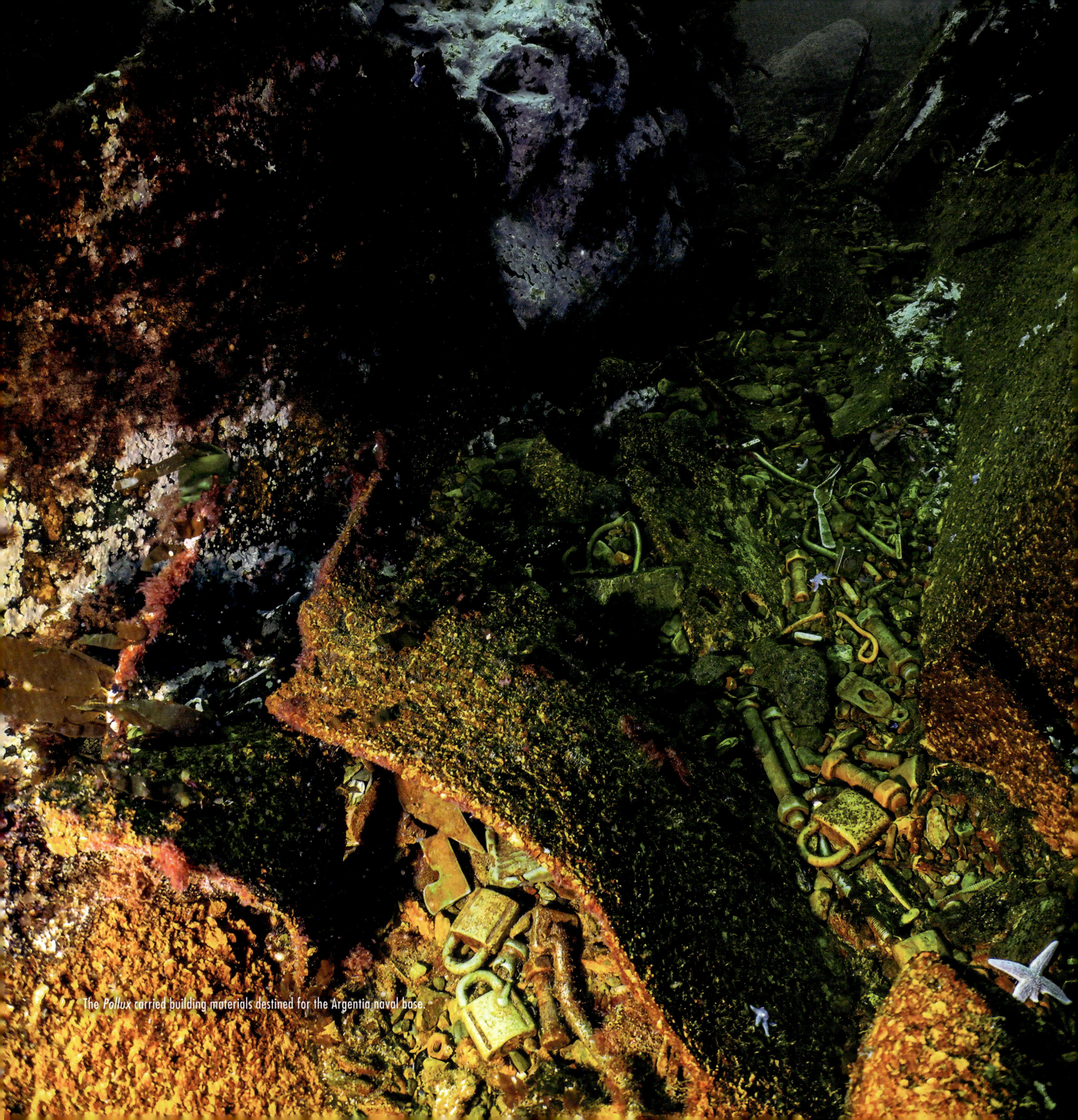

The *Pollux* carried building materials destined for the Argentia naval base.

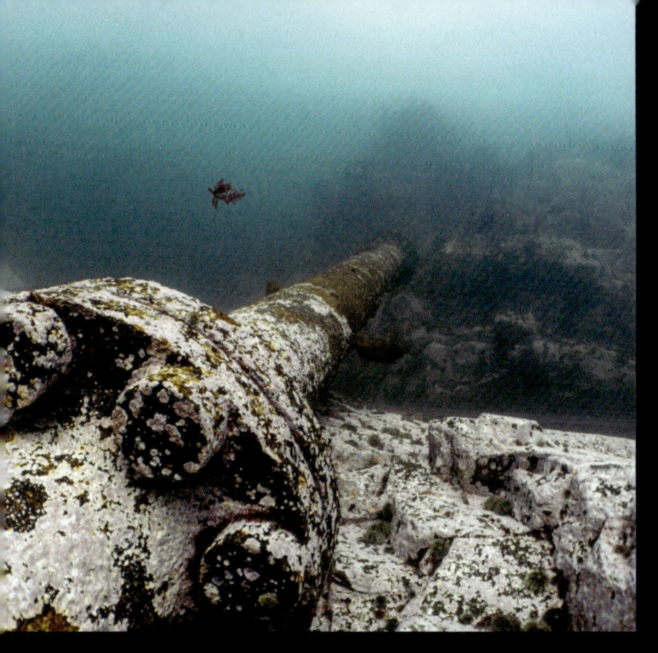

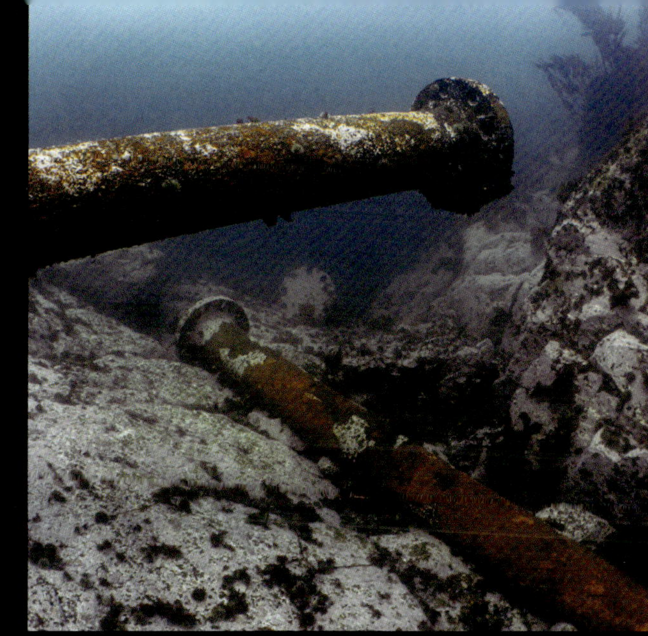

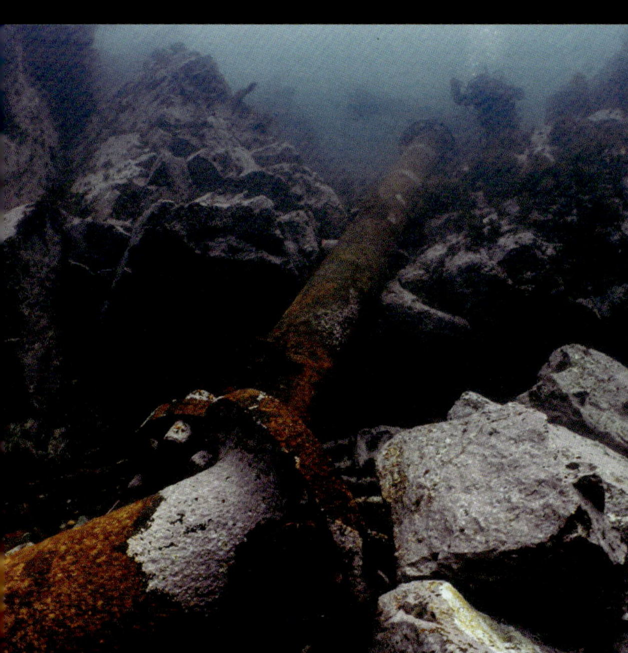

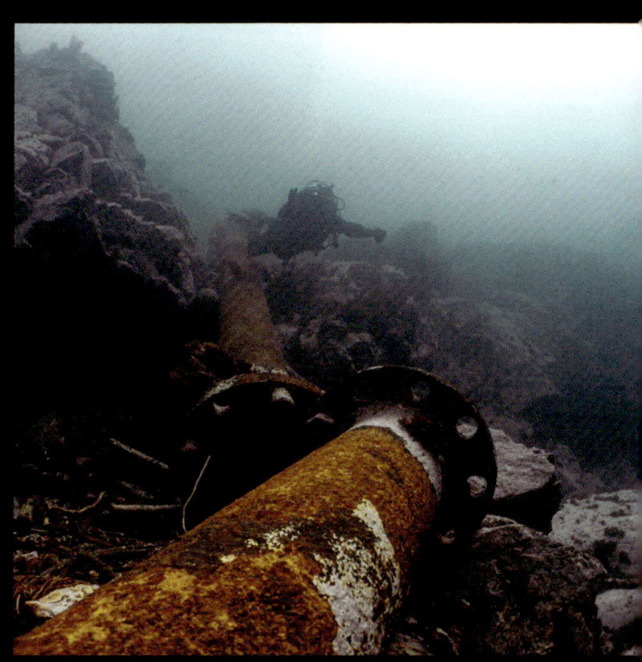

The engine shaft, which led the way to the engine room

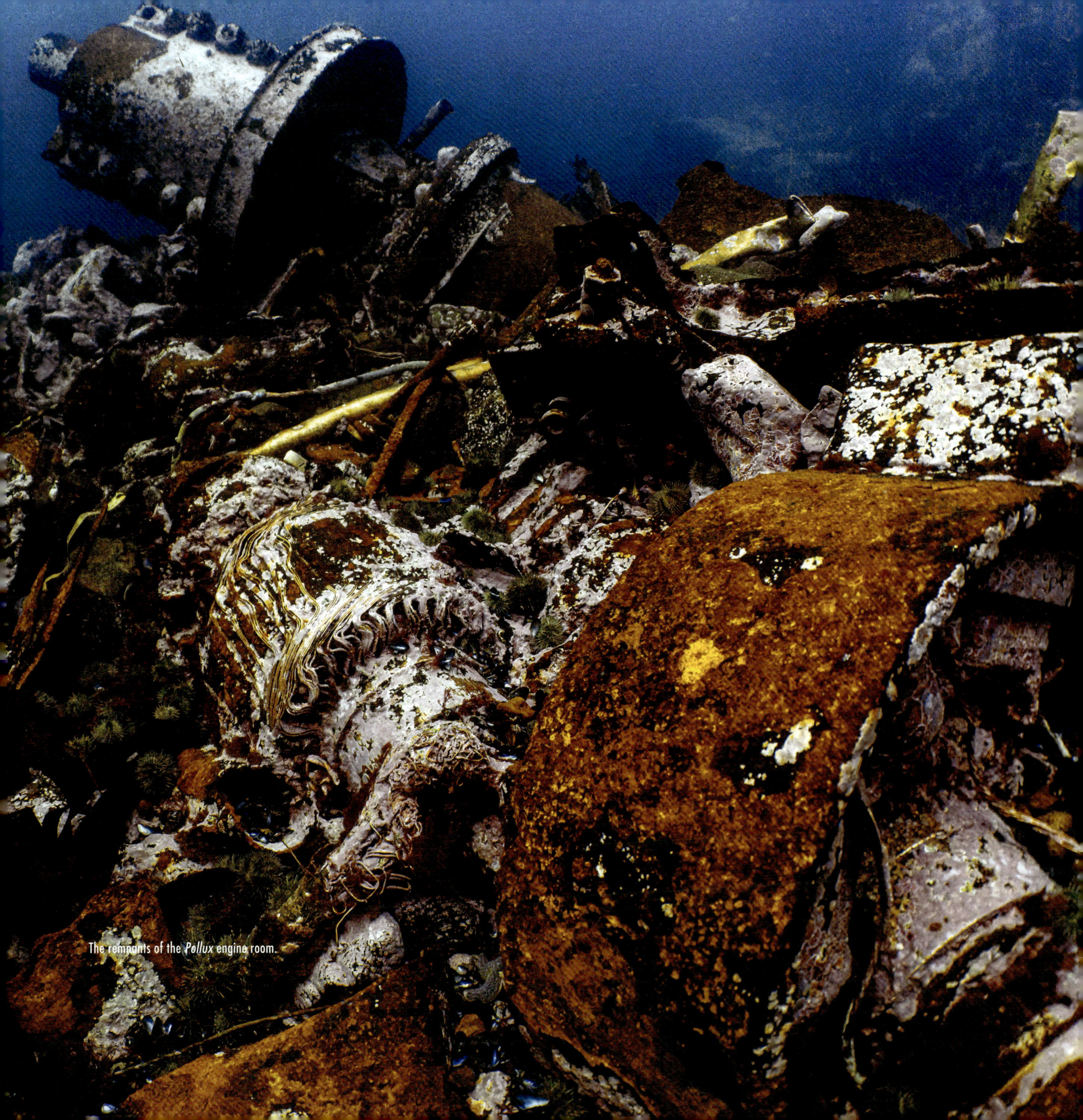

The remnants of the *Pollux* engine room.

shaft would be like the yellow brick road in Oz, leading the way to our highly anticipated goal. Our surface interval felt like an eternity; the anticipation was almost unbearable as we awaited our next dive.

Team one surfaced with nearly as much excitement as they had after the first dive, but this time, success. Soon, my dive buddy and I were back in the water following the directions given to us by the first team. The swim was tough, and I had to protect my camera from the rocks as we navigated through rough waters. The water was relatively shallow and we were tossed around in the surge. But then, there it was: debris and engine equipment scattered everywhere. The scale of the discovery overwhelmed me. As we surfaced, we all shared in the exhilaration. This was the goal that had fuelled our determination and drive. The USS *Pollux* had revealed its secrets, and we felt privileged to have been a part of its story.

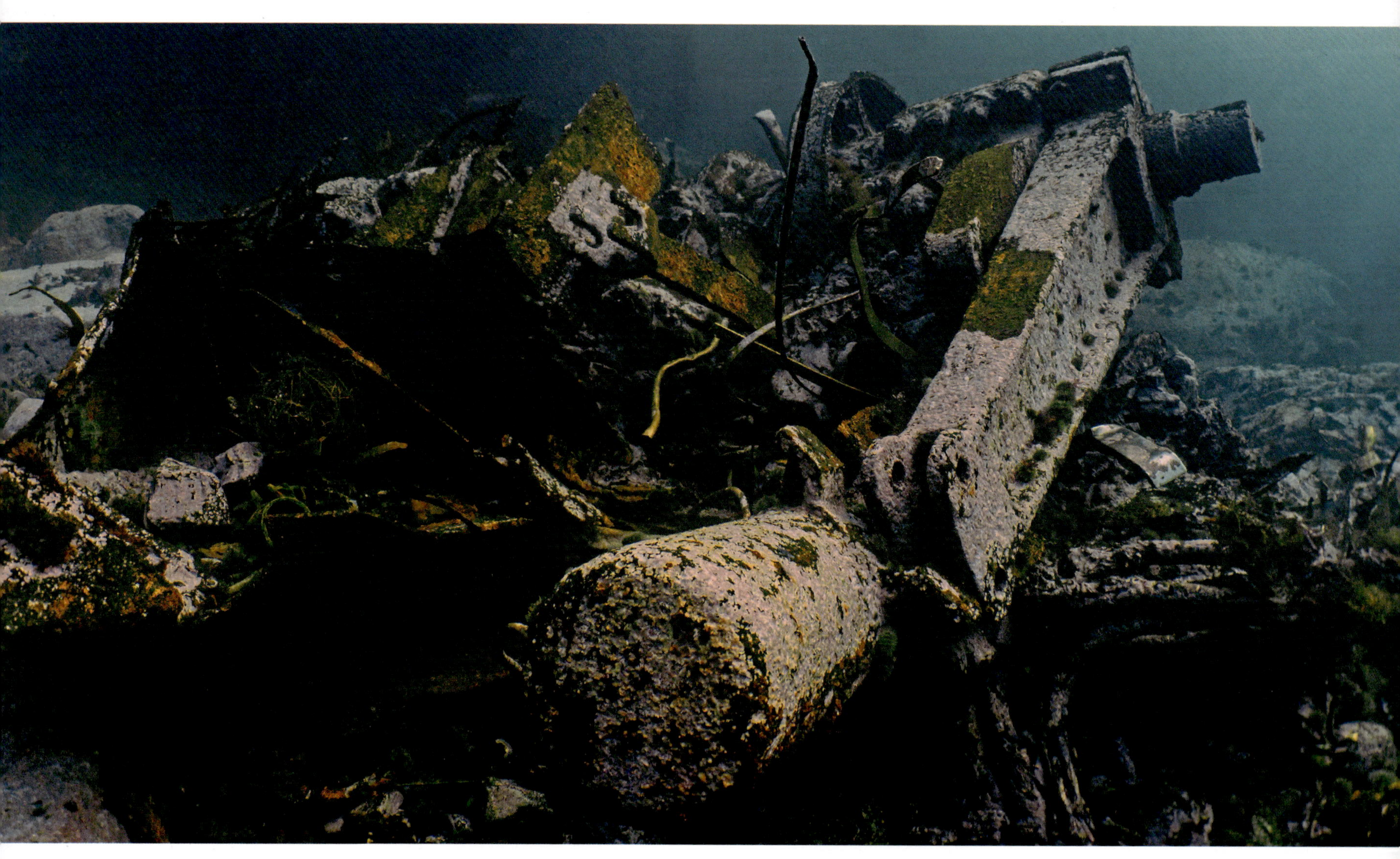

A lever for the rudder of the *Pollux*.

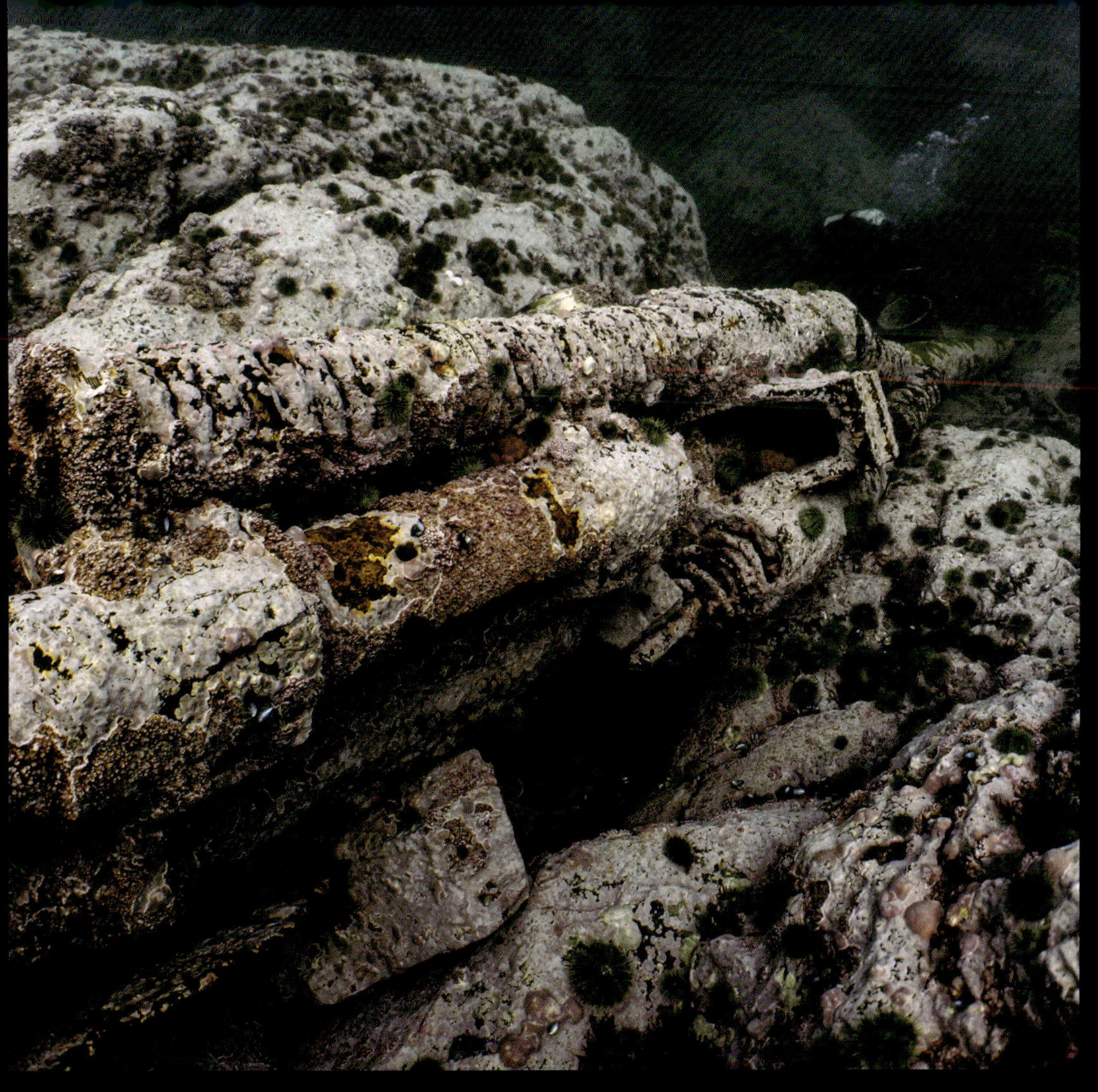

One of the *Pollux's* stern deck guns.

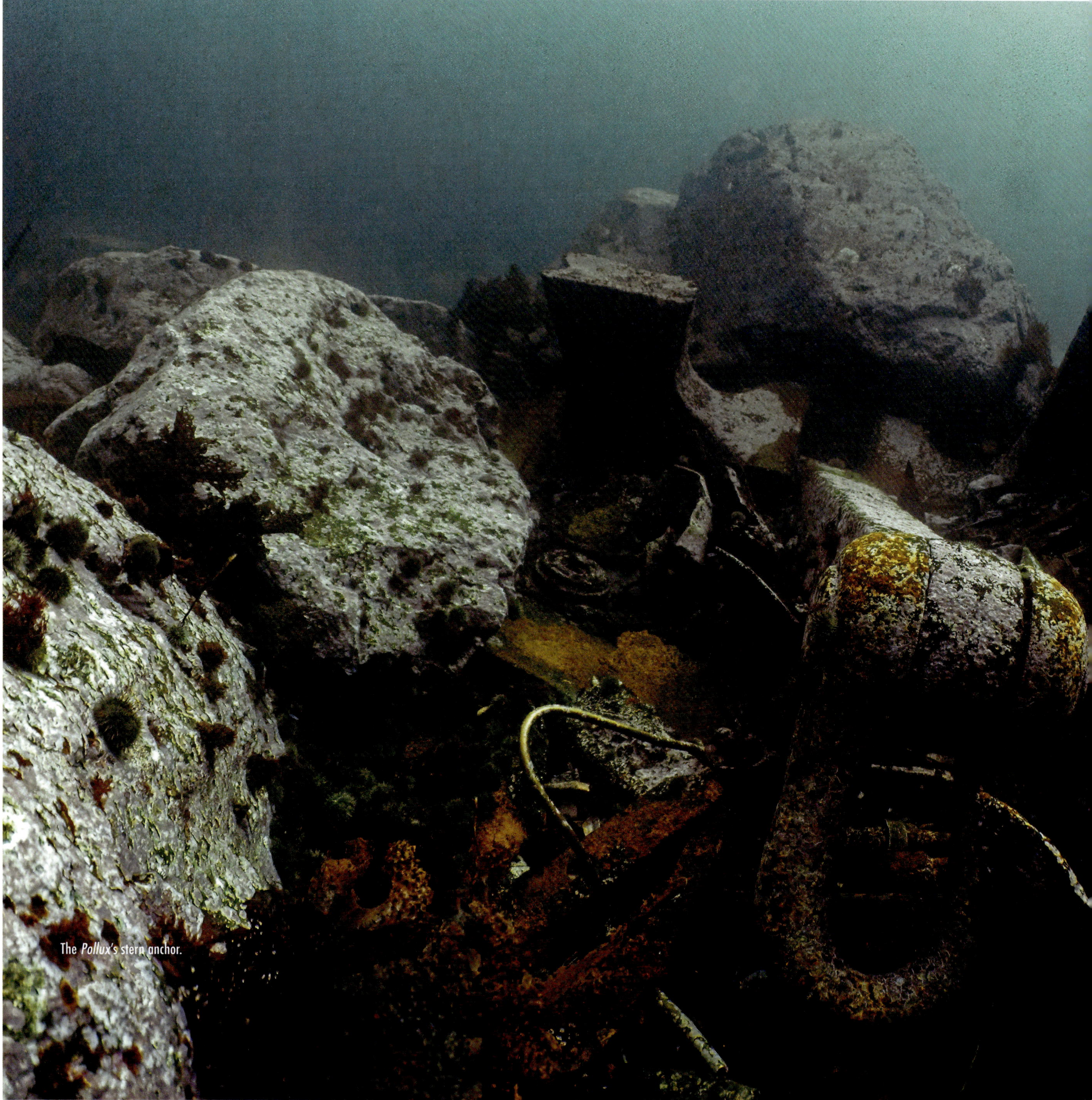
The *Pollux's* stern anchor.

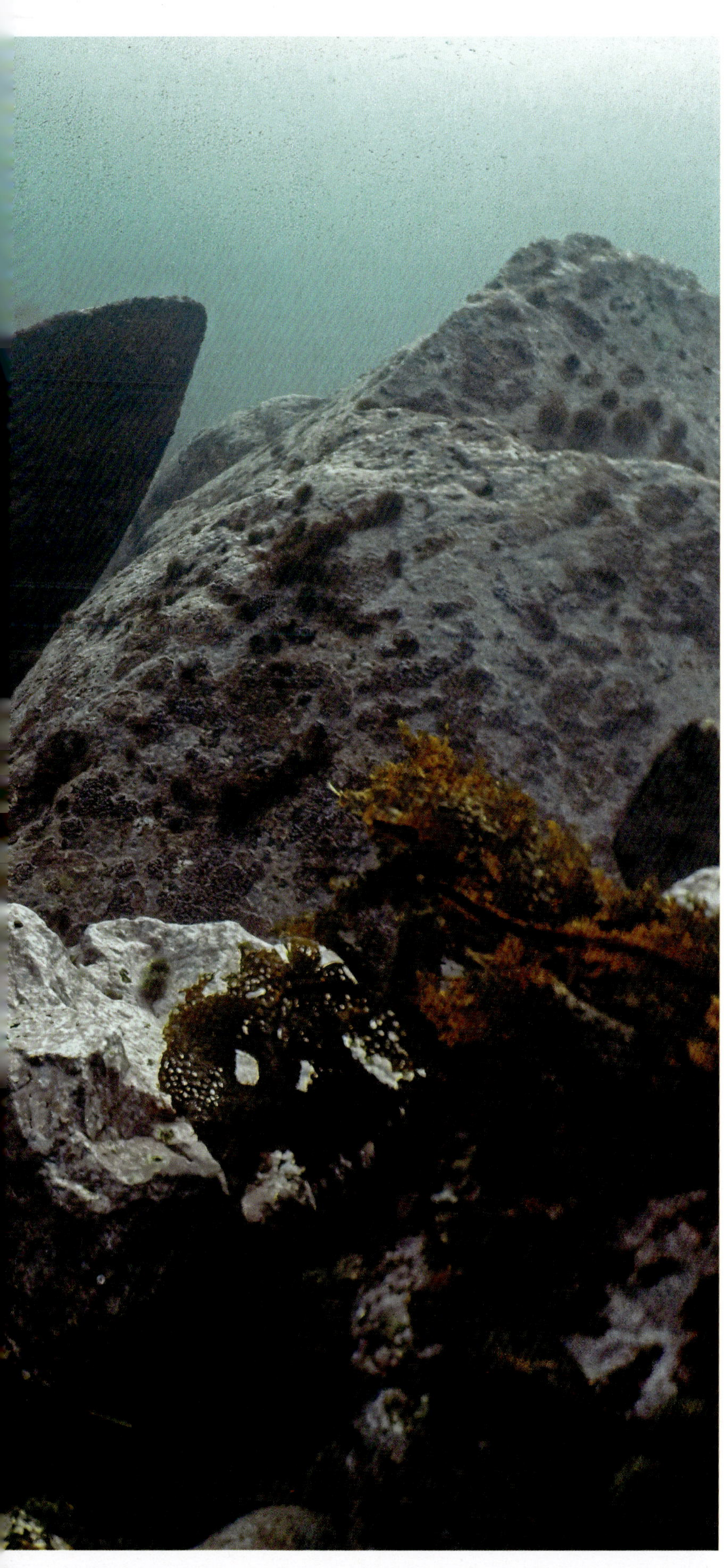

Diving is a way to connect with our sense of adventure and feel the excitement of discovering something new.

—PAUL NICKLEN

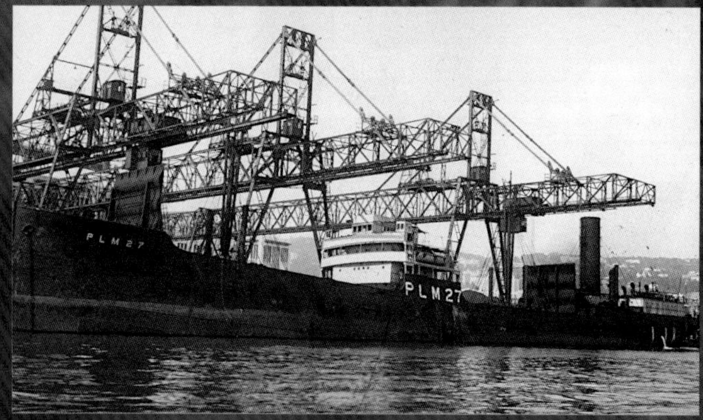

SS *PLM-27*

(Paris, Lyon, Marseilles)

BUILT: 1925, by Sir Raylton Dixon & Co. Ltd., Middlesbrough, England

REGISTRY: British

TONNAGE: 5391 gross tonnage

LENGTH: 123 metres / 400 feet

BREADTH: 17 metres / 56 feet

DRAFT: 8.6 metres / 28.4 feet

SINKING: 3:36 a.m., November 2, 1942, by U518

POSITION: Bow facing west, oriented parallel to Bell Island

MOORING LINE: Port, windless aft of bow; and port stern, aft of torpedo hole

APPROXIMATE DIVING DEPTHS:

- Bridge: 12 metres / 40 feet
- Fore/Afterdeck: 14 metres / 45 feet
- Main Deck: 21 metres / 70 feet
- Keel: 30 metres / 100 feet

HIGHLIGHTS:

- Bow and starboard anchor hanging on the side of the ship at a depth of 24 metres (70 feet)
- A machine gun is visible on the aft deck
- The propeller and rudder: it's the only Bell Island shipwreck with the propeller in place; the propeller is large enough to swim through
- Torpedo hole: swim forward from the propeller and look up at the gaping hole created by the torpedo

HISTORY:

The free French ship *PLM-27* was taken over by the British in 1940. It was at anchor and fully loaded with iron ore from the Bell Island mines when it was struck by a torpedo fired by the German submarine U518, captained by Friedrich Wissman, after the *Rose Castle* sank. Twelve sailors of the 50-person multinational crew lost their lives.

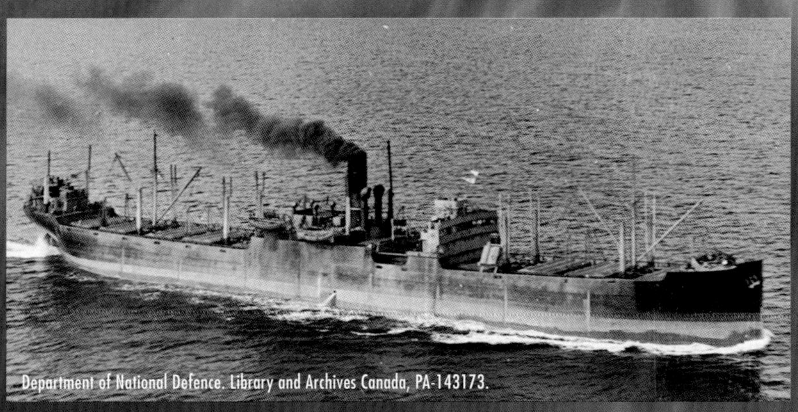
Department of National Defence. Library and Archives Canada, PA-143173.

SS *Rose Castle*

(sister ship SS *Lord Strathcona*)

BUILT: 1915, by Short Brothers Ltd. in Pallion, Sunderland, England

REGISTRY: Canadian

TONNAGE: 7546 gross tonnage

LENGTH: 140 metres / 455 feet

BREADTH: 18 metres / 58 feet

DRAFT: 9.5 metres /31 feet

SINKING: 3:33 a.m., November 2, 1942, by U518

POSITION: Bow facing west, oriented parallel to Bell Island

MOORING LINE: Midship to the top of wheelhouse

APPROXIMATE DIVING DEPTHS:

- Bridge: metres / 105 feet
- Fore/Afterdeck: 35 metres / 115 feet
- Main Deck: 36.5 metres / 120 feet
- Keel: 46 metres / 150 feet
- Torpedo: 46 metres / 140 feet

HIGHLIGHTS:

- Marconi Room above the bridge: not far from the mooring line, inside the Marconi Room the original Marconi Radio is visible and remarkably preserved
- Pointing east, the stern gun sits prominently on top of the vessel, aiming its 4.7-inch barrel into the depths behind the wreck
- 20 metres (60 feet) past the stern in the mud is a German torpedo minus the warhead; in good visibility conditions, the cigar-shaped structure can be seen by hovering next to the gun

HISTORY:

The German submarine U518, captained by Friedrich Wissman, fired two torpedoes at the *Rose Castle*, which was at anchor and fully loaded with 10,200 tonnes of iron ore from the Bell Island mines. She sank in less than 90 seconds; 29 sailors lost their lives.

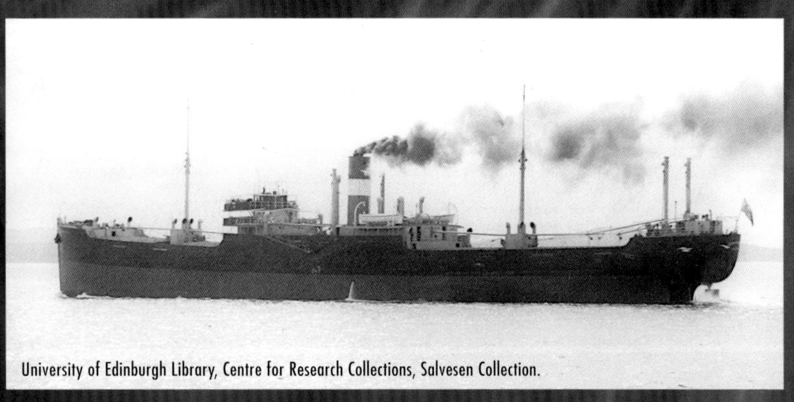
University of Edinburgh Library, Centre for Research Collections, Salvesen Collection.

SS *Saganaga*

BUILT: 1935, by D&W Henderson & Co Ltd., Glasgow

REGISTRY: British

TONNAGE: 5454 gross tonnage

LENGTH: 127 metres / 407 feet

BREADTH: 17.26 metres / 55.6 feet

DRAFT: 8.54 metres / 28 feet

SINKING: 1:46 a.m., September 5, 1942, by U513

POSITION: Bow facing Bell Island, stern facing Little Bell Island

MOORING LINE: Check with divemaster for current position

APPROXIMATE DIVING DEPTHS:

- Bridge: 18 metres / 60 feet
- Fore/Afterdeck: 18 metres / 60 feet
- Main Deck: 21 metres / 70 feet
- Keel: 35 metres / 115 feet

HIGHLIGHTS:

- Passageway swim-throughs
- Large bow anchor now on the main deck had been sitting on the sea floor when the torpedo hit; the explosion launched the anchor into the air and it came to rest on the deck
- Follow the anchor chain from the deck anchor as it weaves forward over the torpedo hole all the way to the bow
- A spare propeller can be viewed by dipping into the cargo hold just forward of the deck anchor

HISTORY:

The German submarine U513 captained by Rolf Ruggeberg fired two torpedoes at the SS *Saganaga* but the captain had forgotten to set the charges and had to launch two more torpedoes, which were successful. She sank in less than 30 seconds. Of the 48 crew, 29 lost their lives.

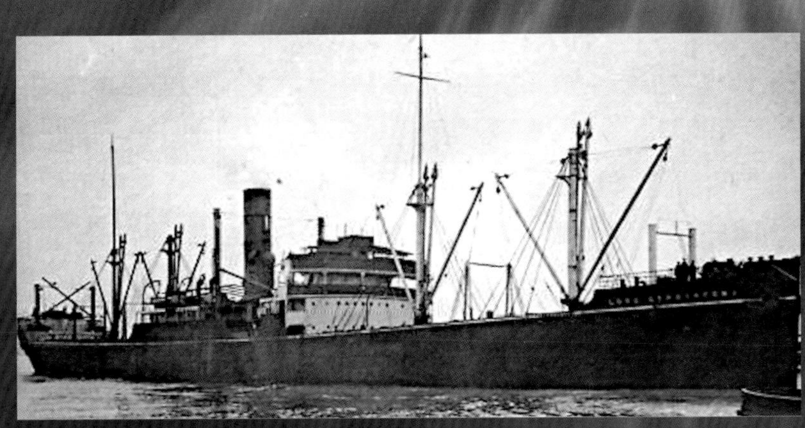

SS *Lord Strathcona*

(sister ship *SS Rose Castle*)

BUILT: 1915, by W. Doxford & Sons Ltd., Sunderland, England

REGISTRY: Canadian

TONNAGE: 7335 gross tonnage

LENGTH: 140 metres / 455 feet

BREADTH: 18 metres / 58 feet

DRAFT: 9.5 metres / 31 feet

SINKING: 12:17 p.m., September 5, 1942, by U513

POSITION: Bow facing Little Bell Island, stern facing Bell Island

MOORING LINE: Forward deckhouse lifeboat davit, starboard side

HIGHLIGHTS:

- Swim-throughs on either side of the deckhouse
- Aft of the deck house is the bathroom, with a collapsed roof
- The 5-metre-long stern gun is still in position, with its 4.7-inch barrel upright on the deck

HISTORY:

German submarine U513 captained by Rolf Ruggeberg sank this ship 30 minutes after the sinking of SS *Saganaga*. This time allowed the entire crew to safely abandon ship. In trying to manoeuvre into position to torpedo the *Lord Strathcona*, the U-boat struck the bottom of the ship with its Conning Tower. Once clear, it fired 2 torpedoes at the *Lord Strathcona*; the ship sank within 90 seconds

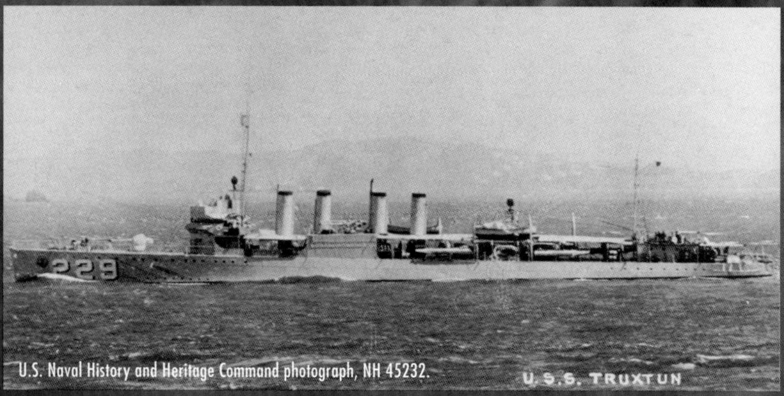

U.S. Naval History and Heritage Command photograph, NH 45232.

USS *Truxtun* DD-229

BUILT: 1920, William Cramp & Sons, Philadelphia

REGISTRY: US, Clemson-class destroyer

TONNAGE: 1215 gross tonnage

LENGTH: 95.82 metres / 314 feet

BREADTH: 9.44 metres / 30 feet

DRAFT: 3 metres / 9.5 feet

ARMAMENT:

- Four 4-inch (100 mm) guns
- One 3-inch (76 mm) gun
- Twelve 21-inch (533 mm) torpedo tubes

SINKING: 4:00 a.m., February 18, 1942

POSITION: Debris field west area of Chambers Cove

HIGHLIGHTS:

- Gear boxes
- Drive shaft parts
- Copper tubing
- Ammunition

HAZARDS:
Shallow depths mean that the area is highly susceptible to surge and wave action.

HISTORY:
After departing Boston, the four-stack destroyer was destined for Argentia, Newfoundland. The *Truxtun* (as well as the *Pollux* and the *Wilkes*, the other boats in the convoy) was hit by a violent winter storm and veered off course, eventually running aground in Chambers Cove. Only 46 of 156 sailors survived.

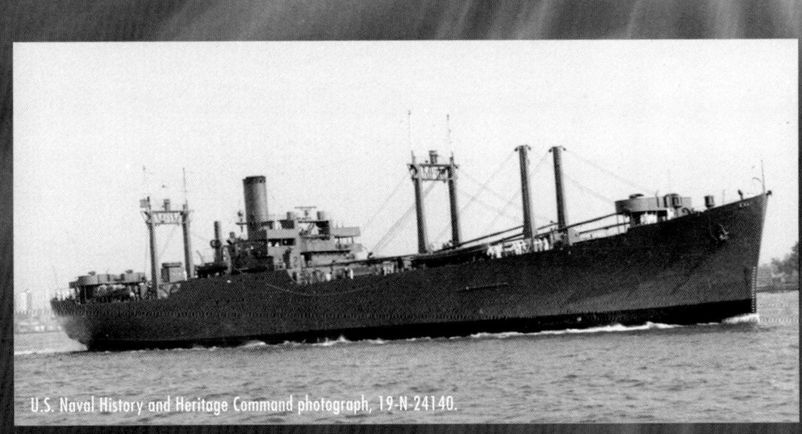
U.S. Naval History and Heritage Command photograph, 19-N-24140.

SS *Pollux* AKS-2

BUILT: 1939, Federal Shipbuilding and Drydock Company, New Jersey

REGISTRY: US, Castor-class general stores issue ship

TONNAGE: 13,910 gross tonnage

LENGTH: 140 metres / 459 feet

BREADTH: 19 metres / 63 feet

DRAFT: 8 metres / 26.4 feet

ARMAMENT:
- One 5-inch (38-calibre) gun
- Four 3-inch (50-calibre) guns

SINKING: 4:00 a.m., February 18, 1942

POSITION: Debris field spread out east and west along the cliffs of Lawn Point

MOORING LINE: N/A

DIVING DEPTHS:
- Inshore 5 metres (15 feet); offshore to 30 metres (90 feet)

HIGHLIGHTS:
- Main reduction gear
- Stern anchor with sheared-off fluke
- Stern guns
- Mangled engine equipment
- Drive shaft
- Boilers and wall panels
- Miscellaneous stores and other brass items
- Forward gun and Hausse pipe

HAZARDS:
Inshore, the shallow rocky terrain is highly susceptible to surge and wave action. In deeper areas, cross currents can be strong.

HISTORY:
After departing Boston loaded with supplies and ammunition for the new base in Argentia, Newfoundland, the *Pollux* and its convoy went off course in a violent winter storm and ran aground off Lawn Point. Only 103 of the 196 sailors survived.

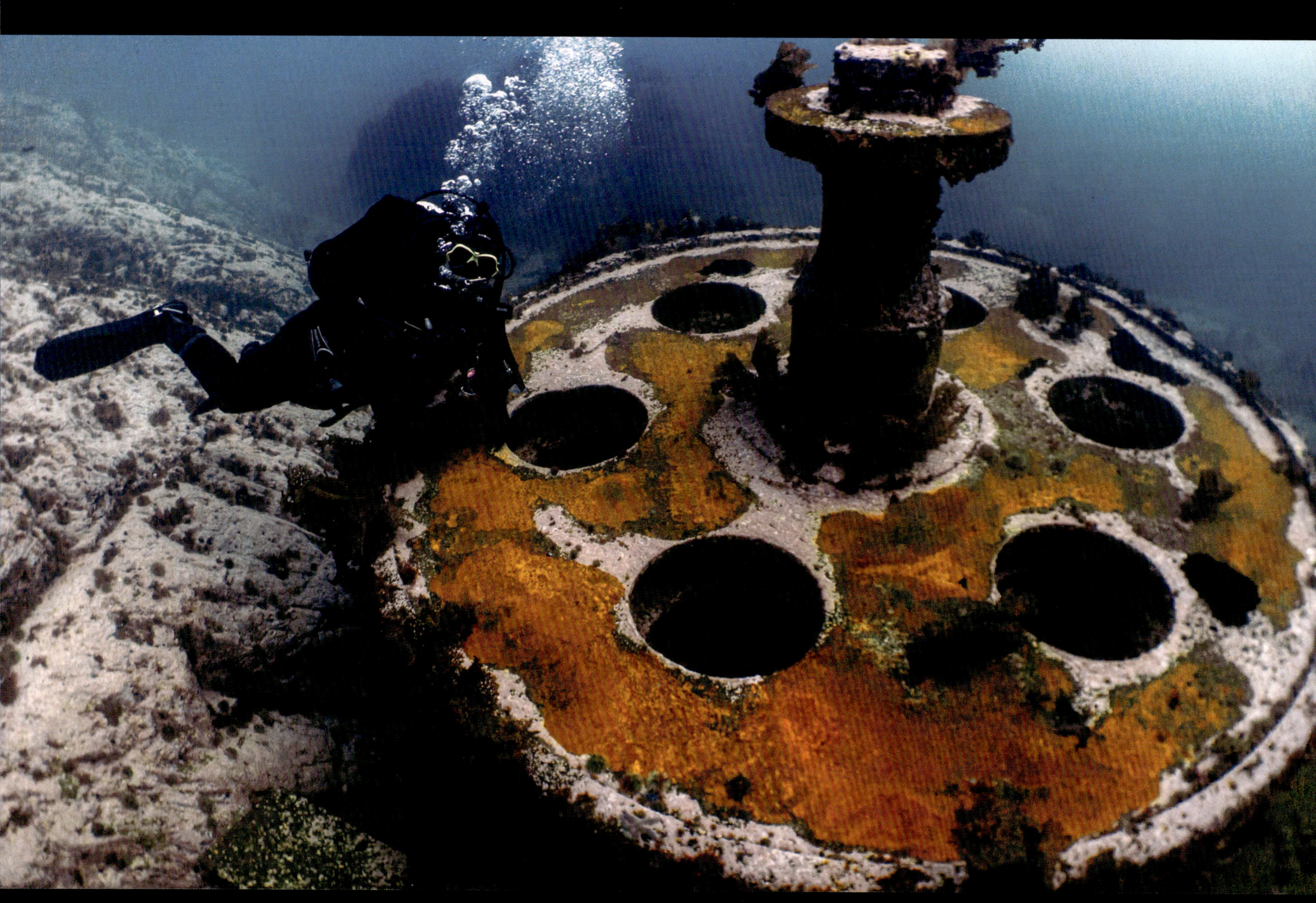

Main reduction gear from the *Pollux*.

ACKNOWLEDGEMENTS

I would like to thank a few people for their help and encouragement. First, Mikaila, the love of my life, my wife, and my best dive buddy. We started diving together on the first day we met. Her passion for diving rivals mine. You can see her hovering over the bow on the cover of this book. She has become my top scuba model, always being in the right place at the right time and, most importantly, putting up with my bright lights in her face. Without her, this book would not have come to be.

My parents, Frank and Shelley Power, have always encouraged my sense of adventure and love of nature. My mother has wanted me to create an album of the photos from my diving adventures. This book is the result of starting that process.

Rick Stanley and John Olivero, thank you for your friendship over many years. Thanks also to the rest of Ocean Quest Adventures family and staff. Without your help and guidance, and the opportunities you have offered me, I would not be the diver I am today.

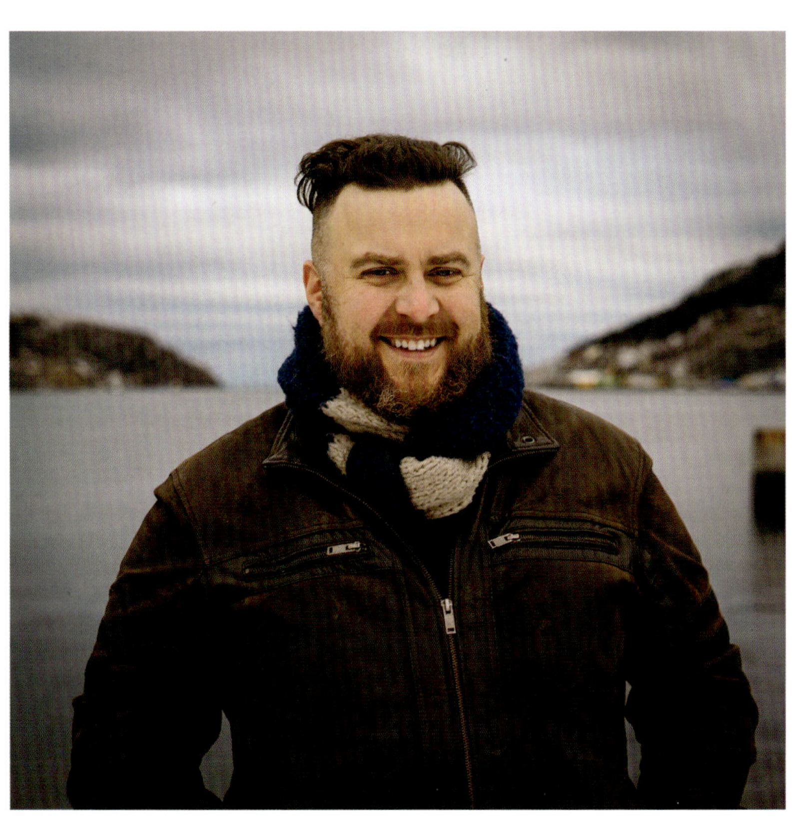

BIOGRAPHY

Chris Power is an avid scuba diver, dive instructor, and award-winning photographer. Based in Newfoundland and Labrador, Canada, Chris is well acquainted with the cold waters of eastern Canada. He spends his free time exploring the underwater world and photographing creatures big and small. An instructor and certified technical diver, Chris enjoys introducing students to the extraordinary underwater realm, and sees every group of students as new dive buddies to adventure with.